JOHAN L. LOTTER
CONSULTING ACTUARY
424 E. 52ND STREET
(212) 832-0646

STRAND PRICE
$5.00

INDIVIDUAL HEALTH INSURANCE

edited by FRANCIS T. O'GRADY, F.S.A.

published by the
SOCIETY of ACTUARIES

Copyright © 1988, Society of Actuaries

All rights reserved by the Society of Actuaries. Permission is granted to make brief excerpts for a published review. Permission is also granted to make limited numbers of copies of items in Individual Health Insurance for personal, internal, classroom, or other instructional use, on condition that the foregoing copyright notice is used so as to give reasonable notice of the Society's copyright. This consent for free copying without prior consent of the Society does not extend to making copies for general distribution, for advertising or promotional purposes, for inclusion in new collective works, or for resale.

NOTICE

The Society assumes no responsibility for statements made or opinions expressed in the articles, criticisms, and discussions published in Individual Health Insurance.

Library of Congress Cataloging-in-Publication Data

Individual health insurance.

    Includes index.

    1. Insurance, Health—United States.   I. O'Grady, Francis T., 1927-

HG9396.I53 1988   368.3'82'00973   88-6349

ISBN 0-938959-00-X

About the Editor

Francis T. O'Grady entered the actuarial profession in 1950 as an actuarial student with Metropolitan Life, immediately following graduation from Queens College, Flushing, New York, with a Bachelor of Science degree in Mathematics. His actuarial career at Metropolitan spanned 38 years, where during that time he rose through increasingly responsible actuarial positions to that of a Senior Actuarial Officer. Mr. O'Grady has served as a member and Chairperson of the Society's Education and Examination (E&E) Committee. He was Chairperson of the Part 7 Committee that in a single year introduced multiple-choice questions to the Fellowship examinations and also pioneered the use of central grading for these examinations. He has more recently served the E&E Committee as a consultant on individual health insurance. He has been Chairperson of the Society's Committee on Individual Health Insurance Experience Studies and has actively participated in the Society's Health Section, serving as its Chairperson. Mr. O'Grady is currently a member of the Research Policy Committee and the Task Force to Revitalize Research in the Society. He is a co-author of the paper "Reserve Principles for Individual Health Insurance," published in TSA XXXVII, and has written discussions of a number of papers published in the "TSA."

CONTENTS

Preface for The Society of Actuaries xi

Editor's Preface xiii

**Chapter 1 Introduction by Francis T. O'Grady, F.S.A.
and Charles W. Kraushaar, Jr., F.S.A.** 1

  1.1   Historical Development of Individual Health
Insurance Benefits 1

  1.2   Life Insurance Companies as Individual Health Insurers .. 4

  1.3   Health Insurance Compared with Life Insurance 5

**Chapter 2 Individual Medical Expense Benefits by
Willis W. Burgess, A.S.A.** 7

  2.1   Types of Medical Expense Benefits 7

      2.1.1   Hospital Indemnity Benefits 8

      2.1.2   Hospital Expense Reimbursement Benefits 10

      2.1.3   Medical Expense Reimbursement Benefits 11

      2.1.4   Surgical Expense Reimbursement Benefits 12

      2.1.5   Major Medical Benefits 13

      2.1.6   Specified Disease Benefits 18

      2.1.7   Medicare Supplement Benefits 20

      2.1.8   Accident Medical Expense Benefits 23

      2.1.9   Dental Insurance Benefits 25

      2.1.10 Maternity Benefits 26

  2.2   Exclusions and Limitations 27

  2.3   Regulatory Concerns 28

  2.4   Long-Term Care 33

**Chapter 3 Individual Disability Income Benefits by
W. Duane Kidwell, F.S.A.** 35

  3.1   Total Disability Income Benefits 35

  3.2   Business Related Disability Benefits 41

  3.3   Supplemental Benefits Available on Disability
Income Policies 43

  3.4   Residual or Partial Disability Income Benefits 49

  3.5   Rehabilitation 54

**Chapter 4 Individual Health Insurance Premiums by
William F. Bluhm, F.S.A. and Spencer Koppel, F.S.A.** ... 57

    4.1   Gross Premium Structures 57

        4.1.1   Rating Classes and Related Claim
Cost Characteristics 57

        4.1.2   Organizing the Rating Classes 60

        4.1.3   Premium Guarantees 60

    4.2   Elements of Premium Calculation 61

        4.2.1   Morbidity 61

        4.2.2   Expenses 63

        4.2.3   Persistency and Mortality 64

        4.2.4   Interest 65

        4.2.5   Profit and Contingency Margins 66

        4.2.6   Other Considerations 67

        4.2.7   Relative Importance of Assumptions 68

    4.3   Experience Data 69

        4.3.1   Sources of Data 69

        4.3.2   Appropriateness of Data 70

        4.3.3   Adjusting the Data 70

    4.4   Profitability 72

        4.4.1   Criteria Used in Setting Levels 72

        4.4.2   Regulatory Measures of Reasonableness of
Benefits in Relation to Premiums 73

    4.5   Calculation Methods 75

        4.5.1   The Asset-Share Method 75

        4.5.2   Formula Methods 77

        4.5.3   The Cash Flow Method 79

    4.6   Experience Monitoring and Renewal Rating 80

        4.6.1   Management Information Systems 80

        4.6.2   Renewal Rate Calculations 81

    4.7   Other Considerations 82

    4.8   Sample Asset Share Calculation 83

**Chapter 5 Reserves and Liabilities for Individual Health
Insurance by Robert Shapland, F.S.A.** 93

    5.1   The Essentials of Accrual Accounting 93

CONTENTS

- 5.2 Premium Reserves 96
  - 5.2.1 Unearned Premium Reserve 96
  - 5.2.2 Advance Premiums 97
  - 5.2.3 Uncollected Premiums 98
  - 5.2.4 Deferred Premiums 98
- 5.3 Policy Reserves 98
- 5.4 Claim Reserves and Liabilities 103
- 5.5 Calculation of Claim Reserves and Liabilities ... 106
  - 5.5.1 Claim Run-out Method 106
  - 5.5.2 Average Size Claim Method 110
  - 5.5.3 Tabular Method 110
  - 5.5.4 Formula Method 111
  - 5.5.5 Individual Claim Estimates 111
  - 5.5.6 Loss Ratio Method 111
- 5.6 Allocation of Claim Reserves and Liabilities to Annual Statement Categories 111
- 5.7 Claim Reserve Testing 112
- 5.8 Reserves for Waiver of Premium Benefits 113
- 5.9 Estimated Expenses of Investigation and Settlement of Policy Claims 114
- 5.10 Contingency Reserves 114
- 5.11 Provision for Policyholders' Dividends Payable in the Following Calendar Year 115

Chapter 6 Underwriting Individual Health Insurance by John W. Hadley, F.S.A. 117

- 6.1 The Basics 117
  - 6.1.1 Field Underwriting 118
  - 6.1.2 Preliminary Screening 118
  - 6.1.3 Medical/Nonmedical Underwriting 119
  - 6.1.4 Conditional Receipt 120
- 6.2 Health Insurance Underwriting Contrasted to Life Insurance Underwriting 120
- 6.3 Actions Available to the Underwriter 122
- 6.4 Sources of Information Available to the Underwriter 123
- 6.5 Effect of Product on Underwriting 125

6.5.1	Medical Expense Insurance	126
6.5.2	Disability Income Insurance	127
6.5.3	Medicare Supplement Insurance	129

6.6 Effect of Renewability on Underwriting 129

6.7 Specific Underwriting Factors 130

    6.7.1 Occupation 130

    6.7.2 Income 131

    6.7.3 Avocations 132

    6.7.4 Medical History 132

    6.7.5 Other Insurance 133

    6.7.6 Other Factors 134

6.8 Issue and Participation Limits 136

6.9 Renewals/Policy Changes/Reinstatements/Rate Revisions/Updates 138

6.10 Special Underwriting Situations 139

Chapter 7 Individual Health Insurance Claims Administration by John W. Hadley, F.S.A 141

7.1 The Claims Evaluation Process 142

    7.1.1 The Basics 142

    7.1.2 Contestability and Rescission 143

    7.1.3 Claim Validity 144

7.2 Claim Payment 146

7.3 Sources of Information Available to the Claim Examiner....................................... 147

7.4 Effect of Product on Claims Administration 148

    7.4.1 Medical Care Coverage 149

    7.4.2 Disability Income Coverage 150

7.5 Tools Available to Challenge Questionable Claims 151

    7.5.1 Incontestable Clause 151

    7.5.2 Preexisting Conditions Exclusion 152

    7.5.3 Good Health Clause 152

    7.5.4 Other Exclusions 153

7.6 Other Factors Affecting Claims Administration 153

Chapter 8   Selling Individual Health Insurance by Noel J. Abkemeier, F.S.A. 159

- 8.1   Markets and Products 159
- 8.2   Marketing Channels 162
- 8.3   Compensation 163
- 8.4   Special Sales Characteristics 165
- 8.5   Summary of Agent Sales and Service Steps 166

Chapter 9   Annual Statement Reporting of Individual Health Insurance by Anthony B. Richter, F.S.A. 169

- 9.1   Background 169
- 9.2   Statutory and GAAP Accounting Principles 170
- 9.3   Most Important Annual Statement Sections for Individual Health Insurance 171
  - 9.3.1   Analysis of Operations by Lines of Business 171
  - 9.3.2   Schedule H: Accident and Health Exhibit 175
  - 9.3.3   Exhibit 9: Aggregate Reserve for Accident and Health Policies 177
- 9.4   Other Sections of the Annual Statement Involving Individual Health Insurance 178
- 9.5   Continuing Evolution of the Annual Statement 181

Chapter 10   Individual Health Insurance Policy Forms by Charles Habeck, F.S.A. and Mark Litow, F.S.A. 187

- 10.1   The Basics 187
- 10.2   The Content of an Individual Health Policy 189
  - 10.2.1   Policy Face Page 191
  - 10.2.2   Back of Face Page 192
  - 10.2.3   Schedule Page 192
  - 10.2.4   Benefit Provisions 193
  - 10.2.5   Schedule of Procedures 195
  - 10.2.6   General Provisions 195
  - 10.2.7   Required and Optional Policy Provisions Under the Uniform Policy Provisions Law 196
  - 10.2.8   Attachments to the Policy 198

Appendices **201**
1 Reserve Standards for Individual Health Insurance Policies 201
2 Uniform Individual Accident and Sickness Policy
  Provision Law 207
3 Restatement of the NAIC Uniform Individual Accident
  and Sickness Policy Provision Law in Simplified Language 225

Index **233**

PREFACE FOR THE SOCIETY OF ACTUARIES

Significant social, political, economic, technological and medical changes have occurred since the Society of Actuaries textbook on Individual Health Insurance was last revised in 1968. Insurance products, markets, distribution systems and the insurers themselves bear little resemblance to the scenario of the 1950s and early 1960s, which was the background for the original Miller and Bartleson texts.

The Health Section of the Society of Actuaries recognizes that the most current study material possible is a necessary part of the examination syllabus. This need is all the greater in light of continuing volatility in demographics, health care delivery, benefit programs, taxation and insurance regulation.

The work that Mr. O'Grady and his associates have produced responds to this need most successfully. The Health Section Council, on behalf of the Society of Actuaries and its members, expresses its appreciation to all the contributors to this text for their time and effort.

Robert J. Dymowski, F.S.A.
Chairperson
Health Section of the
Society of Actuaries

Howard J. Bolnick, F.S.A.
Vice Chairperson
Health Section of the
Society of Actuaries

EDITOR'S PREFACE

This textbook is intended to provide basic training in the fundamentals of the actuarial aspects of individual health insurance. It was planned and written to be compatible with the rest of the syllabus material for the Society of Actuaries Fellowship examinations and at a level of difficulty consistent with that material. While it can, therefore, be considered to be a higher level college text, it should be useful to all health insurance professionals, including actuaries, who want to get back to "the basics."

The original Society of Actuaries textbook on this subject was published in 1956 with John H. Miller as the principal contributor.

A revised edition was published in 1963 with Edwin L. Bartleson as the principal contributor. That edition was further revised and updated by Mr. Bartleson in 1968 after the Medicare system became law in the United States.

As with the previous textbooks, this one was prepared by an outstanding group of actuarial experts in the individual health insurance field. Each chapter of this book was written by a designated author on an assigned topic. The limitation of the assignment to a specific topic facilitated the recruiting of the authors.

While the subject matter of this textbook is, in general, the same as that of the earlier ones, this book is not to be considered merely a revision of them. Rather, each topic was examined anew and the text drafted from a "zero base."

The progression of the chapters was purposely chosen to meet the primary objective of the book, that is, to be used as a basic education tool in the actuarial aspects of individual health insurance.

The first chapter gives a brief history of the development of individual health insurance benefits and some of its similarities and dissimilarities with life insurance coverage.

The second and third chapters give a solid grounding in the benefit structures provided by individual health insurance policies. The first of these two chapters deals with medical expense insurance benefits and the second with disability income insurance benefits.

Chapter 4 introduces the student to the more critical actuarial aspects of individual health insurance with explanations and demonstrations of the development of premium rates for the benefits described in the two previous chapters. Sources of data for premium calculation are explored in this chapter. A detailed asset share example at the end of the chapter illustrates the use of that powerful actuarial tool.

The fifth chapter covers another essential actuarial aspect of individual health insurance. This is the rationale for and the statutory reporting requirements for the reserves and liabilities for this line of business. This subject has been a matter of controversy among actuaries and this chapter examines the different viewpoints.

Chapter 6 enumerates the risk factors to be considered in underwriting individual health insurance and describes the process for evaluating the risk, including comparisons with this process for life insurance coverage.

The claim evaluation process for individual health insurance is described in Chapter 7, including the tools available to challenge and contest questionable claims.

Chapter 8 discusses the sales aspects of individual health insurance which are of importance to the actuary.

Chapter 9 covers statutory reporting for individual health insurance and gives a close-up look at the parts of the Annual Statement which involve individual health insurance.

The design and drafting of the policy contract and related forms for individual insurance are considered in Chapter 10, as well as the impact of regulatory requirements on policy drafting.

There are three Appendices. Appendix 1 is the NAIC Reserve Standards for Individual Health Insurance Policies. Appendix 2 is the NAIC Model Uniform Individual Accident and Sickness Policy Provision Law, and Appendix 3 is the Restatement of the NAIC Uniform Policy Provision Law in Simplified Language.

The idea for this new textbook came from a Task Force appointed by the Health Section at the request of the Society to review the existing portions of the examination syllabus dealing with individual health insurance. The Task Force consisted of John W. Hadley, Charles W. Kraushaar, Jr., John A. Young, and myself.

This Task Force reported that the syllabus for individual health insurance was inadequate in many areas and needed considerable improvement and updating. The Task Force also recommended that a new textbook be written to replace the study material of the current syllabus. This recommendation was adopted, and I was appointed the Editor for this project.

The authors whose names are given in the headings of their respective chapters were recruited. The authors were also most helpful in reviewing each other's drafts and offering valuable comments and suggestions.

In addition to the authors, a number of other Society members and students gave generously of their time in reviewing the drafts of the text or otherwise offering helpful suggestions. At the risk of possibly excluding someone who made a contribution, I am giving the following list: David B. Baldwin, E. Paul Barnhart, Thomas R. Casner, Jon M. Stellmacher, and Linda Fiacco.

EDITOR'S PREFACE

The officers and council members of the Health Section Council, especially Ex-Chairperson Donald M. Peterson, were most supportive of our work.

My associates at Metropolitan Life provided much needed assistance. The word processing was done by Augusta Ulrich, Gladys Walker and Alvera Cleary. The review work was performed by Robert Hansen. The effort was supported by my immediate superiors during this project, Jerrold R. Scher and Stephen E. White.

The Society staff, particularly Linden N. Cole, Millicent Treloar, Susan Pasini, and Donna Richardson, were most helpful at all times. Millicent Treloar did a substantial amount of the professional editing of the text.

And last but not least a special word of thanks to Charles W. Kraushaar, Jr., who from beginning to end served as my right hand man on this project.

Francis T. O'Grady, F.S.A.

Chapter 1

INTRODUCTION

by Francis T. O'Grady, F.S.A. and Charles W. Kraushaar, Jr., F.S.A.

Insurance for medical expenses and for loss of income due to disability has become an important component of economic life in the United States and Canada, as well as in many other parts of the world.

Such insurance benefits are provided by three basic sources:
1. individual insurance policies
2. employee benefit plans (including fully insured, partially insured and self-insured programs) and
3. social insurance, including the Old Age, Survivors, and Disability Insurance (OASDI), Medicaid and Workers Compensation programs.

As this textbook is limited to individual health insurance, the brief history given here is focused on the development of coverage under that particular vehicle. Treated in the discussion are the major social and economic events that have necessitated product revisions and account for the predominance of life insurance companies in this market. Included also in this introduction is a brief discussion of the compatibility of the life and health insurance lines. This introduction is intended to provide the reader with a broad general background of the individual health insurance business. This perspective is basic to the study of subsequent topics.

1.1 HISTORICAL DEVELOPMENT OF INDIVIDUAL HEALTH INSURANCE BENEFITS

The broad scope of benefits now available to protect against the various risks of accident and sickness has developed over a period of well over a hundred years.

The first policies issued in the United States, as far back as 1850, provided benefits only in the event of disability due to accidental injury. Some insurance against loss due to sickness was sold in the following decades, but these early efforts were not successful. In 1890 policies covering disability from certain specified diseases were offered, and from this starting point progressive liberalizations were made. Soon after the turn of the century policies were issued to cover substantially all diseases.

Meanwhile, accident disability income policies had been liberalized and supplementary benefits were introduced providing payments toward the cost of hospital, surgical, medical and nursing care. In 1903 limited surgical benefits were included in some of the policies providing protection against loss due to accident and sickness, and in 1905 hospital benefits were offered in the form of an increase in the benefit for disability payable while the insured was in a hospital.

Benefits for medical treatment first appeared in 1910 and in 1916 insurers began providing benefits toward the cost of nursing care. From this time until the late 1920s the history is one of liberalization and extension of benefits. One of the major liberalizations was the introduction by several insurers of policies that were noncancelable and guaranteed renewable, usually to a stated age such as 65. Due to the economic depression that started in 1929, experience on these policies produced very substantial losses. The unfavorable experience led to a retrenchment, particularly with respect to benefits payable on account of sickness. For some insurers the restrictions adopted put them out of the business for all practical purposes.

A new period of liberalization for disability income coverage then began in the middle 1930s. The advances during this period, however, were made on a more cautious basis. Liberalizations included the elimination or modification of many of the restrictions and limitations such as those relating to foreign travel, residence and air travel.

Rapid developments were also occurring in the provision of insurance against the cost of medical care. Although benefits had been available for hospital, surgical and nursing expenses almost since the turn of the century, these were included as incidental features in policies providing principally for weekly or monthly indemnity payments in event of disability, and were rather limited in amount. In 1930, what was generally called the "blanket accident expense benefit," was introduced. Under this coverage the insured was reimbursed up to a specified limit for all expenses for hospital, surgical, medical and nursing care, including medicine, laboratory charges and other miscellaneous medical expenses, when such expenses were incurred by the treatment of accidental injuries.

In the years following, important advances were made in providing insurance against the cost of medical care resulting from sickness as well as accident. It is important to note that parallel developments were also occurring in group insurance. These were different at first from those in individual health insurance, but their success provided the model for later individual insurance policies. Per diem benefits for hospital confinement were offered with additional benefits toward payment of hospital charges other than for room and board. Comprehensive schedules provided benefits for surgeons' fees. There were also benefits for physicians' calls, either at a stated limit of reimbursement per call and a stated aggregate per injury or illness, or on a blanket basis subject to a deductible or exclusion of the first few calls and a similar aggregate. Such benefits frequently were limited to in-hospital calls. Nursing expense benefits were provided sometimes, either for care in the home or for the cost of private-duty nurses in the hospital. Sometimes these hospital, surgical, medical and nursing benefits were included in weekly or monthly indemnity disability policies but, increasingly, they were offered in a separate contract.

Family policies or riders covering the spouse and dependent children in addition to the insured were introduced in the early 1930s and family coverage grew at a rapid rate. In 1945 special "polio" policies were introduced providing for the payment of as much as $10,000 for the treatment of poliomyelitis. Such benefits were also available as special features or optional riders to policies with more restricted benefits for other causes.

With poliomyelitis all but disappearing after the development of vaccines in the 1950s, such policies and benefits were succeeded by "dread disease" benefits. Such a policy or rider provided $5,000 or more for the treatment of specific diseases such as polio, leukemia, scarlet fever, diphtheria, smallpox, spinal or cerebral meningitis, encephalitis and rabies, for a small annual premium for a family.

Broad coverage "major medical expense" benefits were introduced in the 1950s following the lead established by its successful introduction for group insurance. In its early stages this coverage provided for reimbursement of expenses arising from either sickness or accidental injury, usually on the basis of paying a percentage, such as 75 or 80 percent of all covered expenses in excess of a stated amount or deductible, subject to a specified maximum limit of payment. A common deductible was $500, although sometimes when there was no other coverage, it was written with a deductible as small as $50 and, then, the coverage usually was termed "comprehensive medical expense insurance." The maximum was usually $5,000 or more and was sometimes as much as $25,000. This coverage was usually written with "inside limits" such as a specified daily limit for hospital room and board and specified maximums for surgical operations according to a schedule.

Inflation in medical care costs brought higher maximum benefits and higher "inside limits." Another concept introduced was that of the "out of pocket" maximum. This benefit provided for 100 percent reimbursement of covered medical expenses after the insured had paid a specified dollar amount from his own funds.

Another significant development in the 1950s and early 1960s was the expansion of the availability of medical expense insurance to those at the older ages. This phase of expansion was dramatically modified with the legislation of Medicare coverage in 1966. The emphasis shifted to benefit packages, for those who were eligible for Medicare, to provide, in one way or another, coverage supplementing that available under Medicare.

The early 1970s saw the development and expansion of comprehensive medical expense insurance coverage providing the same in and out-of-hospital benefits as were available under group medical expense insurance. Adverse developments in the mid-1970s, particularly in the areas of rate regulation and mandated benefits, resulted in poor financial results for this type of coverage, and a number of companies that had been active in this area reconsidered their position and left the field.

The same adverse conditions also affected all other medical expense insurance coverage to different degrees and caused some companies that had been marketing only a more traditional type of product to decide to discontinue even those coverages,

1.2 LIFE INSURANCE COMPANIES AS INDIVIDUAL HEALTH INSURERS

The early companies organized to issue accident insurance began to meet growing needs for other forms of protection, forms which neither the life companies nor the fire companies were then providing, such as employers' liability, burglary and theft and, later, workers compensation. Thus the present multiple line casualty companies may trace their origin to the sale of accident insurance benefits. It is not surprising, therefore, that health insurance was, until 1947, classified solely as a casualty line in the Annual Statement Blanks.

Another phase in the development of the business was the organization, in the latter part of the nineteenth century and the first decade or so of the twentieth century, of fraternal societies, mutual benefit associations and assessment organizations that offered accident insurance and, in some cases, accident and sickness insurance. A number of these organizations later changed their organizational form to that of stock or mutual insurance companies, while others continued to write health insurance either as fraternal or assessment organizations. Some of the largest insurers in the business today trace their origin to this form of organization.

The number of life insurance companies also writing health insurance has expanded from just a few companies in the early 1920s to that of representing a major presence in the health insurance business.

The emergence of the life companies as principal writers of health insurance resulted from

- the change in organizational form of many health insurance companies to that of corporate life insurance companies,
- the entry of health companies into the sale of life insurance by expansion of activities or by merger with life companies, and
- the entry of traditional life insurance companies into the health insurance business.

The last reason was the most significant. After the first life companies commenced writing health insurance in the 1920s, the further movement of life companies into this field was discouraged by the unfavorable experience that developed during the 1930s both in sickness insurance and in total and permanent disability income benefits attached to life insurance policies. However, a number of life companies were making considerable progress with group life insurance and there was a natural extension of this interest in the direction of group weekly indemnity benefits. The active development of hospital expense insurance by both insurance companies and Blue Cross organizations dating from the mid-1930s greatly stimulated the interest of life insurance companies in the field of health insurance. While this developing interest on the part of life insurance companies was largely centered in the group business, it carried over to the individual policy side of the business.

1.3 HEALTH INSURANCE COMPARED WITH LIFE INSURANCE

Life insurance with its settlement options protects against the risk of dying during the productive years or of outliving the productive years, while health insurance complements the program of personal insurance protection by providing benefits in partial replacement of income lost because of disability, and benefits toward the expense of medical care and treatment. Any discussion of these hazards to individual person security naturally leads people to a discussion of other hazards, and it was logical, therefore, that both life and health insurance be provided by the same agent and through the same company. Recognition of the complementary nature of life insurance and health insurance is evident in the action of the life insurance business, initiated many years ago, of including disability income and waiver of premium benefits in life insurance policies. Had the practices of the 1920s been directed along sounder lines, and had the problems not been intensified by the economic depression of the 1930s, many life insurance companies would probably have entered the health insurance business earlier then they did.

Not only is there a strong tie between health and life insurance from the standpoint of the needs the insurance agent is trying to supply, but also in the mechanics of selling and administering both kinds of coverage. It is true that there are some areas where the similarities are less apparent than the differences, but on the whole there is much common ground. For example, the application the agent uses to write health insurance policies is similar in form and content to that used for life insurance, although the answers to the questions on a health insurance application often do not have significance to the home office underwriters. This is because there are many impairments of more importance to health than to life insurance. However, the use of medical examination, inspection reports, attending physicians' and hospital statements in the underwriting of health insurance are procedures familiar both to the life insurance agent and to the underwriters of life insurance in the home offices. The processing of applications in the home office is much the same for both types of business. A company engaged in the two operations may be able to use the same clerical staff in processing both kinds of business. For instance, the same underwriters may render decisions on life and health applications, although it is more usual for the two lines to be handled by separate underwriters specializing in their respective fields.

Procedures a company adopts for issuing its policies and setting up its policy records, including its mechanism for the collection of premiums, may be entirely parallel for both lines of business. There is, of course, a wide range of practice among the companies writing health insurance, and it should not be inferred that health insurance business is always done on a basis that is comparable to life insurance. If the background of a company in this business stems from casualty insurance, it is likely that the practices followed on health insurance will be more in keeping with casualty than with life insurance. However, it is practical for a life insurance company to employ similar practices in many areas, should it wish to conduct the health insurance business on a basis familiar to its sales and administrative personnel. This choice of procedure exists, to some extent, in each phase of the operation. For example, a company may decide on a plan of agent compensation patterned after that customary for life insurance, with a high first-year commission and lower renewal scale rather than the level scale more typical of casualty insurance.

Perhaps the area where the greatest difference lies is in claim administration. Not only is the frequency of accident and sickness claims many times that of life insurance claims, but because of the subjective nature of disability and medical care, questions as to the validity and amount of the claim are more likely to arise. Many life insurance companies refused to offer any individual health insurance, or issued only disability income policies, and deemphasized this line of insurance because of the fear of adverse public relations. Investigations are more often required, including in some cases a medical examination or statement from the attending physician. It is extremely important, therefore, that the agent fully understand the terms of the contract and the reason for his company's action on each claim, if misunderstandings and poor policyholder relations are to be avoided. This requires special training of agents and claim administration personnel.

Chapter 2

INDIVIDUAL MEDICAL EXPENSE BENEFITS

by Willis W. Burgess, A.S.A.

The earliest use of medical expense insurance is believed to have been the system for remunerating doctors in ancient China. Members of the upper class would pay the local doctor while they were in good health and stop payment when they became ill. There was even a form of malpractice remedy built into this system. If a powerful Chinese landowner did not recover from an illness and his family felt that the doctor had not done his best, the doctor was executed.

Today's medical expense insurance benefits offered through individual policies are not as simple, nor is today's malpractice remedy quite as costly to the doctor.

This chapter deals with various types of medical expense insurance benefits: hospital indemnity; hospital expense reimbursement; medical expense reimbursement (pays the fees of physicians or other health care professionals); surgical expense reimbursement; major medical; specified disease; Medicare supplement; accident medical expense; dental insurance; and maternity. It provides details of these benefits, some of the more common exclusions and limitations unique to medical expense policies, and regulatory problems and concerns.

There is also a section on long-term care. Financial protection against the cost of long-term care may become the major health financing issue in the coming decades.

2.1 TYPES OF MEDICAL EXPENSE BENEFITS

The earliest form of medical expense insurance was an additional benefit offered under a disability contract. This provided for an increased payment in the event of hospitalization. It was an indemnity payment rather than an expense reimbursement. The difference between the two types of benefits is probably not fully appreciated by most policyholders. However, there are some very important distinctions between the two.

2.1.1 HOSPITAL INDEMNITY BENEFITS

The most common type of indemnity benefit is for hospital coverage. It evolved naturally from the extra payment provided along with a disability policy. Hospital indemnity policies are sold as supplementary coverage to both group and individual plans for persons under age 65. They are also issued as Medicare supplement plans for senior citizens.

Hospital indemnity coverage is available from health insurance agents, and has become increasingly popular as a mass-marketed product. Persons who belong to organizations with large memberships find brochures offering hospital indemnity coverage plans in their mail. Senior citizens are asked to respond to television appeals. Credit card holders are offered an easy way to offset the rising cost of hospital care by purchasing a daily benefit hospital policy for a small monthly charge. Newspaper and magazine readers are told "no salesman will call," and by completing a simple application form, coverage is offered with no medical exam. For some, the policies are guaranteed issue.

To the public, the appeal of so simple a way to purchase insurance is great. For many, the guaranteed issue offer is enticing. By carefully defining how preexisting conditions are to be dealt with, the companies providing such coverage can protect themselves from being inundated with adverse antiselection by potential claimants.

For the company the higher loss ratios expected from this type of appeal, be it guaranteed issue or with limited underwriting, are offset by reduced marketing, underwriting and policy issue expenses. Another advantage to the company lies in the fact that the indemnity benefit is not affected by inflation. Expense reimbursement plans require periodic rate adjustments to keep up with rising costs. This causes policyholder dissatisfaction and resultant policy lapsation. Indemnity contracts have historically had a better persistency record than have reimbursement plans for this reason.

In the 1950s and 1960s most hospital indemnity policies were sold as weekly benefit indemnity contracts with a maximum payment period of 50 or 100 weeks. Thus, a $50 weekly benefit payable for 100 weeks would be advertised as a $5,000 policy. With rising costs and a demand for more benefits, companies expanded their coverages to $100 or $200 per week with an extended maximum benefit period allowing them to advertise $50,000 coverage ($200 per week for 250 weeks). State insurance departments began to clamp down on this type of advertising, especially by direct mail sales organizations. It became necessary to express all hospital indemnity plans in terms of the per diem rate. Because maximum dollar benefits could not be emphasized, it became more popular to offer no limit coverage. Now many indemnity plans will cover the patient for the full hospital stay. This presents very little problem since it is very difficult for a patient to remain as a hospital inpatient for an extended period. Hospital review boards, expansion of skilled nursing care and the use of home health care techniques have reduced the hospital's role as a long-term care facility.

Some of the early hospital indemnity plans called for a three-day elimination period for sickness while providing first day coverage for accidents. This did create some problem in determining whether a given claim was for an accident or a sickness. One marketing advantage of the indemnity plans over reimbursement plans is the simplicity of the policy language. If the policy, and therefore the sales piece, need to set out the difference between a sickness and an accident, this detracts from the basic appeal of the product—simplicity.

Some carriers have offered accident only hospital indemnity coverage. This is generally in conjunction with other accident benefits. Such plans have been popular as credit card solicitations or by companies training new agents who need the financial and psychological lift of a few easy sales.

Besides hospital benefits issued as an indemnity, the other medical coverage most easily adapted to this type of payment is nursing home coverage. Many nursing home plans are sold as indemnity contracts or as combination Medicare supplement and indemnity plans.

When the OASDI program was expanded to provide medical care to the elderly in 1966, and when coverage for nursing homes became effective in 1967, changes in the public attitude toward nursing homes took place. These facilities, especially the newer ones or units of a hospital converted to extended care, became an accepted way of treating patients who were recuperating from a serious condition but were not yet well enough to be sent home.

Medicare was supposed to pay for skilled treatment in an extended care facility or an approved nursing home. Medicaid would often pay for a lesser level of treatment called "intermediate care." This left a third level of care that has been called "custodial care." However, it took a few years for Medicare and Medicaid to settle on a distinction between these. Actually, what is classified as one type of treatment in one state may very well be called something else in another.

All of this attention focused on nursing homes created a demand for the individual insurance industry to offer coverages to the public. The indemnity concept seemed most appropriate. However, the problem of defining what level of care to cover and how to clearly spell out the intent of the company has become a serious one. A few states have mandated specific levels of care for those insurers who do offer the coverage. For many companies, the easiest approach is to pick up only claims that have been approved by Medicare. This limits liability, since the definition of skilled care acceptable to Medicare has become restrictive.

2.1.2 HOSPITAL EXPENSE REIMBURSEMENT BENEFITS

As previously noted, indemnity contracts have certain advantages over expense reimbursement plans. However, there are two big disadvantages of this type of coverage as far as the policyholder is concerned, First, the benefits are limited and should be considered as supplemental coverage at best. Second, the coverage has to be constantly upgraded in an inflationary period if it is to provide adequate funds at claim time.

Thus, reimbursement plans are more suited for basic health care coverage. Today there are many varieties of such plans. These developed swiftly in response to the rapid inflation in medical costs which began in the 1960s, and represent a revolution in product design from the older scheduled policies.

Briefly, scheduled hospital expense policies typically had two benefit sections. The first covered room and board expenses. A fixed per diem benefit could be matched to the charges of the local hospital. Most agents knew the fee schedules of the hospitals in their territories and could package policy benefits to those levels. Benefit durations ranged from 21 to 365 days. Payment would be made for actual charges, not to exceed the daily benefit schedules for a period of confinement up to the number of days specified.

For miscellaneous in-hospital expenses, such as operating room, x-rays, medicines, laboratory services or surgical dressings, there was a schedule of allowable amounts. This represented the maximum amounts that would be reimbursed for each of these items. In most policies, outpatient care was not covered, except in some providing emergency room coverage for accidents only. Maternity was generally excluded unless covered at a fixed amount, or a multiple of the daily hospital benefit, in lieu of all other policy benefits. Some policies would include a surgical benefit as an integral part of the basic hospital plan. If so, it would be a scheduled benefit. Coverage for physician visits was not available as a part of the basic plan, but was offered by some companies in riders. Other companies provided this benefit only in a separate policy.

With the escalation of health care costs, the traditional benefits provided by scheduled policies became increasingly inadequate. The initial industry response was to depart from the scheduled miscellaneous in-hospital expense provisions of many policies. Companies came out with an unscheduled or blanket miscellaneous benefit. Usually there was an overall fixed limit, or a multiple of the daily hospital benefit. Many new policies called for coinsurance of 20 percent. This meant that the company paid 80 percent of the ancillary charges while the patient paid the balance.

Some insurers applied the coinsurance factor after a given level of benefits had been paid, such as $500. Thus, the policy would cover the first $500 of in-hospital miscellaneous expenses and 80 percent of any balance up to the benefit maximum. Other carriers would apply the coinsurance at the front end of the claim. Thus they would pay 80 percent of the first $500 and then pay 100 percent up to the policy limit. Still other contracts called for a fixed-dollar deductible under the miscellaneous expense provision. This could be $25, $50 or even $100. All of these provisions were attempts to introduce an awareness on the part of the patient that he had a share in the hospital bill.

With the change to an unscheduled miscellaneous benefit provision, the fixed daily-room-rate benefit became somewhat of a problem. Limits were raised so that higher and higher coverage was offered. Once sold, however, this benefit did not adjust to inflation as easily as did the unscheduled miscellaneous provision. Some companies solved this by sending out automatic upgrade offers. Periodically the daily-room-rate benefit would be increased for a comparable increase in premium. Some companies offered optional added hospital benefits by rider while others simply sold a separate hospital indemnity contract to update the coverage.

Unpredictable economic pressures continued to force changes in policy design resulting in the development of more detailed and comprehensive structures (see Section 2.1.5).

2.1.3 MEDICAL EXPENSE REIMBURSEMENT BENEFITS

Expense reimbursement insurance that pays the fees of physicians or other health care professionals is commonly called *medical expense insurance*. Its popularity followed that of hospital expense coverage and was developed by the same third-party payers.

Problems that hindered the rapid development of medical expense insurance included the fact that it was impractical to cover the first or second doctor visit. For many conditions, the cost of processing the claim would be greater than the policy benefit. For most sicknesses, only one or two sessions with the doctor would be sufficient to cure the patient. Thus, most early medical expense policies and riders excluded payment for the first two or three visits for sickness.

A second problem in designing coverage for these charges was to avoid setting up annuities for physicians who could schedule periodic visits for patients suffering from chronic conditions. Thus, the early plans had a maximum payment for any one accident or sickness.

Another problem faced by carriers writing medical expense insurance in conjunction with surgical coverage was duplication of benefits. Policies commonly specified that benefits were not payable under the medical provisions if they were payable under the surgical benefits.

Some companies did package medical and surgical benefits together in one contract along with benefits for miscellaneous health care expenses incurred outside of a hospital. These included x-rays, laboratory expenses, injections or other medicines administered in a doctor's office, or electrocardiograms. The amounts for these benefits generally were scheduled, as were the comparable in-hospital benefits. Sometimes maternity benefits were included if surgical expenses were covered. This benefit was paid as an indemnity with double benefits often provided for multiple births. Some early policies experimented with out-of-hospital prescription drug benefits.

Because of the cost of handling claims, some of these policies had a special provision that no claim would be paid for less than a minimum amount. It is not known if this discouraged policyholders from submitting small claims or if they were charged more so that the bills exceeded the policy minimums.

These policy benefits were also increased as costs rose in the 1960s. As medical costs continued to rise, this coverage, apart from medical expenses included in major medical plans, began to disappear. By the early 1980s it was almost impossible to purchase individual medical expense insurance as a separate benefit.

2.1.4 SURGICAL EXPENSE REIMBURSEMENT BENEFITS

As previously noted, many policies combined surgical expense benefits with other coverages. The earliest surgical benefits were included in accident policies. In the late 1930s, surgical benefits were included in group hospital plans covering surgery resulting from illness as well as injury. The first such contracts covered only inpatient expenses. Later the coverage was expanded to include surgery performed either in or outside a hospital. Individual hospital or medical expense policies soon appeared with surgical benefits automatically incorporated or available on an optional basis.

The traditional surgical benefit is based on a schedule containing a list of 100 or more common procedures, with a maximum benefit allowed for each operation. The schedule is usually referred to by the amount payable for the highest listed fee payable for any one operation. Thus, a $500 schedule would be one paying up to that sum for the most serious condition. Other operations would be paid for at a lesser amount.

Early schedules had $100 or $150 maximums. With the escalation of surgical fees, as well as the introduction of more complicated procedures, $5,000 schedules became common. Some more liberal policies paid $8,000 or more for certain heart procedures.

Since a surgical schedule includes only the more common operations, the benefit provision usually includes language to indicate that, for any nonlisted procedure, payment will be made on the basis of comparable severity. The claim department of each company will have a *relative value schedule* listing many more operations than are shown in the policy schedule. This would be used to determine comparable severity for a nonlisted operation. The earliest of these was the *California Relative Value Study* published in 1954.

The original *California Relative Value Study* was updated periodically (1957, 1964, 1969 and 1974) to reflect changing values and to include new procedures. However, a California Court decision held that the use of such schedules by physicians and surgeons was a violation of statutes dealing with unfair competition. Thus the 1974 version is the last one available. Companies now have to rely on their medical directors or other staff for information on new procedures or on changes in the relative severity of older ones.

The surgical benefit generally has a special provision for multiple operations. For two or more operations performed through separate incisions, a typical allowance might be the maximum shown for the most costly surgery performed plus 50 percent of the maximum(s) for any other procedure(s) executed during the same operative session. If the multiple procedures require only one incision, payment would normally be limited to the maximum allowed for the most expensive operation performed.

Other special provisions are found in many contracts covering surgical expenses. These may include payment for anesthesia, for an assistant surgeon, or for a second surgical opinion. The last provision has become an important feature in cost containment. There were claims that many surgeries were unnecessary, thus increasing the cost of medical care. A number of states require that this benefit be included in all newly issued policies.

The earliest surgical policies generally contained a clause that would pay only surgical or only medical benefits, but not both. Now the more common practice is to pay both medical and surgical expenses when two separate physicians are involved. It is rare for a policy to provide both medical and surgical fees to the same doctor.

2.1.5 MAJOR MEDICAL BENEFITS

After World War II, great strides were made in medical technology. New drugs and medical procedures practically eliminated many diseases from the list of potentially fatal ailments. Advancements in therapy turned many patients from invalids into useful citizens. However, this was not accomplished without cost. All of these advances, along with a general inflationary trend and a change in our attitude concerning hospital care, exacerbated the cost of health care.

As hospital costs rose and new therapies developed, it soon became apparent that the traditional form of health care insurance needed to change. In the early 1950s a new form of coverage was developed for the group insurance market, and was soon made available on an individual basis. It was the major medical expense benefit policy.

Originally major medical insurance was designed as a supplement to a basic policy. The two contracts were coordinated through the use of a deductible. Sometimes this was a flat sum, such as $500, which was supposed to eliminate all but the catastrophic situations. The second type of benefit integration was known as a *corridor deductible* under which the patient was responsible for $100 (or whatever the corridor in his policy required) of out-of-pocket expenses over and above the basic contract coverage.

Under either type of major medical benefit, there would be a coinsurance factor, usually 75 or 80 percent. This meant that the insurer would pay this share of the eligible expenses and the insured would have to pay the remaining 25 or 20 percent. The early policies specified maximum sums to be paid over the life of the policy; $5,000 was fairly common. As inflation pushed up medical costs, these maximum benefits continued to be increased. Currently maximums of as much as $1 million are common and some contracts have no set limit.

Some of the more recent major medical contracts are not intended to provide coverage that is supplemental to an existing basic policy. These contracts are intended to provide comprehensive coverage for both minor and serious medical situations. The original concept of a deductible and coinsurance is still applicable with a maximum limit, if utilized, that is comparatively large. The deductible has become a means of introducing cost sharing to the consumer. It is usually set at a level that would be financially manageable, yet high enough to reduce the premium for the coverage to an amount that can be budgeted.

A newer feature of these policies is the *out-of-pocket* limit, meaning that the coinsurance split, usually 80-20, is eliminated after the insured has paid a set amount on a given claim. If a policy is issued with a $500 deductible and a $1,000 coinsurance out-of-pocket limit, this means that the insurance company will pay 100 percent of the eligible expenses incurred over $5,500. The claimant pays the first $500 as the deductible. He pays his 20 percent of the next $5,000, or $1,000, as his coinsurance. He then no longer has to share in the payment of additional expenses. This feature makes this type of policy truly catastrophic coverage.

Some of the earlier major medical plans contained benefit limits or scheduled benefits. For example, a policy might have a $50 limit on daily room expenses and/or contain a $1,000 surgical schedule. When inflation caused medical bills to escalate rapidly, these inner limits became sales and persistency drawbacks, and thus were dropped by some companies.

In the early 1980s, health care costs were escalating so rapidly that the individual major medical carriers found it extremely difficult to maintain an adequate balance between premiums and claims. Cost shifting, which was caused when certain indirect patient costs were not included in the payment formula of large-block payers, also exacerbated this problem. For example, expenses for bad debt cases or certain teaching hospital costs were not reimbursed by Medicare, Medicaid, Blue Cross or Health Maintenance Organizations. These expenses would then have to be shifted entirely to the individual payer or to his insurance carrier. Individual insurance companies deciding to remain in the major medical market attempted to find ways to combat this negative cash flow. Some returned to the concept of inner limits and benefit schedules.

One concept favored by certain carriers was to allow the policyholder the right to select an inpatient room limit and/or a surgical schedule level. The higher the benefit level, the greater the premium. This was supposed to make the policyholder more aware of the cost of health care and thus be a more prudent user of that resource. Some of these plans had limits on inpatient ancillary expenses that were balanced with the scheduled room rate level. Another innovation involved the elimination or reduction of deductibles or coinsurance whenever an out-of-hospital facility was used in lieu of inpatient care. Free-standing surgical centers, emergency medical facilities, and well-equipped physicians' offices began to compete with hospitals for health care dollars. The actuaries and attorneys who designed the newer insurance contracts could see that encouragement to stay out of a hospital would mean a reduction in claims paid.

There are six key features of any major medical policy that must be examined in order to understand the actual policy coverage. These are

1. eligible medical expense
2. deductible
3. accumulation period
4. benefit period
5. coinsurance percentage
6. maximum benefit.

Some of these concepts have been briefly touched on, and will be subsequently defined.

The first key element in a major medical policy is *eligible medical expense,* also commonly referred to as *covered medical expense.* This provision describes the various types of expenses the policy covers and any limitations applicable to certain of these expenses. Such a list includes almost all hospital, medical, nursing services, supplies and equipment necessary to treat sickness or injury. Eligible medical expenses will, however, normally include only charges for care and treatment that are prescribed by a physician.

A few of the early plans paid benefits only if the claimant was hospitalized. Out-of-hospital expenses were excluded. It soon became apparent that this fostered unnecessary confinements. Thus, out-of-hospital benefits were included. Current major medical products now include home health care as an eligible expense. Payment for expenses incurred in settings alternative to inpatient care are not only accepted but encouraged.

The *deductible* can be defined as the amount of eligible medical expense incurred and payable by the insured before benefits are payable under the policy. Unlike a hospital expense policy, the major medical policy usually includes a deductible, sometimes a high one.

The major medical deductible may be on either of two bases. Under the *per cause basis,* the deductible amount must be satisfied by eligible medical expenses attributable to the same sickness or injury. The *all cause basis* is satisfied when all eligible expenses incurred by an individual for any variety of covered sicknesses or injuries are accumulated to meet the deductible amount.

For example, assume that an insured, under a policy with a $500 deductible, incurred $420 of eligible expenses for a broken arm. Shortly thereafter, a skin condition arose, for which an additional $160 of expenses was incurred. If the deductible was of the per cause type, the $500 deductible amount would not have been satisfied. Treatment costs of neither of the conditions alone equaled $500. However, the all cause deductible expense of $500 was exceeded by the two occurrences. Usually, an all cause deductible must be satisfied each calendar year.

Another form of major medical deductible is the *variable deductible*. Under this basis the deductible that applies to a particular sickness or injury will be the greater of either the minimum deductible stated in the policy, or an amount equal to all benefit payments received from any other medical expense coverage for the same eligible medical expenses.

It is customary in the major medical policy for the deductible provision to include a statement that if two or more covered persons are injured in the same accident, the deductible amount will be subtracted only once from the sum of the covered medical expenses for all such covered persons. Sometimes included in this provision is the further stipulation that a specified dollar amount will apply as the policy deductible for the entire family in any calendar year when covered expenses for all family members exceed that amount. Alternatively, some policies provide that if two or three people in a family meet the deductible in one year, no further deductible will apply for the rest of the year.

In the typical major medical policy with a per cause deductible, the deductible must be incurred within a stated *accumulation period*. This is simply a specific time period; it commonly ranges from 90 to 180 days. This time limit is in keeping with the basic purpose of major medical insurance, which is to relieve the financial burden of large, unexpected expenses rather than to take care of the relatively small, repetitive type of expense. The latter expenses can be spread out over a long period of time, and can be budgeted.

With a per cause deductible, however, satisfaction of the deductible amount for a given cause within the accumulation period sets up a *benefit period* during which no further deductible is applied for that condition. The benefit periods generally are 1, 2, 3 or 5 years. The period is usually measured from the date on which the first eligible medical expense was incurred. It is

INDIVIDUAL MEDICAL EXPENSE BENEFITS

customary to provide that if the covered person is hospitalized at the time the benefit period would normally expire, the benefit period will be extended until the end of the period of hospital confinement. After a benefit period expires, the covered person may still be incurring eligible medical expense for the same condition, even though not hospitalized. In such cases, the person may establish a new benefit period by meeting the deductible requirements once again.

Once a benefit period is established, any eligible medical expense incurred (over and above the deductible) during the continuation of the benefit period is shared by the insurer and the insured. This sharing is specified by the policy's *coinsurance percentage,* indicating what percent of the eligible medical expenses the insured is responsible for and what percent the insurer covers.

Different coinsurance percentages may be applied to different types of expenses. For example, in a policy containing inside limits on hospital and extended care facility room/board expenses, 100 percent of those charges falling within the applicable inside limits would qualify as eligible medical expense. The remaining types of expenses covered under the policy (those not subject to inside limits) would be payable on the basis of the usual coinsurance sharing.

The coinsurance principle and the resulting cost sharing is intended to motivate the insured to control expenses.

One additional control on the insurer's liability under a major medical policy is the policy's *maximum benefit*. This simply specifies the maximum amount payable by the insurer. The maximum benefit applies in some policies to each separate sickness or injury, and in others it is expressed as an *aggregate maximum* or *lifetime maximum* that applies to all sicknesses and injuries of each covered person. The former approach is often referred to as a *per cause maximum.* From the insured's standpoint, the per cause maximum is more liberal than the aggregate maximum for the same dollar amount.

To summarize, under a per cause contract, only expenses due to a single condition may be used to satisfy the deductible stated in the policy. The time during which such expenses are accumulated is the accumulation period. Whenever the deductible is satisfied within the accumulation period, a benefit period is established. Thereafter, all expenses relating to the original condition will be eligible for reimbursement. The actual amount paid is governed by the coinsurance factor. If expenses are very large, the maximum limit may apply and terminate coverage for the condition which was the cause of the claim.

For a contract with an all cause provision, expenses from any covered condition may be used to satisfy the deductible. Normally the period used to begin accumulating these charges is the start of a new calendar year. Once the deductible is satisfied, all further expenses for any covered condition will be eligible for reimbursement. Again, the coinsurance factor will be applied. Sometimes an out-of-pocket limit will eliminate the policyholder's copayment once the scheduled limit is reached. At the close of the calendar year claim payments cease unless a new deductible is satisfied. If the total payments under an all cause policy exceed the scheduled maximum, then no more benefits are payable and the policy becomes null and void insofar as that one insured is concerned. If other persons are covered under the policy, it will remain in force. If not, the policy would be terminated.

2.1.6 SPECIFIED DISEASE BENEFITS

Policies have been designed to provide coverage for certain specified diseases. Such policies have been developed to provide an inexpensive form of supplemental insurance providing financial protection against losses associated with the specified diseases. Originally these policies were issued to cover losses from polio.

With the advent of the polio vaccine, many of the companies that had been successful in the marketing of the product added a few uncommon diseases and continued to push the sale of this type of coverage. Applicants were attracted by the modest premium and the high policy limits.

When major medical products eliminated the high benefit appeal, some carriers added cancer coverage to the list of specified diseases. Soon companies were issuing cancer policies without any other specified diseases.

There are two types of cancer policies, schedule and indemnity. The former has specified benefits for each of the various types of expenses. A typical cancer policy providing scheduled benefits would include a daily hospital benefit plus coverage for surgery, doctors' visits, nursing care, radiotherapy, chemotherapy, blood transfusion charges and possibly drugs.

The specified per diem benefit is paid for each day the claimant stays in the hospital. It is paid regardless of the actual hospital charge. A number of variations of this benefit can be found in the marketplace. For example, the daily benefit may vary by the length of the hospital confinement, paying $100 for the first 7 days and $50 thereafter. Or, the benefit might be $100 for the first 90 days of confinement and $200 thereafter. Some plans have a maximum on the amount of total payment under this benefit. This maximum can be expressed for the lifetime of the policy or for the duration of the particular illness.

Benefits paid as the result of a surgical operation are dependent upon the type of operation performed. A surgical schedule lists the amounts paid for each type of operation. Amounts paid for unlisted operations will be determined by the time and difficulty in comparison with similar listed operations.

INDIVIDUAL MEDICAL EXPENSE BENEFITS

Some policies provide additional benefits for an anesthesiologist. These are sometimes based on a schedule similar to the surgical schedule. Others merely specify a percentage, such as 15 or 20 percent, of the surgical schedule.

Doctors' visits are usually paid as a per diem benefit for each day attending physicians call on the claimant while hospitalized.

A special benefit is sometimes paid toward expenses for drugs and medicine rendered while the claimant is confined in a hospital. The benefit may be expressed as a percentage of the hospital confinement benefit, or it may be stated as a per diem amount.

Another common benefit provides a daily allowance for special nursing services while hospitalized (other than those provided by the hospital).

Benefits for radiotherapy and chemotherapy are usually provided on a blanket basis. They are often equal to whatever charges are incurred, subject to a lifetime maximum.

Blood and plasma benefits also frequently equal the charges to the claimant. The benefit usually has a lifetime maximum.

Many policies also pay charges for ambulance services, subject to certain limits. The limit may be a lifetime limit, a per confinement limit, or a combination thereof. Some plans provide a benefit designed to assist with medically necessary transportation expenses, other than ambulance charges. This benefit would generally be subject to some overall lifetime maximum.

Should a hospital confinement last for an unusually long time, many plans will provide for a special benefit during the latter part of the confinement. For example, a benefit of $5,000 or $10,000 may be paid for each month in the hospital after the 90th day. This benefit is paid in lieu of the normal schedule benefits.

The second type of cancer policy is the indemnity plan. It usually provides only a specified per diem benefit for every day spent in the hospital. Some plan designs call for a variation by the length of the hospital confinement. For example, the daily indemnity for the first 90 days of confinement might be $200 and, for days after the 90th, it might be $400.

In addition to the daily hospital indemnity, some plans also provide an outpatient benefit. This often takes the form of a per diem benefit, $100 for instance, for each day certain types of treatment are received on an outpatient basis.

A feature of the indemnity plan is that the benefits paid are not related to actual charges for the medical services rendered. The plans may have some type of aggregate lifetime benefit, but many times there is no dollar limit on total benefits.

2.1.7 MEDICARE SUPPLEMENT BENEFITS

In 1966 the individual health insurance market for persons age 65 and over was drastically changed with the start of the Medicare program. Benefits under this law are divided into two sections. Part A is the Hospital Insurance Program. It was originally available to all persons age 65 and over, but later was available without charge only to individuals eligible for OASDI retirement benefits. Others are able to buy into the program by paying a monthly premium. The coverage is funded through the OASDI system.

Part B, the Supplementary Medical Insurance Program, is voluntary and requires the payment of a monthly premium. However, this pays only a portion of the monies needed to provide the mandated benefits. The bulk of the funds for this coverage come from general tax revenues.

Part A covers hospital, skilled nursing facility (SNF), and home health care, as well as certain therapy services. It is oriented towards acute care, and its coverage provisions are based on the concept of a benefit period or *spell of illness,* a period that begins on the first day an individual has been in a hospital and ends when an individual has been out of the hospital or SNF for 60 consecutive days. In each benefit period, individuals are entitled to up to 90 days of inpatient hospital care, up to 100 days of post-hospital SNF or other acceptable alternative care. If the full 90 days of hospital benefits are exhausted during a spell of illness, a beneficiary may draw on 60 additional lifetime reserve days.

Part B provides coverage for physician, medical and other health services (a wide range of services including diagnostic tests and x-rays, outpatient hospital services, durable medical equipment, ambulance service, prosthetic devices, and physical therapy).

Both parts of Medicare contain cost sharing provisions, that is, deductibles and coinsurance. The law requires that, under Part A, the inpatient hospital deductible and hospital and SNF coinsurance amounts be adjusted annually to reflect the rising costs of health care.

Under Part A there is an initial hospital deductible related to the cost of one day's stay as an inpatient. In 1987 the initial hospital deductible was set at $520. The daily copayment for the 61st through the 90th day of care was 25 percent of this figure, and the copayment for each lifetime reserve day was 50 percent of it. The SNF copayment for each day of care from the 21st through the 100th day was one-eighth of the initial hospital deductible.

Part B of Medicare pays 80 percent of *reasonable charges,* defined as the amount of the actual charge of a physician or supplier that can be recognized for payment under Medicare. The beneficiary pays 20 percent coinsurance. Since actual charges generally exceed the reasonable and customary charges, beneficiaries are responsible for the difference unless the physician or supplier accepts an assignment. In addition, the beneficiary must pay an annual deductible. It originally was $50, and has been increased periodically. In 1987 it was $75.

A number of items and services are not covered under either of Medicare's two insurance programs. These items and services include custodial nursing home care, custodial home care, most out-of-hospital prescription drugs, dental care, eyeglasses and eye examinations, immunizations, most foot care and homemaker services.

When the federal government established the Medicare system in 1966, many insurers felt that the market for health care coverage for persons age 65 and over was gone. Some did not care, because they believed that this was a nonprofit market. A few companies saw Medicare as an opportunity to sell supplemental coverage. Some of them added a rider to existing policies for senior citizens. It provided that the original benefits would be paid, but the coverage would be secondary to Medicare. Thus, hospital expense plans would pick up the first $40 of any confinement (this was the 1966 Medicare Part A deductible) and any coinsurance payable after 60 days. Medical and/or surgical coverage would pay up to $50 (the original Part B deductible) plus 20 percent of any additional expenses. For most policies, this represented a much lower anticipated claims cost than for the pre-Medicare benefits. Thus, premium reductions were offered.

A few companies saw that this new program should not be treated as a minor product. They designed riders or new policies to be fully integrated with the new Medicare program. When the Medicare deductible rose to $44 in 1968 and other changes were made in the program, some companies developed a flexible plan paying benefits that automatically adjusted each year to keep pace with the changes in Medicare benefits. Many of these policies contained a premium formula that allowed rates to rise automatically with benefits.

Most of these early Medicare supplement policies covered hospital expenses only. Some paid for doctors' visits while hospitalized, but did not cover out-of-hospital expenses. They did not provide any coverage for nursing home or prescription drug expenses. Thus, they were rather limited. Some covered the Medicare initial deductible while others picked up expenses only when the coinsurance provision became effective after a 60-day confinement.

Soon senior citizens began to realize that the biggest gaps in Medicare were not in the category of inpatient care. Nursing home expenses, charges by doctors who would not accept a Medicare assignment and prescription drug costs were a serious drain on their limited incomes. A second generation of policies and riders to upgrade the original products was developed.

Some carriers continued the old concept of providing scheduled medical and surgical benefits to senior citizens while others followed the major medical approach with Medicare being considered the basic plan. Most carriers still sold Part A or Part B supplementary benefits as two separate policies. A few carriers also offered nursing home benefits, again as a separate contract. Most of these covered skilled care only, the same as Medicare. This was somewhat misleading, since the vast majority of nursing home confinements were classed as intermediate or custodial. Very few policies covered this level of care.

Prescription drug coverage was also difficult to obtain. Because of the rather high claim handling expense compared to the benefits to be provided, many companies did not consider this a viable benefit. Thus, the prescription drug benefit never was a popular part of an individual Medicare supplement package.

In 1980, as part of the periodic amendment of OASDI, a new law was passed by Congress. It included the Baucus Amendment, named after the senator who sponsored it. It established the date of July 1, 1982 for the various states to enact laws regulating Medicare supplement insurance. These specified minimum benefit standards, minimum loss ratio standards and special advertising limitations, as well as other provisions intended to regulate the sale of senior citizen health insurance.

Among the more important features of the Baucus Amendment was the establishment of 60 percent as the minimum acceptable loss ratio for an individual Medicare supplement policy. Some states required higher standards of 65 percent or more. Another key requirement was that any contract advertised or marketed as a Medicare supplement policy must cover both Part A and Part B benefits. The initial deductibles did not need to be included, but the various copayment gaps of Medicare had to be insured. Benefits were required to escalate with the yearly increases in the Medicare deductibles.

A few companies developed a "bare bones" Medicare supplement policy. Some used this plan as their economy model but pushed the sale of a package that included additional benefits. Popular additions included coverage for the Part A initial deductible, the Part B deductible, some nursing home benefits, coverage for doctors' charges above the level accepted by Medicare or perhaps some type of coverage for prescription drugs. The most common of the drug plans would pay for medication required only after a period of hospital confinement and then for a limited period, such as 30 days. An alternative plan would pay for drugs on an annual all cause basis, but with a $50 or $100 deductible. Each of these drug plans would pay 80 percent of the actual charge, up to a stated maximum.

A common Medicare supplement nursing home plan would pick up benefits in a skilled nursing home only if Medicare approved the stay. Coverage would include the copayment amounts through the 100th day with perhaps additional benefits thereafter so long as the level of care remained the same. A few policies would pay for skilled or intermediate care provided there was a prior hospital stay and entrance into the nursing home following immediately or shortly thereafter. Medicare supplement nursing home benefits usually would cover only 200 days confinement, with some plans offering 365 days coverage.

Some Medicare supplement writers pick up all or a part of the Part B doctors' fees that are not accepted by the federal claims payment agency. As noted, a doctor could agree to take an assignment from the patient. In this case, he would have to accept whatever the government paid and would be able to collect only that portion of the Part B deductible still applicable plus the 20 percent copayment from the patient. By the mid-1980s, the amount of surgical or medical fees allowed by Medicare had been reduced to a lesser amount than what most doctors felt adequate. Therefore, fewer and fewer of them were accepting assignments. Most were billing their patients for an extra 20, 30 or 40 percent over and above what Medicare said was proper. For those persons treated by doctors who would not accept an assignment of fees, insurance for these excess fees was practical. An example of such a benefit, in addition to paying the 20 percent Medicare copayment, would also pay all (or a share, such as 50 percent) of the difference between what the doctor charged and what Medicare allowed. The actual charges would still have to meet a reasonable and customary test. Thus, a surgeon could not bill the patient $5,000 for an operation that should have cost no more than $1,000 and expect to be paid the extra $4,000.

These Medicare supplement plans are generally available with either very large or unlimited maximum sums. Some contain limitations or restrictions on certain benefits. For example, coverage for in-hospital care might end after 365 days, nursing care after 200 days and doctors' fees after $5,000 per year. Some of these limits were used to conform to the minimum standards of the Baucus Amendment. Most companies, however, decided that the fewer the limitations the easier it was to sell a product. Since the federal government was extremely anxious to move patients out of hospitals and provide for only urgent skilled nursing care, very costly confinements have been minimized. Insurance carriers benefited from this philosophy and reduced their policy restrictions and monetary limitations in order to remain competitive with companies that had taken a more liberal attitude in this regard.

Projection about the future funding of Medicare benefits indicate that some rather drastic changes will have to be made in the amount of funds, the benefit level, the payment system or a combination of all three. Thus it is very likely that some rather severe changes in the program will be forthcoming. This will affect companies heavily involved in the Medicare supplement market. As in the past, there will probably be a number of individual insurers ready to fill the gaps with a whole new generation of policies.

2.1.8 ACCIDENT MEDICAL EXPENSE BENEFITS

Even though the earliest form of medical reimbursement insurance offered to individuals was for accidental injuries, this type of coverage is no longer a major line for most health insurance companies. The emergence of broad coverage hospital and medical policies and major medical products has made the need for accident medical expense coverage largely redundant.

There are three categories of individual accident medical plans available at the time of this writing. The first is travel accident coverage. These plans are a throw back to the earliest health insurance contracts. An individual can purchase coverage for a single trip, for a few days or weeks, or as a continuous policy form. Most of these plans are sold basically as accidental death coverage with medical reimbursement benefits provided as fringe benefits. These generally contain blanket medical expense reimbursement provisions with comparatively high limits.

The most common form of single trip policies are those available for air passengers. A few years ago these were very popular, with sales machines or booths scattered throughout airport passenger terminals. The appeal of this type of coverage seems to have worn off, perhaps because the frequent flyer has found that for the price of coverage for four or five flights he can obtain coverage for a few months or perhaps the whole year. These plans are offered by specialty agents or through the mail, particularly to persons who belong to travel organizations or who use credit cards.

Another form of accident plan that is often sold through the mail or by specialty agents is the all-accident or 24-hour-accident policy. It features accidental death and dismemberment benefits with secondary medical coverage. A few companies have built up a very profitable block of business by concentrating on the sale of a simple accident policy through an agency force that found this coverage easy to sell and useful as a door opener for other products.

The third type of accident medical expense product is the student accident or sports accident contract. Much of this coverage is sold on a group basis, but it is also available as individual coverage. Some insurance agents use these plans as an entry into homes where there is a potential for other sales.

The student plans may be 24-hour coverage or only for school time plus an hour before and an hour after school to allow for getting to and from class. These plans provide blanket coverage with moderate dollar limits. Many plans have an exclusion for benefits paid or payable under automobile insurance contracts. These are the most serious and costly injuries involving school children. This exclusion eliminates duplicate coverage and potential claim problems. Many of these plans exclude coverage for injuries incurred while engaging in organized school sports.

School sports policies, as well as other sports coverages, are almost always sold on a group basis. However, some individual student accident plans will cover injuries for any sport other than football by paying an extra premium. Also, a few companies will insure individual athletes for amateur competition.

Closely akin to this coverage is camp insurance that covers young people while away at camp. Most of these plans are offered through the camp, either on a group basis or through a local agent who specializes in this coverage.

2.1.9 DENTAL INSURANCE BENEFITS

Dental expense insurance provides reimbursement for the cost of dental services and supplies and encourages preventive care. The coverage normally provides for oral examinations (including cleaning and x-rays), fillings, extractions, inlays, bridgework and root canals, as well as oral surgery. Orthodontia may be covered with special dollar limits, coinsurance or both. This coverage was introduced in 1959 on a group basis. In recent years a few individual carriers have experimented with comparable coverage. It has not really caught on, but there are contracts available in the individual market.

The principal problem with offering dental insurance on an individual basis is one of antiselection. This is a concern not only when the policy is issued, but any time a contract comes up for renewal. Only those who know that they have some necessary dental work would be eager to purchase a plan. Once the work was completed, the incentive to renew the coverage would be diminished.

Following are the benefits available under one dental expense policy currently available on an individual or family basis. (The company will not insure children unless they are included as dependents under the family policy.) Note the waiting periods for the various benefits and the fact that there are no benefits for the preventive care or routine maintenance coverage found in most group contracts.

- All benefits are subject to a $25 calendar year deductible.
- For dental work resulting from injury, benefits are payable for all reasonable and customary expenses with a 20 percent coinsurance and a $750 limit per accident.
- For dental expense resulting from disease, there is a general surgical schedule for procedures such as root canal. These are covered after a 3-month waiting period. Also, conditions necessitating fillings are payable based on a schedule with a 6-month waiting period. For crowns there is a 9-month waiting period with a limit of two during the first policy year. This is doubled on the second policy anniversary. Bridgework or dentures are payable according to a schedule, also with a 9-month waiting period.
- X-rays are payable only when necessitated by some procedure included in one of the other parts of the policy. Diagnostic x-rays are not included.
- Payment will be made for general anesthesia when required in connection under either the accidental injury or the disease sections of the contract.

2.1.10 MATERNITY BENEFITS

Pregnancy and childbirth are not insurable risks under the usual definition of the term, and many health insurance people would wish that these benefits had never found their way into the general scheme of coverage. Maternity benefits got their start in the 1930s and 1940s when the initial growth of hospital expense coverage was viewed more under the concept of prepayment than as true insurance.

Under the prepayment concept, it becomes logical to prepay hospital maternity expenses along with other forms of confinement, but the idea remains basically foreign to a true insurance concept of medical coverage. Nevertheless, the public has come to expect hospital benefit plans to include maternity benefits and the industry has, for the most part, felt obliged to meet this expectation.

Originally insurers attempted to avoid offering any option to the policyholder covering the inclusion of pregnancy coverage. The pregnancy benefit was automatic under all family policies covering husband and wife, and automatically excluded unless both were covered, without exception. Later, some companies covered married women whether or not the husband was covered.

Some insurers provided maternity benefits if both husband and wife were insured on the same contract, but they would allow the purchase of separate individual contracts with no maternity benefits.

The original maternity benefit was a blanket sum. It was not uncommon to double the basic benefit if the delivery involved a caesarean operation or a multiple birth. Some carriers offered a graded benefit. This was common where the benefit was optional. Later, some hospital expense policies replaced the small lump-sum benefit for maternity with a provision that provided a pregnancy benefit equal to 10 times the scheduled daily room benefit.

It would be possible for a policyholder to have three different policies—a hospital expense plan, a medical-surgical plan and a hospital indemnity plan—each with a maternity benefit. Even though each contract stated that the maternity payment contained therein was in lieu of all other policy benefits, there was no coordination of benefits between contracts. Thus, it was possible to obtain comparably substantial pregnancy coverage through the use of multiple policies.

Early individual major medical contracts avoided any problems with maternity coverage because the large deductibles were high enough to exclude all but the most complicated claims. As medical costs rose and major medical plans were offered as comprehensive coverage, the deductible was not sufficient to eliminate childbirth and pregnancy related claims. The immediate solution was to eliminate all such conditions.

This was changed, however, in the late 1970s with the promulgation in many states of a mandated benefit dealing with complications of pregnancy. Because of the widespread applicability of these requirements, most carriers included this coverage in their contracts. This provision requires normal policy benefits for any condition that is considered a complication of pregnancy.

Another benefit directly related to the maternity benefit is coverage for newborn children. The earliest individual medical expense policies would not cover newborn children even under family policies. Although some carriers provided automatic coverage upon notification of birth, congenital defects were excluded.

By the early 1970s there was enough concern about insurance protection against congenital defects that the National Association of Insurance Commissioners (NAIC) endorsed a model bill providing for regular policy benefits to be paid for the "treatment of medically diagnosed congenital defects and birth abnormalities." This coverage was to provide for any children born to an insured under any policy providing either expense-incurred or indemnity-type benefits. By the mid-1970s almost every state had promulgated laws or regulations mandating this coverage. The benefits were included in existing policies by rider or endorsement and in all new policies as a separate benefit.

By the early 1980s a few states had gone so far as to amend the required coverage to include well-baby care. A typical requirement states that coverage must include "routine nursery care and pediatric charges for a well, newly born child for up to five full days in a hospital nursery, or until the mother is discharged."

2.2 EXCLUSIONS AND LIMITATIONS

All individual medical expense policies contain exclusions and limitations. Some are characteristic of all lines of insurance and some are particular to medical expense policies. Exclusions common to all insurance products are losses resulting from preexisting conditions, war, full-time active military duty and intentionally self-inflicted injuries.

Some of the more common exclusions and limitations unique to medical expense policies are:

- Workers Compensation: Under workers compensation laws, insurance protects workers against medical expenses resulting from occupational illness or accident. To avoid duplication of coverage, sickness or injury covered under this type of law is excluded from most individual health policies.
- Government Plans: Care or treatment paid for through any federal, state, or other government plan or law is excluded. This also applies to services

and facilities provided in a hospital owned or operated by the government unless the covered person is legally required to pay for the care.
- Normal Pregnancy and Routine Well-Baby Care: These were discussed in Section 2.1.10. Special benefit provisions offer coverage of expenses associated with normal pregnancy and some states have mandated coverage for well-baby care.
- Cosmetic Surgery: In the absence of a specific policy provision, cosmetic surgery would not come within the scope of coverage because it is neither a sickness or an injury. However, many insurers specifically exclude expenses resulting from cosmetic surgery so that there can be no misunderstanding. Reconstructive surgery following an injury, disease or previous surgery is not considered cosmetic surgery.
- Dental Care or Treatment: Dental insurance was discussed in Section 2.1.9. Most individual medical expense policies exclude dental care or treatment except when it is necessitated by an injury, because it is considered to be an expense that can be budgeted. In some policies, coverage is provided for hospital charges when hospitalization is required for a dental procedure, such as a difficult extraction.
- Eyeglasses and Hearing Aids: Medical expense policies generally exclude coverage for eye-glasses and hearing aids, as well as examinations for prescribing and fitting them. These are considered to be expenses that can be budgeted.
- Mental or Nervous Disorders: This is discussed in Section 2.3. Specific coverages for these conditions are mandated in several states.
- Drug Addiction: This is discussed in Section 2.3. Insurers have tended to exclude coverage for drug addiction on the theory that the condition is at the control of the insured.
- Alcoholism: This is discussed in Section 2.3. Insurers have tended to exclude coverage for alcoholism on the theory that the condition is at the control of the insured.

2.3 REGULATORY CONCERNS

The history of health insurance is replete with regulatory or judicial action and company reaction. An example of this interaction is in the definition of terms. Consider the definition of a doctor. It is easy to draft a policy that reads: "We will pay for all doctors' expenses incurred...." However, what the policy pays for can vary considerably from state to state. Each jurisdiction has its own law or regulation defining the term. Most of these are due to legislative action resulting from lobbying efforts of the various allied practitioner groups. Thus, in various states, payment for doctors' expenses could include the fees of podiatrists, dentists, optometrists, chiropractors, physical therapists, psychologists, social workers, speech pathologists, audiologists, marriage counselors, nurse midwives, nurse practitioners, osteopaths or practitioners of oriental medicine. Some states merely require payment for all licensed practitioners of the healing arts.

The major concern companies have is that of control. A carrier needs to be aware of the regulations in each state in which it operates. This includes knowing not only which of these allied practitioners is approved for payment, but also the scope of the treatment they may perform. For example, some of these health professionals use hypnosis or special diets as parts of their treatments. If their state licenses do not provide for those types of practice, then insurance payment is not required.

"Hospital" is another term that needs to be clearly defined in a health insurance contract. There was a time when some doctors, especially in remote rural areas, would have a few beds available for patients who needed a place to stay overnight or for a day or two because travel between their homes and the office was inconvenient. These were called hospitals and the charges for accommodations would be billed to the patient's insurance company. There were instances of children being left to spend a few days at these facilities in lieu of hiring a baby sitter while parents were out of town. Insurers, therefore, used restrictive language to limit payment to hospital confinements that were medically essential. The following is a definition of a *hospital:*

> An institution which is operated pursuant to law for the care and treatment of sick and injured persons at the expense of the patient, has organized facilities for diagnosis and surgery, and which has continuous 24-hour nursing service by or under the supervision of a registered nurse. It does not mean convalescent, maternity, nursing, rest or extended care facilities, or facilities operated exclusively for treatment of the aged, drug addict or alcoholic, whether such facilities are operated as a separate institution or as a section of an institution operated as a hospital.

Certain states would not allow this type of restrictive language to be used. In some cases the objection was to the requirement that surgical facilities needed to be contained within the four walls of the institution. At least one state objected to the 24-hour nursing requirement. Most of the objections were related to the language eliminating facilities or special units of a facility set up to treat drug addicts or alcoholics. A few states have mandated benefits for the treatment of these conditions. Thus, a definition of hospital that excludes this coverage is not acceptable.

When state insurance departments first objected to a specific definition or insisted that special language be used, the carriers generally would use a special rider or endorsement to modify the objectionable wording. This was because individual health insurance contracts were printed on one large sheet of paper folded over to make an 8.5"x 14" document. To have a special form for each state would have been complicated and expensive. In the 1960s and

1970s, many companies changed over to a different contract format. The new structure consisted of an 8.5″ x 11″ cover page followed by any number of individual pages containing a schedule, a list of benefits, policy definitions, required provisions and so on. It was then a rather simple task to have special pages for those states requiring special language or benefits. Many companies began using computer issued policies, so control of the forms was further simplified.

As mentioned previously, some states will not allow health contracts to exclude payment to facilities that treat alcoholism or drug addiction. This is because the legislatures in these states have seen fit to mandate special benefits for the treatment of these conditions. One of the reasons for these statutes is to pass along the expenses of treating patients with alcohol or drug problems from the public to the private sector. Another reason is that it is supposed to be cheaper to treat these patients for their addiction rather than to wait and pay for the more expensive conditions that may arise if they are not cured. One positive feature of these laws is that they require outpatient as well as inpatient benefits. In the past, many persons who needed treatment for drug or alcohol addiction were hospitalized with some other diagnosis. The inpatient charges were much greater than the cost of care rendered to the insured as an outpatient.

Some states have mandated coverage for care provided in special state owned or operated facilities. This places insurance companies in a very awkward position. Certain state agencies have paid insurance premiums on behalf of individuals who are then confined in state institutions. Insurers end up paying the bills for these persons who would otherwise be cared for at taxpayer expense. This is especially true where mental illness benefits are mandated.

A number of states require some coverage for mental conditions. However, there is no uniformity among states. This makes claims handling very difficult. It also complicates underwriting. For example, it is difficult to prove that a parent had prior knowledge of a drug or mental problem his or her teenager showed symptoms of shortly after a family policy was issued. When mental illness coverage is mandated, it can be very costly.

It is becoming common practice for companies to include some sort of mental illness coverage in their hospital expense reimbursement or major medical plan, even in states where such coverage is not required. However, there are usually limits on both inpatient and outpatient benefits.

Two other benefits not included in policies a few years ago are now usually provided because of mandated coverage requirements. Those are home health care and ambulatory surgical-center coverages. Individual state laws and regulations regarding home health care are as varied as are the rules governing other mandated benefits. The logic behind each regulation is the same, however. When a licensed home health agency can provide care or treatment equivalent to that available as an inpatient, then the policy must provide for reimbursement of the home health care expenses. Some states allow for deductibles and/or coinsurance. Most have a limit on the number of treatments that need to be provided. Some make a distinction between coverage to be provided for patients who are terminally ill and those who are not. Most states are not specific about what constitutes home health care, but some very carefully enumerate the services to be included.

The other recent addition to mandated coverages is ambulatory surgical center expense. For years, surgery was performed in a hospital except for a few minor procedures such as suturing a small wound. These took place in a physician's office. When hospital costs rose to the point where one day's stay cost hundreds of dollars, it became apparent that some surgery could be performed outside the hospital at considerable savings. A number of surgical procedures require only the use of a fully equipped operating room with facilities for general anesthesia and a room for the patient to rest for six or eight hours after surgery. These surgeries had always been performed in a hospital with the patient remaining overnight in a regular hospital room.

Some surgeons realized that if they could have a fully equipped operating room and a few recovery rooms in a facility separate from a hospital, the cost would be considerably reduced and patient control would be increased. Thus, the concept of the free-standing or ambulatory surgical center was born. At first, one major drawback to the spread of such facilities was the reluctance of insurance carriers to pay for many of the expenses incurred in these surgical centers.

In 1971, Arizona became the first state to mandate the inclusion of coverage for these facilities on the same basis as if the procedure were performed in a hospital. Other states followed over the next few years. Many insurance carriers then began to pay these claims in all jurisdictions by administrative practice. Now, this benefit is found in almost all hospital and major medical policies.

Several states have passed legislation mandating the offering of benefits for *hospice* care, a palliative and supportive care rendered to persons with terminal illnesses. It also includes counseling for families to help overcome emotional suffering. The hospice care usually must be under the supervision of a physician, and must meet standards established by a public health agency.

Another regulatory action that dates back to the mid-1970s is the establishment of minimum standards for health insurance products. Besides the special mandated benefits already mentioned, about half of the states have now adopted a version of the Accident and Sickness Minimum Standards Model Bill first adopted by the NAIC in 1975. This model bill has been revised several times since then, and will probably be updated periodically in the future.

As has been noted, the 1970s and 1980s brought a rapid increase in state regulation of health insurance. This was due in part to pressures from the federal level. The Baucus Amendment mandated that the state take regulatory action with regard to Medicare supplement products. Consumer groups have pushed the various state legislatures to pass laws having a drastic effect on the what, how and to whom of health insurance sales. Coverage for persons who are unemployed, divorced, widowed or disabled has been mandated in some states. It is likely that this activity will increase.

In a few states, there are special coverage pools for persons who are unable to obtain insurance through normal channels due to disability or handicap. It is very likely that more of these pools will be established. Bills authorizing similar programs are pending in numerous state legislatures. The main feature of these pools is that they are open to anyone who has been rejected for standard coverage. Rates are set at no more than 35 or 50 percent above standard premiums. This means that there needs to be a subsidy for the balance of the claims cost and all of the administrative costs of the program. These expenses are borne by all the insurance carriers (in some states self insurers are included) who write health insurance in the state.

The benefits under these plans are fairly comprehensive, with a carve out for any Medicare coverage. The plans generally include all of the benefits a liberal group major medical policy would offer, including an out-of-pocket limit on the coinsurance provision.

In some states, there are proposals to open these programs to any state resident, regardless of medical condition. It is reasoned that this would attract many standard risks, thus spreading the cost for substandard insureds over a broader base. In turn, this would mean a lower premium for pool participants and, perhaps, this would eliminate the need for private insurance. Obviously, this is just one step away from a national health care program.

Another proposal being considered by some states is the requirement that insurance coverage be expanded to include certain medical or surgical procedures that have been excluded in the past. Organ transplants are an example. The industry's reasoning behind the denial of such coverage in the past has been that the American Medical Association did not recognize these as traditional forms of medicine. However, now that certain organ transplants are becoming more common, many insurers are paying for them. This still leaves unresolved whether or not the implantation of an artificial heart would be paid for. It is possible that the states will mandate this coverage, taking the decision out of the hands of insurance executives.

Also to be decided is what to do about alternative forms of cancer treatment or the use of diet as a medical means to control various conditions. In some states the political climate is such that the legalization of almost any type of so-called medical procedure is possible. Thus, in a few years health insurance may have to pay for a large number of new procedures and disciplines currently excluded.

2.4 LONG-TERM CARE

The treatment of Medicare patients in alternative sites has become exceedingly important. The senior citizen segment of the United States population is growing much faster than any other. The number of persons over age 80 is increasing by geometric proportions. This is due in part to the medical care and attention being given to our elderly. Senior citizens who once would not have survived are now becoming octogenarians. But many are in frail health and in need of special treatment.

Nursing home and other long-term care alternatives are much in demand. If funding was available, many more facilities than currently exist could be filled. Insurance would seem to be in demand and easily marketed. However, very few insurance carriers offer nursing home or alternative care beyond the 100 days coverage of Medicare or the added 100 or 265 days of skilled care offered by some carriers.

One reason private insurers have not entered the long term care market is Medicaid. This is a companion to Medicare. It became effective at the same time in 1966 and provides medical benefits for the poor, near poor, or those who become medically indigent. The program is partially funded by the federal government, but is administered by each state. Many senior citizens have been able to qualify for Medicaid nursing home benefits by using the "spend down" procedure. Under this procedure, a senior citizen can dispose of property and transfer assets until remaining income and assets are below the Medicaid eligibility level.

Now Medicaid funds are being reduced at the same time as demand for long term care is increasing. There has been a tightening of the rules for eligibility, so that it is much more difficult now to qualify for Medicaid nursing home benefits. Various government and community groups are looking to the private insurance sector for an expansion of the number of carriers offering long-term care policies. The insurance industry has examined this market and has developed some recommendations. The following is taken from a report made by a Health Insurance Association of America committee on long term care.

> Financial protection against the cost of long term care may well become the major health financing issue in the coming decades. From an insurance perspective, factors which must be considered in any insurance decision are more difficult to resolve in the long term care area than with respect to acute medical coverage in the under age 65 population. To protect companies from undue risk, precise policy language and plan design are critical if the product line is to be successfully marketed. Anticipated high premium

levels and the potential for adverse selection may be minimized if products were attractive to younger individuals. Capital accumulation products with cash settlement options and/or the ability to convert to a combination retirement and long term care benefit may stimulate demand in younger age categories.

Another consideration is the potential for cost escalation. The accelerating growth in the nursing home industry during the 1970s was, in large measure, due to the expansion of public programs that finance long term care. The concomitant pressures on government budgets have been well documented. New products may fuel another round of inflation in the long-term care area, threatening the financial integrity of private programs and creating additional pressures on the public sector.

Finally, changing demographics and budgetary constraints may force a reexamination of the question of responsibility and the extent of individual and family obligation to meet long term care needs. Tax incentives and other public measures should be considered as stimuli for increased consumer involvement.

Chapter 3

INDIVIDUAL DISABILITY INCOME BENEFITS
by W. Duane Kidwell, F.S.A.

The individual health insurance business encompasses all forms of policies providing benefits in the event of accident or illness. Chapter 2 dealt with policies that reimburse the insured for medical expense. This chapter describes contracts to reimburse the insured for income lost while totally or partially disabled and for business expenses incurred while disabled. It also includes policies providing advance payments against economic losses that a thriving business suffers from a permanent loss of a key employee.

In this chapter the major disability income benefit plans are described, and the nuances of defining disability and of determining eligibility are highlighted for the reader's examination. The discussion concludes with considerations regarding the emerging role of rehabilitation coverage in disability income plans.

3.1 TOTAL DISABILITY INCOME BENEFITS

Disability income insurance is primarily designed to provide income on a monthly basis. Benefits begin after an initial period of disablement following accident or injury, called the *elimination period* or the *waiting period,* and continue until the earlier of recovery, death or the end of the benefit period. The benefit period is determined at the time of policy issue. It can be as short as a few months, but more frequently benefits are payable to age 65 and in some circumstances for life. The amount of basic monthly income benefit is also determined at the time of policy issue, often by a formula relating the benefit amount to the income actually lost.

The benefit clause in a disability income policy specifies the contract coverage and conditions. The terms "income" and "disability" are defined along with the elimination and benefit periods and the method of computing the benefit amount.

The definition of income is usually restricted to earned income, including salaries or wages, bonuses, commissions and any other compensation the person receives or is entitled to receive from daily vocational efforts. In contrast to this, income that is not considered insurable under these policies is unearned income, such as investment income, royalties, gifts or annuities received independently of daily occupational efforts.

A measure of the amount of income lost is sometimes helpful in determining whether a person is truly disabled and entitled to receive benefits. A *compensable loss* can be defined to have occurred only if the earned income while disabled is less than a given percentage, such as 75 percent, of the predisability income. A *total loss* of earned income is sometimes defined to have occurred if the corresponding percentage of lost income is more than a stated amount, such as 80 percent, of the predisability income. Such measures are used to limit the definition of the qualifying disability to one providing reasonable amounts of benefits and easing the effort of determining the amount of benefits when the amount payable is tied by formula to actual earnings.

An insurable disability occurs when, due directly to an injury or sickness, a person is under the care of a physician and has a reduced capacity to work. A person can be totally or partially disabled. The degree of disability is viewed in terms of the degree of reduced capacity to work. Although it would seem to be fairly obvious when a person is or is not disabled, or even partially disabled, honest differences of opinion arise when an ailment is difficult to diagnose, for example, a sore back. A sore back might well prevent a surgeon from working, but may have little effect on a business manager's ability to work. The definition of "work" also accommodates a degree of flexibility. Therefore, contract language must be carefully written. A statement of the training or licensing required and a precise description of the usual physical performance of duties are often used as more specific criteria to identify the insured's occupation.

A few impairments, because of their nature, are singled out for special attention in disability income policies. Usually these include irrecoverable loss of speech, loss of hearing in both ears, loss of sight in both eyes or loss of the use of two limbs and are referred to as resulting in *presumptive total disability*. These impairments are easily recognizable and clearly result in major changes in the impaired person's working lifestyle. They require a minimum effort to establish existence and time of occurrence, and are permanent in nature. Even though many persons will adjust to such conditions and resume an active career, they are considered to be totally and permanently disabled and presumptively qualified to receive disability income payments.

A provision in some disability income policies specifies that the full monthly indemnity benefits for total disability due to sickness are payable only if the insured is confined to his house or to a hospital. Such policies provide a reduced monthly indemnity, or a shorter indemnity period, for a disability which does not require such confinement. The confinement clause is becoming increasingly unpopular and is now illegal in several states, since it is felt that such contracts are too restrictive to provide a useful economic value, and since they can be so easily misunderstood by the insured.

Total disability is generally defined as one or more of the following:

1. The inability of the insured to perform the principal duties of his/her own occupation. This is called the *own occ* definition.
2. The inability of the insured to perform the duties of any occupation for which he/she is suited by training and experience.
3. The inability of the insured to engage in any form of significant gainful employment, considering the insured's prior economic status.
4. The suffering of a loss by the insured of some amount of earned income solely as the result of an accident or illness.

Competition has forced a trend towards emphasizing the more specific own occ definition in policies sold to white collar and professional people. This causes some concern that the policies are being used to insure specific jobs rather than to replace lost income. This results in the insurance risk being more subjective than objective, less controllable by the insuring company and more controllable by the insured. Each of the definitions has its advantages and disadvantages, largely stemming from the amount of control transferred from the insurer to the insured. Clearly definition 3, while less appealing to the insured than definition 1, gives the insurance company greater control over possible antiselection by a claimant who may want to postpone recovery. However, insurers have been relinquishing a substantial degree of control in order to provide coverage in line with the concerns of professional clients. Professional people have fewer work options as they become progressively more specialized in their training and experience. Thus, professional people are concerned about their ability to return to work in their own field and are requesting that insurance benefits be designed accordingly. The cost for this insurance increases relative to the greater benefit provided, and so more careful claims procedures have been designed to retain control. Telephone reviews with the claimant are now common procedure and direct personal service in the field is a rapidly growing practice.

Definition 3, used widely twenty years ago, is now rarely offered. Skeptical public attitudes and the leaning of the courts make it difficult to sell and to administer. Furthermore, very few claims administrators would feel qualified to prescribe a substitute area of employment. Nevertheless, quite frequently, a physical impairment that prevents an insured from performing in his own occupation, for instance, surgery, does not prevent the insured from working in a different occupation requiring the use of different skills, such as an administrator, teacher or consultant.

Some policies restrict covered disabilities to those resulting only from accident. These policies are becoming less popular as the public and the courts find it increasingly difficult to distinguish between accident and sickness disablements, particularly when benefits are greater, or are payable for a longer period for an accident than for a sickness. Although policies are still available that provide lifetime benefits for accidents, and benefits for shorter periods (5 years or to age 65) for sickness, most insurers believe that there is no justifiable difference in insurance needs among the different causes of disability. These insurers are promoting policies with *coterminal benefits,* where the same benefits apply for accident as for sickness disability.

Cost considerations influence the length of the elimination period. According to the *Metropolitan Statistical Bulletin,* at least one person in three will experience one or more sick days per year. About 60 percent of illness episodes are for durations of less than one week. Another 20 percent are for durations of one to two weeks and about 10 percent are for durations of two weeks to a month. Although these numbers are not applicable to each insured class, they indicate the potential for very high volumes of small claims which would be expensive and impractical to administer. Furthermore, small amounts of income lost during a short period of disability can be budgeted by a prudent policyholder. Therefore, it is more logical that the insurance premium dollars available from a particular household be used to provide larger benefits for longer periods of disability, with short-term losses being covered by the insured's own savings. Also there is substantial evidence of greater antiselection among insureds with policies containing shorter elimination periods of 0, 7 and 14 days than among those with policies containing longer elimination periods of 30, 60 and 90 days. Additionally, there is a very heavy administrative cost element on short-term benefits, making the premium so expense burdened that it is not possible to provide a reasonable loss ratio on such policies. Some state regulations specifically require that benefits be reasonable in relation to premiums, thus enforcing a relationship between benefits and expenses that can best be obtained with longer elimination periods. Elimination periods of 30 days or longer are now considered necessary to provide insurance at a reasonable cost.

Periods of recurring disability from the same cause are sometimes applied toward satisfying the waiting period. Most policies provide that if the insured suffers a recurrence of disability from the same cause within 6 months of recovering from the prior episode of disability, the recurring disability will be considered a continuation of the original disability. Also, many policies waive the elimination period in the event of a presumptive disability.

Maximum benefit periods are generally for 2, 3 or 5 years, or to age 65. As an example, consider an insured who owned a policy with a 5-year benefit period and a 30-day elimination period and who became totally disabled. Income benefits would begin to accrue to the insured on the 31st day of disablement and would be paid for the next 5 years (until the end of the 61st month) or until the insured's recovery or death, if earlier. Occasionally, benefits for accident, and even less frequently for sickness, are payable for life. Usually, shorter benefit periods are associated with shorter elimination periods and smaller amounts, and are sold to persons in the lower income brackets.

The rationale for lifetime benefit periods is that if a person was disabled, his contributions to retirement savings would be suspended. Accordingly, this type of policy provides income to age 65 as reimbursement for the inability to work and then provides pension benefits while the insured remains totally disabled. This is not a complete program because an insured may recover at age 68 and be without pension benefits thereafter. Claims administration after retirement is difficult, as disability is not easy to determine for retired policyholders. Currently, underwriters allow adequate maximum monthly benefits in relation to earned income to permit the insured to continue funding a retirement program while disabled, if he so chooses, and so lifetime benefit periods are not often necessary. A few companies do offer lifetime accident, and sometimes lifetime sickness, benefits for marketing attractiveness rather than for economic reasons, but with reduced benefits after age 65. Lifetime benefits are relatively expensive because it can be assumed that there will be very few recoveries from disability after age 65. Furthermore, OASDI benefits are now payable to retired persons and they may also receive an income from preplanned pensions. This can result in a serious overinsurance problem.

Lifetime benefit period riders offered today are for disabilities occurring prior to age 65. Full benefits are paid to age 65, but the amount payable after age 65 is reduced if disability occurred after some specified earlier age, such as 55. The amount of the reduction is usually defined by formula, such as 10 percent for each full year of age in excess of 55 at the time of disablement. In this example, if disability occurred at age 57, full benefits would be paid to age 65 and 80 percent of that amount would be paid for the year in which the insured attained age 65 and for later years. Benefits are sometimes reduced or eliminated after age 65 if the disablement was from sickness. Support for this distinction between accident and sickness disability is in the reasoning that an insured cannot preselect an accident, while sickness at older ages may be more subjective. Therefore, if the insured wants to buy lifetime benefits, the company wants some protection against antiselection for sickness.

A more conservative approach frequently followed is to provide lifetime benefits only if disability occurs before age 55. On these policies, full benefits would continue to age 65, but would be paid after age 65 only if the insured became disabled prior to age 55.

The monthly income, the basic amount provided by a disability income policy, commences at the end of the elimination period and continues through disability for the stated maximum benefit period. The amount of basic income is an option of the insured, but it must not exceed the company's issue limits. Issue limits are designed to control the possibility of overinsurance. They vary from 75 percent of gross earned income for incomes of $20,000 or less, downward to 30 percent, or even less, for larger earned incomes. Table 3.1 is an illustration of issue limits. These limits are intended to cover about 85 percent of the insured's after-tax earned income. Short-term limits are estimated at approximately the amount of maximum monthly income that would be provided to a person fully insured under the OASDI program. Monthly income limits are composed of 2 parts: a base policy amount of long-term benefits (benefit periods of 2 years or more), and a short term benefits amount. The short-term benefits are provided by a rider attached to the base policy.

Table 3.1
(1985)

Annual Earned Income	Maximum Monthly Income Benefit*		Total
	Basic Long-term	Additional Short-term	
$ 15,000	$ 200	$650	$ 850
20,000	550	750	1,300
30,000	1,100	750	1,850
40,000	1,600	750	2,350
60,000	2,500	800	3,300
100,000	3,850	850	4,700
150,000	5,050	850	5,900
200,000	6,400	850	7,250
300,000	8,700	850	9,550

* The amount limit for basic long-term benefits will be increased by 20 percent in policies for which the full premium is paid by the employer.

Occasionally, when monthly income benefits are substantial and the period of disability is very long, the insured will ask to have his benefits commuted and paid in a lump sum. Reasons given by the insured or his attorney are that the insured wants to fill an emergency need for a substantial amount of cash. Under the own occ definition, or other situations where continued disability is a certainty, a lump-sum payment may help a person start a new business or train for a different career. An insurance company will sometimes accommodate such a request, but generally prefers not to do so for several good reasons:

- Insurance companies are in the business to replace income lost due to disability. The incidence of the loss is fully as important as the magnitude in pricing and designing the product.
- There is too much of an opportunity for the insured to select against the company. Commuting with adequate risk margin at a high interest rate could reduce the amount available to an unattractive level.

- Once the lump-sum benefits are spent, an insured or his beneficiary might become seriously concerned that the company had not really acted in good faith in allowing benefits to be commuted.
- Insurance companies have an obligation to try to guard insureds against receiving large amounts of cash that may become attractive to creditors or used for high risk cash schemes. Thereby, the company permits the insurance policy to fulfill its true intent of replacing lost income as it would have been earned.

3.2 BUSINESS RELATED DISABILITY BENEFITS

While replacing the insured's personal income forms the core of disability insurance products, disability often creates wider financial problems. Losses are further compounded for professional people by the continuing incurral of normal business expenses. Rent, insurance, utilities and, possibly, a staff must be paid to preserve a business through a period of disablement of a key employee. Money for continuing expenses can be insured through an *overhead expense* benefit policy.

The overhead expense benefit is issued specifically to cover the normal and customary costs of maintaining the insured's office during a period of total disability. This benefit covers the insured's share of actual expenses incurred, up to a predetermined maximum, each month until a multiple of the monthly maximum has been paid. An example is an overhead expense benefit policy where the maximum monthly benefit is $ 10,000 and the maximum multiple number of monthly benefits is 15, with a 2-year limit. If the disabled insured validates $12,000 in expenses each month, the benefit will be $10,000 monthly (the maximum) until he recovers or until 15 months' benefits ($150,000) have been paid. If he can validate only $6,000 each month, then only $6,000 will be paid each month, but that amount will be paid for up to 24 months as long as the expense is incurred each month and the insured remains alive and disabled. A validation of $7,500 would be payable for no more than 20 months ($150,000). Benefits cease if the business is sold.

The amount of overhead expense benefit is independent of any other disability income policy that might be in effect for replacing earned income but it is not independent of any other overhead expense policy. The amount payable is generally prorated among all policies that cover the insured's disability and provide similar overhead expense benefits. This is to prevent the possibility of overinsurance where benefits from several companies might exceed the actual expenses incurred. Overhead expense benefits are offered to professional people in small offices of one to five professionals or to sole proprietors. The insured's direct expenses must be preidentified using a prescribed formula for expense distribution among all members of the office professional staff. Covered expenses might include rent, insurance premiums, interest payments, taxes, utilities, depreciation and salaries of employees other than members of the insured's own family or the families of other members of the professional staff.

A surrogate salary benefit is available that will provide payment of the salary of a substitute person employed to perform the duties of a disabled person. However, to prevent antiselection the person employed cannot be a member, by blood or marriage, of the insured's family.

The elimination periods for overhead expense benefits are usually long (90 days or more) and the benefit periods offered are usually short (6 to 24 months) on the theory that short periods can be insured more economically by the business and that other arrangements will be made by the business when it becomes evident that the key person will be disabled for a long period.

Business partners are often concerned that in the event of the death or permanent disability of one of them, the remaining partners will find it difficult to carry on normal business. Frequently, therefore, partners in a small business enter into buy/sell agreements which obligate a disabled partner to sell his interest to the continuing partners who are likewise obligated to buy that interest. Buy/sell agreements were originally developed to cover the contingency of death, but progress in the design of business insurance policies now makes it practical to include provisions for disability as well. Life insurance is a practical way to fund the death buy-out provisions, while disability income insurance covers the disability portion.

Disability buy-out insurance is made available only in situations where a formal buy/sell agreement is in place. The agreement must require that continuing partners purchase the insured's interest in the business at a predetermined price at the end of a specified period of disability. The benefit is provided either as a lump sum or as an equivalent monthly income benefit. The purchase price must be determinable from the terms of the buy/sell agreement. The maximum insurable percentage of an individual's worth in a business is about 80 percent for a lump-sum benefit. This insurable percentage reduces rapidly after age 60 (for example, 50 percent at age 61 and 25 percent at age 62) as it is logical for the partners to begin planning for transition at the insured's retirement. Buy/sell disability insurance policies are designed to terminate 2 or 3 years prior to anticipated normal retirement. Policies providing monthly payments for 3 years or 5 years in lieu of a lump sum also reduce the benefit substantially for ages near retirement.

Elimination periods on buy/sell policies are very long, from 1 to 3 years, and the maximum underwriting limit usually increases with the length of the elimination period. An insurance company may feel that because of the opportunity for antiselection it must restrict its maximum amounts on buy/sell (or buy out) policies to $150,000 lump sum for a 1-year elimination period and $500,000 lump sum for a 3-year elimination period. The policy may permit the coverage of active working stockholders as well as operating partners. The use of this benefit is usually restricted to a business with two to five working partners and/or working stockholders. Where more than five partners are involved in a business the loss of one partner is relatively less severe and insurance is not necessary.

The policy insuring the contingency of one partner's disability is owned either by a trustee or jointly by the other partners since it is they who will actually incur the expense of the insured's disablement.

A *future buy-out expense* option is usually available. This provides the insured the option to increase the maximum buy-out expense benefit without evidence of insurability on specified option dates, usually scheduled every 2 or 3 years from the date of policy issue to the next option date after age 50. The normal company buy/sell financial underwriting rules still apply and premiums for any increase in amount are on an attained-age basis.

3.3 SUPPLEMENTAL BENEFITS AVAILABLE ON DISABILITY INCOME POLICIES

The amount of monthly income benefit needed to remain adequately insured normally increases from year to year as a person's income increases. Increases in discretionary income that occur from regular progress in a career or as a result of salary increases are insurable. During active employment the insured has ample opportunity to increase the amount of monthly income benefit in his policy and has the responsibility, along with his insurance representative, to remain adequately covered. Adequacy of benefits is therefore within the insured's control, provided he is insurable and pays the premium.

Once disabled, however, the insured has no further control over the possibility that his purchasing power will become eroded by inflation. Therefore it often happens that what was an adequate benefit at the time of disablement becomes progressively inadequate the longer a person is disabled. That this situation needed attention was clearly brought to light in the late 1970s when inflation was so high. The policy feature designed to maintain adequacy of benefit while disabled is called the *cost of living benefit (COL)*. It is often embodied in the basic description of benefits but is more often available as an optional rider that may be purchased and included at the time the policy is issued. This feature provides that after a disability has lasted for 1 year the amount of benefit will be automatically increased, and that subsequent increases will occur while disability continues and benefits are payable. It will not extend the benefit paying period, but will increase only the amount of periodic benefit payments.

Some policies express the COL benefit as a flat amount payable in addition to the basic periodic benefit payments. The flat additional amount is a fixed percentage of the basic periodic benefit, multiplied by the number of full years for which benefits have been paid. As an example, a policy with a $2,000 per month basic benefit and a 7 percent flat COL benefit would provide total benefits of $2,000 per month during the first year of disability,

$2,140 per month during the second year, $2,280 per month during the third year and so on. The added flat COL benefit is 7 percent of $2,000, or $140 per month for each full year of disability. In contrast to this, other policies specify a total benefit for the next year as a multiple of the current year's benefit. A factor compounds the basic benefit at an assumed rate of increase which is expected to approximate the annual increase in the cost of living.

The consumer price index (CPI) is often used for the specified percentage under the COL benefit. The CPI varies from year to year and is more likely to provide benefits that match the true needs of the disabled person. Two types of CPI are published by the United States Department of Labor, CPI-W and CPI-U. CPI-W is an index of purchases made by wage earners and clerical workers, and is less comprehensive than the CPI-U that is based upon purchases made by all urban consumers (CPI-U will be the CPI referred to in the remainder of this text). The major problem with using the CPI for the COL benefit factor is that the method used to compute it may change at the discretion of the United States Department of Labor, and may become unreliable for insurance purposes. Generally when the CPI is used, a maximum and minimum annual increase is specified in the policy.

COL benefits are sold both with and without caps. A cap is a maximum overall limit on benefit increases for any one disability. Usually a cap is set at two or three times the basic benefit. The purpose of a cap is to prevent the buildup of excessive overinsurance over a long period of disablement occurring during a period of economic stability. A cap is particularly significant where the COL is increased on a compounding basis. A CPI annual maximum such as 10 percent, or a minimum such as 6 percent, is used to keep the contingency more predictable for pricing purposes and less likely to be disputed in administration. If the COL benefit is payable beyond age 65, as might occur with lifetime benefit periods, the limit of the amount payable may be frozen at the age 65 level or it may continue to increase to the limits of any cap.

An example, Table 3.2, of how the COL-indexed benefit works begins with a particular policy providing benefits for two-thirds of the earned income of an insured who becomes totally and permanently disabled. Although the inflation rate and the CPI will seldom match exactly, this illustration will assume an inflation rate of 7 percent each year to exactly match the CPI index.

Table 3.2
COL-Indexed Benefit Example

Pre-disability monthly earnings (Pre-Dis.) $3,000
Total disability monthly benefit purchased (Dis. Ben.) 2,000
COL 2X Cap 7% compound annually

Year of Dis.	Pre-Dis. Earnings	Earnings While Disabled	Total Dis. Ben. With COL
1	$3,000	0	$2,000
2	3,000	0	2,140
3	3,000	0	2,290
4	3,000	0	2,450
5	3,000	0	2,622
6	3,000	0	2,805
7	3,000	0	3,001
8	3,000	0	3,212
9	3,000	0	3,436
10	3,000	0	3,677
11	3,000	0	3,934
12	3,000	0	4,000 (Cap of 2X 2,000)

The total amount payable under this policy with the COL-indexed benefit is the monthly income otherwise payable multiplied by the COL factor, 1.07 compounded annually.

Since a 2X cap has been included, benefits in the 12th and later years are $4,000 per month.

In summary, COL benefits may be based on simple or compound rates, and may be offered with or without a maximum cap. Although the annual increase is sometimes tied to an index, such as the CPI, it is more often a stated amount such as 7 percent or 8 percent of the first-year benefits. It is easy to see that compounding a flat rate could lead to substantial amounts of overinsurance and to very high claim costs. Over insurance situations are partially prevented by the use of a flat amount increase and by limiting the maximum amount to a 2X or a 3X cap.

Frequently an applicant has needs for short-term benefits as well as needs of a long-range nature. This might occur where there is a desire to provide higher benefits during an adjustment period or for the balance of a mortgage period or to integrate with OASDI or other anticipated benefits. *Additional monthly* income benefits are available as riders on longer-term policies to fill this temporary need. The elimination period of the short-term benefits is equal to or greater than that of the base policy because the relatively smaller amounts would not otherwise be practical to administer.

Underwriters frequently use this benefit on certain high risks to permit issuing larger amounts of insurance for short periods of 3 to 5 years than they are willing to allow for longer periods. Such high risks could involve chronic disorders that are impossible to evaluate.

During a very long period of disablement there is an inherent adjustment in life-style by the claimant to one requiring lower financial needs, so that what was initially considered adequate insurance becomes overinsurance. Through the use of short-term additional benefits the insured can tailor his coverage to make the best use of his available premium dollar.

OASDI benefits in substantial amounts, of upwards of $1,000 per month, are available to persons who qualify as being disabled under the program. The elimination period for OASDI benefits is 5 full consecutive calendar months.

If basic insurance benefits are set high enough to be adequate at the onset of disablement, they will become excessive as soon as the OASDI benefits begin. To prevent this from happening, companies offer two forms of additional monthly income benefits to program around OASDI benefits. The first of these provides amounts of additional monthly income approximately equal to OASDI benefits, beginning with the regular benefit payments at the end of the elimination period and running to the 180th day. The second benefit is similar to this in amount, but does not begin until the 181st day, providing OASDI benefits are not then payable. This latter benefit continues while basic benefits are being paid, but only while OASDI benefits are not being paid.

Some states have cash sickness programs that provide somewhat lesser amounts than OASDI and are designed to cover the first 180 days until OASDI coverage begins. The possibility of overinsurance from this source is allowed for in setting issue limits by reducing the short period (1 year or less) maximum amounts by approximately the amount of any available cash sickness benefit in the applicant's state of residence.

A *waiver of premium benefit* in individual disability income policies provides that premiums are not payable during a period of qualifying disability. A policy may or may not include retroactive benefits to the date of disablement. Retroactivity provides that once a person has qualified for the waiver benefit, any premiums paid since the date of disablement will be refunded. Most individual disability income policies contain a built-in waiver of premium provision. In contrast, life insurance policies include the waiver of premium provision as an option to be elected at the time of policy issue. The reason for the difference in structure is that, in a life insurance policy, the underwriting requirements for waiver are somewhat different than the underwriting requirements for basic life insurance coverage. Frequently persons who may be eligible to purchase life insurance on a substandard basis are not eligible to buy the waiver of premium benefit on any basis. In a disability income policy the incidence of these benefits parallels, and the underwriting requirements for waiver are identical to those for disability income. Accordingly it is more economical to include the benefit in all disability policies.

Waiver benefits may begin with premiums falling due after the end of the elimination period or, as is more usual, after a period of 90 days of disability. Waiver benefits usually extend to the limiting age of the policy (age 65) even though basic monthly income benefits may be for a shorter period.

The *accidental death and dismemberment benefit*, once very popular in individual disability income contracts, provides a lump-sum benefit in the event of accidental death or dismemberment. It is provided in addition to any disability benefits, usually in moderate amounts of $50,000 or $ 100,000, for accidental death, or for the loss of both hands or both feet, or the loss of one hand and one foot, or the loss of sight of both eyes. The amount payable is often referred to as the principal sum. Benefits of one-half the principal sum are payable in the event of the loss of one limb or the sight of one eye.

Originally this benefit was provided in amounts of 50 to 100 times the monthly indemnity and was included as an integral part of most policies. As monthly income benefits grew, the amounts of principal sum in such proportions became a severe burden on the disability income premium dollar. Marketing considerations required that it be offered separately from the base contract with separate premium charges. As the costs were more visible and significant, the principal sum lost its appeal.

Some disability income policies will continue the disability income benefit payment for two or three months after the death of a person receiving benefits. This is to provide adjustment period insurance to help with the immediate extra expenses of the family or, in the case of business overhead policies, to allow for the winding up of the business. Benefits sometimes grade out over a three-month period to 75 percent, 50 percent and 25 percent of the monthly indemnity being paid at the time of death.

Frequently, disability income policies may be continued in force for a few years beyond the normal expiry age of 65, while the insured remains actively and regularly employed on a full-time basis. Benefits are usually reduced to a maximum of two years. Premium rates are reset at age 65 and may be guaranteed at a level rate thereafter. Usually, because disablement after age 65 is so unpredictable, rates are offered on an experience basis, subject to the change in premium for an entire underwriting class at each attained age.

Policies are also available that provide for the return of a portion of the premiums paid less any benefits paid out, during a specified initial term, usually 10 years. This feature was designed to discourage large volumes of small claims and to encourage persistency.

The *guaranteed insurability option (future-income option) benefit*, though the details vary among different policies, takes the standard form of providing for periodic increases in monthly benefits while the insured is not on disability. Such scheduled increases are optional to the insured, and the amounts must be such that the total benefits are still within the company's underwriting participation limits for the insured's current earned income. Benefit increases are limited to maximum amounts of about $500 at each option, and the enrollment period is restricted to 30 days before or after an option date in order to retain some control on antiselection. Generally the option periods are scheduled at 1-, 2- or 3-year intervals with a maximum of five to ten options and a maximum age at option under 55. Maximums are sometimes also set at one or two times the initial amount of indemnity with no more than one-third of the maximum permitted in a single option, in order to keep the guaranteed insurability risk reasonable in relation to the initial risk. The theory here is that the degree of thoroughness in initial underwriting is greater for larger policies, and so the risk of insurability is kept proportional to the initial risk.

Evidence of current earned income is required at each normal option date in order to satisfy financial underwriting standards. An option that is passed up may be picked up at the next option date, but may not be carried beyond. Thus up to two times a normal option amount might be exercised at one time, if earnings qualify.

Some policies provide that if a person is disabled on an option date, the option may still be exercised, subject to the amount limits permitted by the net earnings immediately prior to disability, and the added benefit will become payable 90 days later if the insured is still disabled. In this case, only one option may be elected during a period of disability. Other policies permit the election of any or all options that occur during a period of disability, but do not pay benefits on the newly elected options during the current period of disability. Premiums for the additional options are the attained-age premiums, since servicing is usually required and new business commissions are usually credited.

A special future-income option in many policies gives the insured the opportunity to buy additional coverage without evidence of insurability upon recovering from disability and returning to work. The added coverage amounts to the difference between the monthly benefit last paid under disability and the amount that would have been payable in the absence of the COL benefit or other indexing features. This permits the insured to modernize his coverage under the assumption that he would have done so had he not been disabled. Application for the additional coverage is restricted to a short period, such as 90 days after recovery, to prevent antiselection.

Some renewable future-income option riders automatically increase the basic indemnity by a flat percentage or a flat amount each year for a period of 3 or 5 years without requiring evidence of insurability. The rider may then be renewed for an additional period subject to regular underwriting requirements.

3.4 RESIDUAL OR PARTIAL DISABILITY INCOME BENEFITS

Disabilities are not always total and permanent. Frequently, a disabled person will pass through stages of gradual recovery on the way back to a fully active status, or may be only partially disabled by either a temporary or permanent condition.

Residual or partial disability is much more common than total disability, and is much more subjective. Such disabilities are easier to establish and, in fact, are inherent in occupations where acute senses are required because the senses often tend to become less responsive as a person ages. Airplane pilots should have excellent vision and hearing for safety reasons. Inherently, sight and hearing deteriorate with age and would frequently lead to an own occ disability. This deterioration is insurable to the extent that it may result from an accident or illness, but to the extent that it is inherent it should be part of career retirement planning.

As an extension of the own occ definition of disability, companies offer *residual benefits* designed to provide full benefits while the insured is totally disabled and partial benefits while the insured is partially (residually) disabled. Below is typical definition of *residual disability*.

Because of an injury or illness,

1. a. you are unable to perform all of the important duties of your regular occupation but you are performing some of them, or
   b. you are necessarily engaged in another occupation, and
2. your monthly earnings are less than 80 percent but more than 20 percent of your predisability earnings, and
3. you are under the care of a physician.

Another popular insuring clause, sometimes referred to as the *dual definition,* recognizes situation 1.b as qualifying a person for total disability. In this instance residual benefits are payable if a person is partially disabled in his regular occupation, but full benefits are payable if he cannot perform all of the important duties of his regular occupation even if working in another. Problems of control are evident in each of these definitions. Under either the own occ or dual definitions, a person could qualify for total disability, collect benefits, and work full time at a less demanding occupation. As an example, a partially disabled surgeon could become a hospital administrator while using the dual definition to continue to collect total disability benefits. Considering that disability benefits are not taxable in the United States when purchased with premiums from after-tax personal income, the insured could possibly receive a higher net income than he was earning prior to his disability. This would influence claimants to choose alternate employment options and remain disabled longer than necessary.

The pure own occ definition, in contrast, may discourage an insured from returning to work on a partial basis or even on a trial basis for fear of losing all benefits. Not only is control lost, but the insured may be discouraged from reentering the labor market, even though he is capable of entering another occupation. The surgeon in the illustration should be encouraged to elect other meaningful work, since he cannot perform his regular duties.

Many polices providing residual benefits are issued with a qualification period of prior total disability and offer a reduced benefit period if disability begins after age 60. The inclusion of a qualification period requires that an insured be totally disabled for 30, 60, or 90 days in order to collect residual benefits. When the residual benefit was first introduced, there was great fear of its being used for early retirement or being abused by easy access. Since partial disability is so subjective, insurance companies try to retain a greater element of control by requiring that residual benefits be treated as intended, for financial assistance during recovery. The intent is to permit a more gradual return to work or to promote rehabilitating a person to another line of work. There are, of course, disablements that are degenerative, multiple sclerosis for example, and there are disablements such as a broken arm that may be partial disablements from the start. In order to allow for coverage where partial disability precedes total disability, or where total disability may never develop, the zero-day qualification period, though expensive because of the speculative nature of the risk, is frequently an option. Although this effectively eliminates the qualification period, it is called a zero-day qualification period in order to keep a standard policy form flexible for options of 30, 60 or 90 day qualification periods. Premiums, of course, are progressively higher with age the shorter the qualification period, because of the concern for its influence on early partial retirement and because of inherent physical deterioration in some disabilities. The length of the qualification period is, therefore, frequently automatically increased toward 60 or 90 days beginning at age 55 or 60 in order to control this possible misuse of the insurance.

A few policies limit residual benefits to no more than 12 months of partial disability after age 60 in order to limit the amount of benefit exposed to the risk of use for early retirement.

A typical monthly amount payable as a residual benefit equals

$$\frac{A - B}{A} \cdot \text{(regular monthly indemnity for total disability)}$$

where A = prior (predisability) earnings, and

B = earnings for the month for which benefits are being claimed.

If B is less than 20 percent of A, total disability is assumed, if B is greater than 80 percent of A, disability is assumed not to exist and no benefits are payable.

Some policies use 25 percent-75 percent limits or some other range instead of 20 percent-80 percent. Many policies provide a minimum of 50 percent of the regular indemnity during the first 6 months of the period for which the insured qualifies for residual benefits. A 3- or 6-month 50 percent minimum residual benefit assures the continuation of meaningful benefits as further encouragement to the insured to return to work. It is also a practical expedient to solving the difficulty of measuring the true lost income in the early stages of recovery. This feature does not change the qualification requirements but only limits the benefits payable.

Prior monthly earnings are sometimes defined as the average monthly income for the most recent full tax year prior to disability, but the more common definitions are monthly earnings averaged over the 6 or 12 calendar month period immediately preceding the date of disablement or the highest monthly average over any 2 successive years during the 5-year period immediately preceding the date of disablement. The longer optional period more adequately protects a person in the event of a gradually debilitating physical condition, or a recent bad economic swing, or a disability occurrence closely following a vacation period when earnings may have been abnormally depressed.

Table 3.3 contains an example of a residual benefit payment structure. Note that if the policy had contained a 50 percent minimum during the first 6 months of partial disability, the insured would have received $2,000 in March and $2,000 in April, instead of $1,778 and $1,222.

Relating residual benefits to the insured's earnings immediately prior to a claim works well in partial disability cases during periods of low inflation, but becomes progressively inadequate during periods of high inflation. The reason for this is that the proportion of recovery, as measured by the relationship of current (partial) earnings, to prior earnings, increases as the earnings under partial disability inherently increase with inflation, even though the insured's ability to work has not improved at all. This is illustrated in the first six columns of Table 3.4 containing an example based upon the results of a person becoming totally disabled, then returning to work at 50 percent of his original capacity at the end of a year. The policy terms are similar to those of the example illustrated in Table 3.2 (for comparison purposes). In the absence of inflation, the insured would receive $2,000 per month during the year of total disability and $1,000 (50 percent) each month thereafter. Inflation, however, acts to reduce the disability income benefit because the earnings from the original occupation will inflate from $3,000

Table 3.3
Residual Benefits Example

Basic Insurance – $4,000 per month
Elimination period – 30 days
Residual Corridor 20% to 80%, 6 month average prior earnings
Date of disablement – August 1
Returned to work on part-time basis – November 1

Month	Monthly Earned Income	Monthly Insurance Benefit	
January	$6,000	0	
February	5,600	0	
March	8,000	0	Average Prior Earnings (APE)
April	7,000	0	(last 6 months)
May	7,600	0	$7,200 per month
June	8,000	0	
July	7,000	0	
August	2,000	0	Elimination Period (dis. Aug. 1)
September	400	4,000	
October	0	4,000	
November	600	4,000	
December	1,000	4,000	Earnings are less than 20% of APE
January	1,600	3,111	Earnings are more than 20% of APE
February	2,000	2,889	
March	4,000	1,778	
April	5,000	1,222	
May	6,000	0	Earnings exceed 80% of APE

per month to $3,210 per month at the end of the first year and, since he works at 50 percent capacity, the insured will earn $1,605 in the year he returns to work. Income lost is compared to predisability earnings, amounting to only 46.5 percent (1,395/3,000) the year he returns to work and the benefit is $930 instead of $1,000. Since the percent of lost income reduces each year, the residual benefit becomes less each year, actually disappearing in the eighth year when lost earnings are only 19.7 percent of predisability earnings.

Even though the insured is partially disabled, the earned income continues to grow at 7 percent per year as illustrated, to $2,758 in the tenth year. The basic residual benefit fails to recognize that the insured is still working at only 50 percent of capacity, measuring instead a loss of only 8 percent. Adding the COL increases, the monthly benefit is somewhat more adequate (see last column), but the relation of benefit to lost earnings still decreases.

Table 3.4
Residual Benefits With COL Example

Pre-disability monthly earnings (Pre-Dis.) $3,000
Total disability monthly benefit purchased (Dis. Ben.)   2,000
Cost of Living index (COL)   7% compound annually
Residual Benefit Clause (Resid. Ben.)
Benefits in this illustration are assumed not payable if earnings while disabled are more than 80% of predisability earnings.

Year of Dis.	Pre-Dis. Earnings	Earnings While Disabled	Total Dis. Ben	Percent Income Loss	Resid. Ben.	Resid. Ben. with COL
1	$3,000	0	$2,000	100.0%	$2,000	$2,000
2	3,000	1,605	0	46.5	930	995
3	3,000	1,717	0	42.8	855	979
4	3,000	1,838	0	38.7	775	949
5	3,000	1,966	0	34.5	689	903
6	3,000	2,104	0	29.9	597	837
7	3,000	2,251	0	25.0	499	749
8	3,000	2,409	0	19.7	0*	0
9	3,000	2,577	0	14.1	0*	0
10	3,000	2,758	0	8.1	0*	0

* Earnings while disabled exceed 80% of pre-disability earnings and no benefits are payable.

A special feature, indexing of prior earnings, is offered that will combat these effects of inflation in measuring the lost capacity to work. For purposes of determining prior earnings in the calculation of the percent of income lost, the previous year's earnings will be increased by a stated percentage for each full year of disablement. This is consistent with the theory that as a result of inflation a person returning to work while partially disabled will, over time, receive a correspondingly higher income for the same relative performance.

If the prior earnings indexing feature is now added to the previous COL illustration, a more consistent relationship between lost earnings and benefits emerges. The extended example in Table 3.5 assumes indexing of prior earnings at a CPI rate of 7 percent compounded annually in order to match the COL ratio, and better illustrates the theory of this design. Observe that indexing, in this ideal situation, keeps the residual benefit at the level it would be if there were no inflation.

Table 3.5
Residual Benefits with COL and Indexed Pre-Dis. Earnings Example

Year of Dis.	Pre-Dis. Earnings Indexed	Earnings While Disabled	Income Loss	Resid. Benefit with Index	Ben. with Index + COL	Replacement of Lost Benefit Ratio
1	$3,000	0	100%	$2,000	$2,000	66.7%
2	3,210	1,605	50	1,000	1,070	66.7
3	3,435	1,717	50	1,000	1,145	66.7
4	3,675	1,838	50	1,000	1,225	66.7
5	3,932	1,966	50	1,000	1,311	66.7
6	4,208	2,104	50	1,000	1,403	66.7
7	4,502	2,251	50	1,000	1,501	66.7
8	4,817	2,409	50	1,000	1,606	66.7
9	5,155	2,577	50	1,000	1,718	66.7
10	5,515	2,758	50	1,000	1,839	66.7

In this illustration, since the inflation and the CPI rates were the same as the COL and indexing rates, the replacement ratio originally indicated in the policy has been preserved; the insurance was designed to replace two-thirds of the income lost to disability. Neither the COL nor the indexing of prior earnings feature alone can adequately stabilize the replacement ratio; thus, these options are usually sold in combination, as shown in this illustration.

3.5 REHABILITATION

Disabled persons sometimes want to join a rehabilitation program. Since the ability to join such a program implies something less than total disability the insured may become concerned that in so doing he might not qualify for total disability benefits. An insurance company, being interested in the claimant's return to an active status, would normally encourage such a program and would work with the insured to develop it. Nevertheless, such a program is open to differences of opinion about the insured's status. The element of uncertainty is eliminated with the inclusion of a specific rehabilitation clause. This clause provides that if the insured chooses to join a rehabilitation program while receiving total disability benefits, the company will consider him to remain totally disabled.

A few conditions need to be specified in order to assure that such programs are in fact true rehabilitation programs. Generally the definition of a qualifying program of rehabilitation would include one or more of the following:

- The program is a professional retraining or education program at a graduate school level.
- The program is sponsored by a federal or state government agency.
- The insurance company approved the program in advance of the insured's joining.

Although the insured may not have to continue under the care of a physician to qualify, he must still be unable to perform the important duties of his regular occupation and must actively participate in the rehabilitation program.

Benefits will be restricted to a short period, typically 36 months, but they will not be payable beyond the remainder of the normal benefit period. If the insured drops out of the rehabilitation program, he must requalify under the regular total or residual disability requirements to continue to receive the income benefits. Any continuation of benefits is still, of course, part of the original disability period.

Rehabilitation benefit riders are also available to provide small amounts of monthly income during a shod period of rehabilitation in addition to the regular total disability benefits.

Recovery from disability is further assisted and encouraged by payments of two or three extra months benefits upon returning to work. If, after the two or three months the insured remains disabled, the claim is reopened and regular monthly income payments are resumed.

Chapter 4

INDIVIDUAL HEALTH INSURANCE PREMIUMS

by William F. Bluhm, F.S.A. and Spencer Koppel, F.S.A.

The process of gross premium formulation for individual health insurance is discussed in this chapter. The process is followed through choice of data, modeling techniques, regulatory limitations, strategic considerations, and actual calculations. The major methodologies in use today by mutual, stock, and nonprofit carriers are described. A detailed profit study (asset-share) calculation, illustrating the major calculation method in use today, appears at the end of the chapter.

4.1 GROSS PREMIUM STRUCTURES

A critical element of gross premium structure is the underlying rate classification system, the system under which rates are determined based on characteristics of the insured population. Basic to this system is the recognition of features representing statistically significant claim cost variations. While such features are predominantly medical, demographic and geographic, legislation and regulation can limit the extent to which they can be used in rating. Once the rating variables are chosen, they are organized into a rating system which will be used throughout the company. In addition to the rate classification system, the gross premium structure will also depend on policy provisions regarding rate guarantees.

4.1.1 RATING CLASSES AND RELATED CLAIM COST CHARACTERISTICS

The major rating classes used for health insurance parallel those used for life insurance: age, sex, occupation, and medical history. Separate rates for smokers and nonsmokers, pioneered in the life insurance industry, are also emerging as important in the health insurance field. Area rating factors are common for health insurance products offering benefits with costs dependent on local hospital, surgical, and medical cost levels. For example, the variations in hospital room and board costs between two cities such as New York City and Springfield, Illinois will result in quite different premium rates. The disparity in costs between one area and another can be in a ratio of 2 to 1 or greater.

Many companies develop rates that vary by state of issue. These rate differences may be due to differences in claim costs by state, to mandated benefits, or to minimum loss ratio standards. A commonly used contract provision provides for changes in renewal rates subject to state regulatory requirements. This provision can be an important factor in pricing, since each state uses its own rules and guidelines in determining the appropriateness of rate increases.

More and more state regulators are asking to review experience data on policyholders from their state, and prefer to ignore nationwide experience in the evaluation of an insurer's results.

The age structure of the insured population is an important rating factor in virtually all forms of health insurance. Claim costs for coverages such as hospital room and board benefits, miscellaneous hospital benefits, and disability benefits for periods of 2 years or longer, rise steeply by age. A less steep slope has been observed for surgical and short-term disability benefits.

In many states, minimum anticipated loss ratios are higher for particular age groups, such as persons over age 60 or 65. This may result in a gross premium structure which is less steeply sloped by age than would otherwise be the case.

Health insurance pricing commonly differentiates by sex. The size and direction of the the differential depends on the type of benefit. Hospital room and board benefits have historically shown a pattern of female claim costs being lower than male claim costs at the youngest ages, higher by age 30, and then lower again at age 50 and over. Claim costs for disability benefits show a pattern by sex similar to that for hospital benefits.

At the time of this writing, the National Organization for Women has a pending lawsuit against an insurer, charging that the insurer is discriminating against women by charging different health insurance rates for females than for males. The outcome of this case will likely affect practices in the health insurance business. Actuaries generally believe that the evidence supporting the existence of sex differences in expected claims is very strong. Female claim costs are lower than male claim costs for some coverages and are higher for others. The principle of equity in pricing, in the absence of other concerns, would support the use of sex as a determining factor in setting rates for individual health insurance policies. It is a common concern that the pricing of insurance products on a unisex basis might create an antiselective marketing situation which might force insurers to charge higher than average rates. For example, if females aged 27 had 50 percent higher claim costs than males aged 27 for a comparable coverage, and an insurance company was required to charge a unisex rate, the company might feel it necessary to charge a rate closer to the female premium rate. This is because the proportion of business to be issued to females at an average unisex rate might be higher than expected, due to the antiselection incentive of the lower price.

Occupation classifications are common under disability insurance coverage, but not under medical care coverage, which usually excludes losses covered by Workers Compensation Laws. Insurance experience with accident disability income benefits for Male Occupation Group II (hazardous or blue collar occupations) shows claim costs approximately double those for Male Occupation Group I (nonhazardous or white collar occupations) at all ages. For sickness benefits, there does not appear to be any difference in claim costs between Group I and Group II at attained ages under 30. Above age 30, the Group II experience tends to be about 50 percent higher than the Group I experience. This may be due to the difficulty of returning to a hazardous job after a disability, or possibly due to different motivation levels.

The insured's personal medical history will have an important impact on expected claim costs, much as it does in life insurance. Unlike life insurers, however, health insurers can often control this effect by using waivers and preexisting condition exclusions, rather than by charging substandard premium rates. The existence of an ulcer, for example, can readily be seen to have a much greater impact on the claim cost of a medical expense insurance policy than on a life insurance policy. Use of an exclusion for treatment related to ulcers, for an insured with such a history, is an effective means of controlling claim costs and this makes coverage for catastrophic illnesses more affordable for that insured.

A commonly used policy provision, which excludes coverage of conditions existing at the time of issue, is the *preexisting conditions exclusion*. This provision is usually limited to conditions for which the insured has had advice or treatment during the 12 month period preceding the policy issue date, and applies only to coverage during the first 1 or 2 policy years. For Medicare supplement policies, this exclusion is often limited to 6 months before and 6 months following Policy issue.

Area rating factors that assign percentage loads or discounts to national average rates are commonly used for medical expense policies. This is because of the wide variations in medical care costs by geographic area. Companies may define areas as states, by counties, or by zip codes. Care must be taken that the insurer has adequate administrative procedures to control an area rating system. The insurer will want to keep experience data according to the same classifications used for rating. The insurer must make decisions regarding an insured's rate if he moves from one area to another, as well as making adjustments between areas over time.

Consideration must also be given to the reasonableness of rating based on the insured's residence as opposed to where he might go for hospital treatment. An insured living in a low cost Dallas suburb may well use a hospital in high cost downtown Dallas. Claim costs tend to vary along the lines of urban versus rural treatment settings. Insureds treated in major metropolitan areas tend to have higher hospital, medical and surgical claim costs than those receiving treatment in rural areas.

4.1.2 ORGANIZING THE RATING CLASSES

Rates classified by factors discussed in the previous subsection can be thought of as a multidimensional array, with each dimension representing one of the rating elements. Rates could be developed for each cell, representing one combination of age, sex, plan, area and so on. However, unless representative cells are chosen, this method can be cumbersome, due to the potentially large number of cells. Inevitably, representative cells (such as quinquennial or decennial ages, rather than each age) are chosen, and rates for the missing cells are later calculated by interpolation.

The method used to develop premiums need not match that used in developing claim costs. For example, claim costs might be derived by applying a set of age/sex factors to some overall level of claims, and then interpolated, while gross premiums could be based, at least initially, on competitive considerations.

4.1.3 PREMIUM GUARANTEES

When a new policy form is introduced, an insurer's rate manual will usually show rates by individual issue age. The length of time over which those premium levels remain unchanged is usually determined by experience trends, renewal and/or rate guarantee provisions in the policy, by regulatory restrictions, and by management considerations.

It is important to conceptually distinguish between structural, age-related changes in rates, such as with attained age or step-rated rates, and changes in rates due to changes in the overall *schedule* of rates.

The weakest form of renewal and rate guarantee is the *optionally renewable* provision. This clause was originated by casualty insurance companies which traditionally issued coverage on the basis of annual renewal at the option of the company. The use of this provision for individual health insurance is quite rare today and is often limited by statute or regulation.

The next stronger renewal and rate guarantee is the *conditionally renewable* provision. The company agrees that it will not cancel an individual's coverage because of deterioration of health, but reserves the right to refuse to renew all insureds of the same class. A variation is to agree that the company will not cancel the coverage of an Individual insured unless it cancels coverage of all insureds in the state in which the insured resides. Such policies are also referred to as *nonrenewable for stated reasons only*.

The next higher level of guarantee is the *guaranteed renewable* provision, which guarantees the insured's right of renewal, although it still reserves the insurer's right to change premium rates, subject to the approval of the state insurance department (where applicable and required).

The *noncancelable and guaranteed renewable* provision provides that the insurance company may not cancel the policy, nor may it change the premium rate schedule at any time during the life of the policy. This is the strongest form of renewal and rate guarantee.

Both the insured's right to renew and the duration of any rate guarantee affects the level of risk accepted by the insurer and therefore must be considered in determining premiums.

4.2 ELEMENTS OF PREMIUM CALCULATION

The major elements in a rate calculation are morbidity, expenses, lapsation, mortality, interest, and contingency and profit margins. Whether a particular element is used in a calculation depends on the method of calculation, the type of coverage, and the significance given to the element by the actuary making the calculations.

4.2.1 MORBIDITY

The term morbidity is used to describe measures of claim costs. Each claim cost calculation can be thought of as a product of two random variables:

the occurrence of a claim in the specified period; and the size of the claim, given that a claim occurs.

For disability income insurance, hospital insurance, and other coverage involving claims which occur over time, the random variable representing the size of the claim can be subdivided into the product of two variables:

the periodic payment amount; and the duration of the claim.

The level of claim costs is affected by a number of variables. The major ones are described below. However, the pricing actuary should be alert for additional factors unique to a given situation.

1. **The marketing method used for the product:** The overall level of claim costs and their incidence by duration can vary significantly, depending on whether the product is issued through agents, brokers, or through mass-marketing or other nontraditional channels.
2. **Other existing coverages:** The level of existing insurance covering a policyholder population can have a significant impact on the level of claims, and should be considered in setting morbidity assumptions. Overinsurance of individual policyholders can be controlled by careful underwriting at the time of issue.

Careful underwriting at issue, however, does not always make good business sense, as it can be relatively costly, especially for policies with small average size premiums. Also, coverage under other insurance programs which begins after issue cannot be anticipated in initial underwriting. In these cases, insurers often use policy provisions for protection against overinsurance.

3. **Underwriting and other durational effects:** The sale of guaranteed-issue products, without medical underwriting, produces substantial antiselection. Often these products are sold on a mass-marketing basis, in which case antiselection will be a function of the response rate to the marketing effort. Such products are usually issued with a preexisting conditions exclusion. This tends to mask the effect of antiselection for the period of the exclusion. In contrast, policies sold with full medical underwriting can often be expected to have an identifiably lower level of claim costs in the early durations (beyond the period of exclusion) due to underwriting.

Cumulative antiselection is the cumulative effect of the higher persistency of poorer risks. Historically, initial underwriting selection factors have been accounted for in rate determination, but cumulative antiselection has not been sufficiently recognized, especially with regard to inflation-sensitive policies. There is, however, increasing recognition of it in the rating of certain coverages.

Disability income products have other intrinsic antiselection effects. Consider a disability income insurer who has a product with both a 7-day elimination period and a 30-day elimination period. The morbidity under the 30-day plan will usually be better due to the availability of the 7-day plan. This is because policyholders who perceive their own claim experience as worse than average will choose the plan with the largest possible benefits. This would be the 7-day plan. However, if the 7-day plan is not available, they will purchase the 30-day plan, thereby worsening the experience under that plan.

The antiselection effect described above is often difficult to measure, due to the existence of another effect referred to here as the "elimination period effect." Again, consider the insurer with the 7-day and 30-day elimination period plans. A claimant who has the 7-day plan is more likely to be disabled on the 31st day than a claimant with the 30-day plan. This is because the 30-day plan claimant will not have been receiving benefits for days 8 through 30, and therefore has more income to lose in that period if he remains disabled. Thus there is more incentive for him to recover during those 23 days than for the claimant under the 7-day plan.

Tables summarizing data by length of claim are called *continuance tables*. Because of the effects described above, modern continuance tables for disability income insurance are usually developed separately for different elimination periods.

Inpatient hospital coverage is also subject to a continuance effect since the claim amount depends upon the length of stay in the hospital. However, hospital benefit pricing usually does not recognize differing elimination periods.

4.2.2 EXPENSES

The treatment of expenses in rating calculations is subject to widely varying levels of sophistication. For the same coverage, one company may apply a single percentage of premium in all rating categories while another may allocate its expenses by means of a complicated formula. Generally, expense allocations can be categorized in the following ways:

- percentage of (gross) premium;
- per policy;
- per benefit unit, such as per $100 of monthly income for disability income insurance; and
- percentage of claims.

Each of these categories can be further subdivided between first year and renewal levels. Increasingly, the subdivision of expense allocations is becoming more complex, especially in renewal years.

The pricing actuary should choose an expense allocation method meeting the following criteria:

- The overall expense level expected to be incurred by the block of policies will be equal to aggregate expense charges expected to be collected by the company for those policies.
- The formula expresses, as much as possible, a reasonable and rational allocation of the expenses by rating cell within the block of policies. This is aimed at achieving equity and fairness.
- No competitive problems are created due to the resulting slope of premiums.

It should be noted that the expense method chosen for pricing purposes need not mimic that used by the company to allocate expenses by line of business. As deviations occur between the two, however, the resulting overall expenses to be collected will become increasingly sensitive to the expected distribution of the business, so care must be taken to analyze this risk.

The expenses most often recognized are the following:

- *Acquisition expenses:* These are charges attributable to acquiring the business, other than commissions. This would include underwriting and issue costs, which often must be converted from a "per application received" basis to a "per policy issued" basis.

- *Commissions:* When commissions are present, for other than medical coverages they are usually high in the first year, moderate and level for a limited number of renewal years, then drop off to a minimal service fee. For medical coverages, commissions tend to be much more level.
- *Agency expense*: When agency costs are separated from other expenses, they are often expressed as percentages of premium received (as opposed to premium *earned*).
- *Claim administration expenses:* These are often expressed as a percent of claims, or on a per claim basis.
- *Policy administration expenses:* These represent the ongoing cost of maintaining a policy on the company's books. These expenses are most likely to be expressed as a per policy or per unit expense.
- *Premium tax and other state taxes:* These are usually expressed as a percent of premium.
- *Company overhead:* This would include company operating expenses not otherwise allocated. These are often expressed as a percent of premium, or as a percent of premium in combination with per policy or per unit expenses.
- *Federal income tax.*

This list is not intended to be exhaustive, nor is it necessary that all these breakdowns be used. As always, the benefit to be gained by a particular level of sophistication must be weighed against the cost of obtaining it.

4.2.3 PERSISTENCY AND MORTALITY

Lapsation is the term used to describe the ratio of the number of policies voluntarily canceled or not renewed to the total number of policies. The *persistency* rate is one minus the *lapsation* rate and measures the proportion of policyholders persisting to the end of a designated time period. Lapsation might also be defined to include policies which end their coverage because the term of the policy or a limiting age has been reached.

Mortality among health insurance policyholders is usually minor relative to lapsation, and most companies do not differentiate between the two in their experience studies or premium formulas. For example, a typical lapse rate for a 45-year old male with a 10-year old disability income policy might be .05; the mortality rate for that age based on the 1958 CSO Table is .0054.

The magnitude of lapsation, and its behavior by duration, varies by the following:

- Younger policyholders tend to have a higher lapse rate than older policyholders, except at ages just prior to retirement.
- Most blocks of policies will have lapse rates that decrease by duration. Lapse rates will usually become level after a period of time. They will often

be expressed as a constant level after a specific duration. Depending on the type of benefit, an increase in lapse rate may occur as policyholders reach the age bracket for early retirement. Changes in lapse rate by duration also can occur within a calendar year when premiums are not paid annually. These changes tend to occur most heavily in the first few years a policy is in force, and can have a significant impact on premium rates.

- Lapse rates will differ by product type. For example, the buyer of a noncancelable disability income product is paying a higher premium for the guarantee that his premiums will not increase in the future. Presumably, if he intended to lapse the policy shortly after buying it, that guarantee would not be worth much to him, and he would be more likely to buy a policy without such a guarantee at a lower rate. Medical expense products will have significantly different persistency than disability income products. Even within a particular product, blocks of policies representing different benefit packages may have different lapse rates.
- Premium levels can have a significant impact on lapsation. If policyholders can find equivalent coverage elsewhere for less money, they are much more likely to lapse a current policy than otherwise. Premium increases can have a drastic effect on lapsation. Some insurers have experienced situations in which the entire expected aggregate increase in premium was offset by increased lapsation.
- The mode of premium payment can impact on lapsation. A policyholder with monthly premium payments has twelve times as many opportunities for lapsation as one paying annually. On the other hand, when premiums are collected automatically through a checking account, cancellation requires a positive action by the insured, and persistency is therefore usually increased significantly.
- The occupation of the policyholder can have a significant impact on persistency. While this is usually considered in analysis of disability income coverages, it is usually not considered for medical coverages.

4.2.4 INTEREST

Interest is included in premium calculations in a number of ways:

- In discounting present values in the profit study (asset share) model: The choice of an interest rate for this purpose may depend on the company's method of measuring profit.
- In modeling statutory reserves: The interest rate used in statutory reserve calculations affects the size of the reserve held, and thus modeled profit. Since this portion of interest earnings will likely be treated differently for federal income tax purposes, it is important that it be separable from the rest of interest earnings.

- In estimating investment income on reserves and/or the accumulated fund: The rate of investment earnings on assets is projected into the future, based upon many considerations, most of which are beyond the scope of this chapter. Care should be taken to consider the risks involved in the investment process, including the risk that future interest rates will not equal what is being projected. Assumed interest earnings rates may decrease over time, which is often a conservative assumption. Since the portion of these earnings that match statutory reserve interest earnings may be accounted for separately, care should be taken that they are not counted twice.

Of equal importance to determining interest rates is the determination of the amounts that will have interest earning rates applied to them. Usually, it costs more to issue a policy than is returned as earnings in the first year. This implies an investment by other policyholders or by stockholders in the new block of business. If either the ROI (Return on Investment) or the ROE (Return on Equity) method of calculating earnings is utilized, the investment will be discounted at the same rate as later positive earnings.

If, rather than using either the ROI or the ROE method of earnings measurement, a fund is accumulated from initial issue, with all cash flows accounted for in each year, the early negative earnings will be accumulated at the appropriate interest rate. (This is essentially equivalent to discounting such cash flows to the issue date.) The interest rate should be chosen carefully, and the choice should take into consideration whether the initial rate is "pre-tax" (Federal Income Tax) or "post-tax." If a fund is being accumulated, and is assumed to be earning investment income in each year, then income tax can be considered to be incurred with respect to those earnings. If the fund accumulation takes into account the income tax on those investment earnings, then the discount rate should likewise reflect that taxation. If the fund accumulation does not, then the discount rate should not. This is the only way that a year of zero earnings will result in zero changes in the present value of earnings (as it should), since the fund will be accumulated and discounted for one year at precisely the same interest rate.

4.2.5 PROFIT AND CONTINGENCY MARGINS

Two types of dividends can occur with respect to individual health insurance policies: policyholder dividends if the policies are participating; or stockholder dividends if the insurer is a stock company.

In both cases, dividends represent a payout of unneeded funds from margins to the recipient. There are different ways to account for margins in premium calculations. These methods can be reduced to two approaches, the implicit method and the explicit method.

The *implicit method* provides margins in the premium structure by means of conservative assumptions. No margins are directly included in the premium calculation. In the early years of health insurance, the development of such margins was often a matter of art, and was not well quantified. Today, actuaries tend to adopt what they call "realistic" assumptions, and then determine appropriate explicit margins to be added to the assumptions. These "realistic" assumptions may still tend to be somewhat conservative. Over time, as emerging experience is measured against the original assumptions, surplus amounts are gradually released. For participating policies, the expected pattern of release of these funds forms the basis of the policyholder dividend scale. For stock companies, released margin amounts are part of generally accepted accounting principles (GAAP) earnings.

Under the *explicit method*, margins are quantified in advance of the premium calculation. These margins constitute the expected profit level, chosen by management, and are usually measured in one or more of three ways:

1. The present value of future profit is set as a percentage of the present value of future premiums,
2. Profit is set at an amount sufficient to provide a particular investment return on the initial investment (negative cash flows) in the block of policies. This is the ROI method.
3. Similarly to ROI, the ROE method considers the initial investment to also include the investment of some company surplus (by allocation).

Under any method, the size of the margins is chosen to suit the philosophy of the company. One company may set a profit target for the company as a whole, another may set the target by product. The actuary should keep the following considerations in mind when setting margin levels:

- the profit philosophy of the company;
- the dividend philosophy of the company;
- the company resources available to analyze actual results, including management information systems;
- the methods used for prior company products; and
- the risk level associated with each of the assumptions.

4.2.6 OTHER CONSIDERATIONS

While the benefit provisions of a policy are the primary determinants of the assumptions used in developing premiums, other policy provisions can also have a significant effect.

In disability income policies, provisions that reduce benefits under certain circumstances, such as a "relation of earnings to insurance" provision can have a significant effect on claim costs. The magnitude of this effect will depend on a number of things, including the specific wording of the provision and the characteristics of the policyholders.

Disability income insurance premium assumptions will also be affected by how the policy defines "disability."

One consideration that can have significant impact on the level of rates is the competition's rates. The actuary's assumptions with regard to morbidity, lapsation, expenses and investment earnings should not depend upon what the ultimate premium level is, at least with regard to profit testing, since the purpose of that testing is to obtain a measure of what is realistically expected to happen, within the chosen definition of "realistic." Profitability and contingency targets can and often are modified, however, to meet competitive premium levels.

Premium rates calculated for an annual premium payment mode can differ significantly from rates calculated for other payment modes. Most companies have standard modal loadings (for monthly, quarterly, semiannual, and perhaps preauthorized check modes) that are used with all products. The modal loading can be a percentage, a flat fee per collection or a combination of the two. For example, a formula might call for the quarterly premium to be 26 percent of the annual premium plus $1.50 per collection.

4.2.7 RELATIVE IMPORTANCE OF ASSUMPTIONS

Since most actuaries have only limited time available to create and analyze premium levels, it is important to determine how significant each of the assumptions is to the overall process so that time can be allocated accordingly. This determination cannot be well defined, since it is subject to change for each product and for each company. Some basic considerations, however, are common to the decision making process.

The premium setting process is essentially a forecast of the future. Therefore, a prime consideration is the result on profitability of significant variation in each of the assumptions. Some questions which should be asked are

- what is the company's future outlook? Will competition and regulation be tougher or easier?
- what will the company's surplus position be?
- are the premium rates subject to revision? If they are, will regulators allow them to change when necessary?
- what premium calculation method is being used? For example, if the cash flow method is used, only one or two years' projection is involved. The effect of interest in such calculations becomes minimal, and projections have a large degree of confidence.
- what are the results of sensitivity tests? The importance of preciseness in choosing an assumption depends on how much the final result changes when the assumption changes.

The overriding consideration is the overall reasonableness of assumptions, rather than the absolute correctness of any individual assumption. Of course, the best way to arrive at the best assumptions in the aggregate is to have that aggregate composed of the best individual assumptions. And, since short-cuts and approximations will almost always be used, the results emerging from the assumptions may not be exactly matched by the results of the approximations. Hence, the need to monitor the aggregate effect.

Another important reason the aggregate assumptions need to be examined is that there may be unintended interactions between differing assumptions, which might produce unintended results. Close attention should be paid, for example, to the differences among various assumed interest rates by duration. Also, assumed inflation rates should be consistent among claims, expenses and interest projections. These are not the only interactions possible, therefore each assumption should be examined in relation to all others.

4.3 EXPERIENCE DATA

Sources of data that can be used to develop premiums, the appropriateness of data relative to expected experience and the types of adjustments that should be considered before data is actually used are discussed in this section.

4.3.1 SOURCES OF DATA

In attempting to develop a basis for premium rates on any product, the actuary will want to search out available statistics as a starting point. The most useful source, if it is available, is the experience of the actuary's employer company on similar products. This experience has already been affected by the company's underwriting, sales and claim practices and is therefore most reliable as a guide to the results that the company can expect to experience on a new form. Of course, if the company is just starting out in the health insurance field, is entering a new market, or is embarking on a new line of business, such company experience would not be available. In such cases the actuary will need to rely on intercompany data, government data, or other published statistics.

A search of papers and committee reports in the *Transactions* of the Society of Actuaries (*TSA*) will give the actuary an indication of available information. For most coverages, and especially for those affected by inflation, the more recent the data, the more useful it will be. The Society of Actuaries periodically compiles intercompany studies in the *TSA Reports* on both individual medical expense and individual loss-of-time policies. In compiling these reports, the Society attempts to homogenize and to translate the data to standard deductible, coinsurance, and benefit levels.

There is a wealth of statistics available from government sources. The United States and Canadian governments publish significant volumes of material, as do many state governments. Indexes of the available data can be found in libraries. These types of studies are most helpful when devising new types of coverages or modifications to existing coverages for which company or industry data is not available. The United Nations publishes mortality and morbidity statistics and rates by country. These may be useful to an actuary with a company that has worldwide operations.

Some insurance departments publish state-specific statistics on loss ratios, premium rates and other financial data. This information is especially useful when the actuary needs to develop a special rate for a single state, either due to regulatory requirements or otherwise.

Industry associations, such as the Health Insurance Association of America, periodically publish statistics on insured and general populations.

The National Safety Council annually publishes "Accident Facts" which provides information on rates and trends of accidents, by type, for the general population.

Another valuable source of information is the "Statistical Bulletin" published by the Metropolitan Life Insurance Company.

4.3.2 APPROPRIATENESS OF DATA

Once the actuary obtains data that relate to the type of coverage being considered, the real challenge begins. The actuary must determine the appropriateness of the data relative to the actual experience that will develop based on the company's planned underwriting, sales and claim philosophies.

Ordinarily, an insured population will not experience the same rates and patterns of morbidity as the general population. Medical underwriting will exclude many impaired lives from the insured population. The company may market its products in a particular socioeconomic group (such as white collar executives) that has different morbidity characteristics than the population underlying the available data. The actuary must adjust the published statistics to take into account any material differences he perceives will exist between the experience of the proposed coverage and the experience of the coverage underlying the available statistics.

4.3.3 ADJUSTING THE DATA

If a coverage is to be fully underwritten, some adjustment for early duration experience is likely to be necessary. Intercompany studies published by the Society of Actuaries usually do not include experience for the first policy year. Similarly, population data must be viewed as aggregate experience, and adjusted for any effects of underwriting selection (or antiselection) expected in the insured population. Similar adjustments would need to be made to reflect preexisting condition limitations.

The determination of such adjustments requires considerable judgment and is based on the degree of anticipated savings from the proposed policy provisions or underwriting rules.

The actuary must investigate the levels of benefits underlying the data he intends to use. He must analyze the impact of actual benefits on experience. If, for example, an intercompany disability income study excluded claims in excess of $5,000 per month, the actuary must consider what impact offering issue limits up to $10,000 per month will have on the experience.

Provisions in the proposed policy may be different than those incorporated in the experience being used to set premiums. With respect to disability income coverage, for example, the definition of disability has an important impact on the claim costs. Defining disability as the inability to perform the duties of any occupation will exclude some disabilities that would be included in a definition requiring the insured to be able to perform the duties of his own occupation. Another example, in accidental death insurance, is the length of time permitted between the date of the accident and the date of death for the claim to be payable. Obviously the longer the length of time permitted, the higher the claim cost will be.

The actuary will want to consider other factors which may have an impact on the level of claims relative to the data being studied. These might include the method of sale (direct response, controlled agents, brokers and so on), market penetration, geographic distribution and so on.

If the available data is not categorized by age and sex in the way the actuary needs to calculate rates, it will be necessary to assume the proportions of these categories that are included in the data, and therefore the effect the actual distribution will have on emerging experience. For example, the actuary may feel that his insured population will tend to be somewhat older than that incorporated in a study of the general population. Or he may feel there will be relatively more blue collar or white collar exposure than that incorporated in the underlying study.

The time periods of exposures and claims in the experience studies being used should be carefully considered. The actuary must consider the difference between economic conditions at the time the study was made and current conditions, and he must consider possible future conditions for the policies he is planning.

Several of the morbidity tables developed by the Society of Actuaries and the NAIC are loaded for contingencies, and are intended to be used for reserve calculations rather than for premium rate calculations. It is appropriate to incorporate margins in calculations of reserves for statutory solvency that would not be appropriate in calculations of premium rates for pricing. The actuary, therefore, should use reserve tables with caution.

Many studies, especially those that are not related to insurance experience, are published in forms not readily usable for claim cost purposes. A published disability table, for example, may show all disabilities for durations of benefits less than one year without identifying the actual durations. In cases like this, the actuary will need to make certain assumptions or modifications to the data base in order to use it.

For inflation sensitive coverages, or at uncompetitive rate levels, healthy policyholders will tend to have higher lapse rates than unhealthy ones. Over time, this effect can accumulate in a significant way. Also, if the actuary is reviewing experience for the purpose of developing a rate increase for existing policyholders, he should take into consideration the effects of the antiselective lapsation that will be caused by the increase. A rate increase will usually result in a greater proportion of healthy than unhealthy lives lapsing coverage. The result may be an increase in the average claim cost for the insureds who remain, generating a rate increase spiral. For a complete discussion of this topic, see the article, "Cumulative Antiselection Theory," *TSA XXXIV.*

4.4 PROFITABILITY

Criteria for determining profit levels and the impact of regulatory considerations on the realized profitability are considered here.

4.4.1 CRITERIA USED IN SETTING LEVELS

In setting premium levels for an individual health insurance policy, another primary task is that of determining a profitability component. The profit objective selected will depend upon factors such as the type of coverage, the marketing method, renewability, competition, incidence of claims and expenses, and the regulatory environment. It will also have to be consistent with overall company objectives and with the profit expectations on past and current products.

Historically, most actuaries have felt that the required level of a profit margin built into the premium rating structure should be higher for coverages that involve a greater risk of fluctuation in claim costs.

Note that the profit margin should not be confused with the loss ratio. While the two are related, it is not necessarily true that high loss ratio products generate low profit margins or vice versa.

Profitability of individual health insurance policies has been the subject of long discussions. Some health products have traditionally not been profitable, at least when measured in terms of underwriting profit exclusive of investment income. Regulators and company personnel alike have long sought a measure of reasonableness of benefits in relation to premiums. Such a reasonableness test is required in the statutes of many states.

4.4.2 REGULATORY MEASURES OF REASONABLENESS OF BENEFITS IN RELATION TO PREMIUMS

The first official position taken by the NAIC, with regard to use of loss ratios as a means of measuring benefits in relation to premiums, was in 1953. The NAIC adopted a bench-mark loss ratio schedule of 50 percent with a 5 percent reduction for accident only policies and additional reductions for policies with annual premiums of $10 or less. The committee recommending this proposal was careful to state that this loss ratio structure was to be considered only as a bench-mark, which would be a presumption that benefits were reasonable in relation to the premiums charged. Individual states would then consider such action as they might deem proper under their statutes. Furthermore, the loss ratio was defined as an *ultimate credible loss ratio*, meaning one based on a significant premium volume on substantially similar policy forms over a reasonable period of time, with weight given to higher first-year expense trends and other relevant factors. Interestingly the NAIC disavowed any intention to regulate premium rates with this proposal. However, history has shown that loss ratio regulation has evolved into a means by which states have regulated individual health insurance premium rates.

The 50 percent bench-mark for most individual health insurance policy forms was widely accepted for many years following its adoption. The next significant loss ratio regulation was adopted by the State of New York in 1973. Known commonly as Regulation 62, it originally required an anticipated loss ratio of 50 percent for most individual health insurance policies. For policies providing accident only coverage, the requirement was 45 percent, and for policies providing "substantially full coverage" for specific accidents the requirement was 40 percent.

Federal minimum standard regulations for Medicare supplement policies require a 60 percent loss ratio for all such forms, regardless of renewability or premium size. The NAIC guidelines incorporated this 60 percent requirement for Medicare supplement forms.

In 1978, the NAIC, working with the Health Insurance Association of America, developed new guidelines for the approval of premium rates for individual health insurance policies. These guidelines set forth criteria for reasonableness of benefits in relation to premiums. These guidelines established anticipated loss ratios as high as 60 percent for optionally renewable policies. Adjustments are permitted to recognize different renewability provisions, the differences between medical expense coverages and loss of income coverages, and policies with low average annual premiums.

4.4.2.1 Current NAIC Guidelines

The current NAIC guidelines set forth requirements for loss ratios with respect to filings for premium rate revisions for previously approved forms as well as for premium rates for new issues. Essentially these requirements are that the minimum loss ratio standard be met for both the *entire lifetime* of the policies from inception as well as the entire *future lifetime* of the policies (from the date of the rate revision).

The requirement that the future loss ratio equal the minimum standard precludes a company that has a higher than anticipated past loss ratio on a policy form from recovering the loss. Some companies have felt this to be a harsh constraint; however, a premium level that would recoup past losses could be actuarially in excess of that which the group of insureds under the policy could expect on the open market for a policy offered at the current minimum standard loss ratio, if they were all still insurable.

The NAIC guidelines allow a company to justify anticipated loss ratios lower than the standards in cases of special coverages such as accident only, short term nonrenewable coverages, specified perils such as cancer and other special risks. It also provides that special consideration be given to marketing methods, extraordinary expenses, high risk of claim fluctuation, product features such as long elimination periods, high deductibles, high maximum limits, and debit policies.

The NAIC guidelines do not, of themselves, apply in any jurisdiction until adopted by that jurisdiction. Many states have addressed concerns about specific provisions through modifications or substitutions of the NAIC guidelines.

4.4.2.2 Loss Ratio Monitoring Under New York Regulation 62

The NAIC loss ratio guidelines apply to the filing of initial premium rates, and requests for premium rate revisions. The minimum loss ratios in the guidelines are those anticipated at the time of the filing. There is no requirement to review the actual experience under the approved rates to determine if the actual experience is better or worse than expected.

In 1983 the New York Insurance Department amended Regulation 62 in a significant way by establishing a procedure for monitoring the actual experience generated under the approved premium rates, to determine whether rate reductions or other actions would be necessary in order to meet the loss ratio minimums. This monitoring compares actual experience with anticipated loss ratios, to determine whether a rate revision should be considered. If a revision should be considered, the company is charged with the responsibility of either filing an action plan with the insurance department or justifying why no revision should be made.

For example, suppose a company filed a policy form with a 50 percent anticipated loss ratio. Suppose further that after five years it became apparent that the lifetime loss ratio on the policy was going to be less than 45 percent. Under the amended Regulation 62 the company would be required to calculate a rate decrease (or take other equivalent action) so that the 50 percent lifetime loss ratio would be achieved. Policies with guaranteed premium levels are subject to less severe corrective actions.

Since Regulation 62 in essence does not allow insurers to keep excessive unexpected profits, in that it requires them to be returned to policyholders, the pricing actuary should consider an additional contingency margin in order to take into account the fact that there will be no savings from those forms which have significantly lower than expected loss ratios.

4.5 CALCULATION METHODS

In this section methods used to calculate the premiums and to test the profitability inherent in a specific premium level are described. One of the methods, the cash flow method, is not commonly used by insurance company pricing actuaries but is included to acquaint the student with its existence.

4.5.1 THE ASSET-SHARE MODEL

The asset-share model is used to study a hypothetical group of policies. The model follows the group for a number of years, and analyzes in detail each important characteristic of the group for each year of the projection. The model is created for a number of representative cells, a cell being a particular combination of rating classifications. For example, a disability income product might have representative cells for issue ages 25, 35, 45 and 55, for males and females, for four occupation classes, for four elimination periods, and for three benefit periods.

Even when broad premium classes will be used in the final rating structure, an actuary may want to use the asset share model to study subclasses separately. This is recommended when final premiums will be calculated on a unisex basis. Although the final premiums will not differentiate by sex, the expected claims will be different by sex and proper measurement of profit would suggest that cells should be analyzed separately by sex.

A large number of assumptions must be made, implicitly or explicitly, in order to define the asset-share model. The first and most important choice to be made is whether the model will be a policy year model or a calendar year model.

The *policy year* model measures time from the simultaneous issue of the entire block of policies. However, since most companies analyze their actual experience on a calendar year basis, direct comparison of results from this model with actual results is difficult. On the other hand, the formulas used in the policy year model are far simpler than those in the calendar year model.

The *calendar year* model measures time on the basis of a calendar year. Since policies are issued at various dates throughout the year, this model requires complicated formulas for tracking exposures and claims. Once these formulas have been developed, however, results from this model are far easier to compare against actual results.

Once the model has been developed and checked, it can be used to test "what ifs." That is, assumptions can be modified to determine the effect on profitability of specified deviations from expected values. For example, if an assumption of 8 percent level interest was made in the model, a test might be performed to see what would happen to profitability if interest turned out to be 7.5 percent, or 8.5 percent. Even a worst case scenario could be created to test what would happen if all assumptions were too optimistic. This type of analysis is important information for upper management, as it helps to quantify a comfort level with respect to the assumptions. This process is often referred to as *sensitivity testing*.

The choice of profit measure used with the model dictates which columns of calculations to set up. The policy year model illustration at the end of the chapter demonstrates results using both the ROI and the percentage of premium profit measures. The appropriate columns for the respective measures are self evident in the illustration, however, the actuary should give some consideration to which choice is better suited to a particular company's operations and philosophy.

When policies are initially issued, there is usually a necessary investment by the company, since the initial cash flow of the policies is not sufficient to meet the associated costs. As time goes on, there will be a positive cash flow arising from the policies. If we think of this cash flow process as being similar to a loan, then the repayments that occur over time due to the positive cash flows will constitute the equivalent of interest earnings on the initial loan. The ROI is then the rate of return earned by the loan, that is, the ROI is the interest rate at which the present value of negative cash flows equals the present value of positive cash flows. Usually, a company using this measure of profitability will have a preset target applicable to all products, not just the one currently being priced.

The *percentage of premium method* of measuring profitability compares the present value of profits with the present value of premium income. Just as in the ROI method, most companies will develop a generalized target of necessary profit which will not vary between particular products within a specific line of business.

In the past in taking present values, the assumed interest rate could be either pre-(federal income) tax or after-tax. When pre-tax interest was used, recognition of tax was made explicitly in the asset-share model. When after-tax interest was used, the smaller interest rate was intended to implicitly account for the lower profits resulting from taxation. With the revised tax law of 1984, and with the short-term tax law which preceded it, there has been an increasing tendency toward using pre-tax methods, with explicit recognition of taxes. The single-phase structure of the new law is much more amenable to explicit recognition of income tax.

INDIVIDUAL HEALTH INSURANCE PREMIUMS

In the asset-share calculation shown at the end of this chapter an initial, or a "test" premium is chosen. If this test premium is the result of calculations described in Section 4.5.2, it may in fact be the premium which will be used. In this case, the asset share calculation is performed only to test the profitability of the premium, and is not used to derive it. However, if some other method is used to derive the test premium, it may be treated as an approximate figure. For example, it may be chosen after examining competitors' rates, and it is not intended to be the final premium. The results of the asset share model then can be used to adjust the premium to its final level.

4.5.2 FORMULA METHODS

Before the availability of computers, actuaries relied on commutation functions and various other techniques to reduce repetitive calculations. The classical development of gross premiums using commutation functions is as follows:

S_x = annual claim cost at age x. This is benefit-specific, but may vary according to the rating classes already described.

$$H_x = S_x \cdot \frac{D_x + D_{x+1}}{2}$$

$K_x = \Sigma H_x$ (summed over the benefit period).

D_x = the normal life commutation function, but including lapsation.

$N_x = \Sigma D_x$ (summed over the premium paying period).

The normal health insurance notational conventions apply. For example, the post-subscript [x]+t represents a point in time t years after issue for a policy issued at age x, the brackets indicating the existence of durational selection (or antiselection). A pre-superscript is sometimes used with S_x, H_x, and K_x to indicate the benefit combination being calculated. For example, $^{30/65}K_x$ might represent a disability income plan with a 30 day elimination period and a benefit period to age 65.

The net single premium at age x then is K_x/D_x, the net annual premium is K_x/N_x, and so forth. The net premiums developed in this way are combined with expenses in a formula to produce gross premiums.

The advantage of this method is that the summations used in calculating the commutation functions are often duplicative, allowing the premium to be calculated directly from them.

The simplest formula method of premium construction is the *loss ratio method*. In this method, expenses are treated as a flat percentage of premium, which usually does not vary even by duration. The net premium is divided by a target loss ratio to produce the gross premium. The loss ratio is the ratio of the present value of claim to the Present value of premiums over the life of the policy. The difference between the loss ratio and 100 percent represents that portion of the premium which is available for expenses and profit.

The formula is

$$\text{Gross Premium} = \frac{\text{(Net Premium)}}{\text{(loss ratio)}}$$

or

$$= \frac{\text{Net Premium}}{(1 - \text{expenses and profit})}$$

The formula method can be as sophisticated as desired, recognizing as many elements of expense and morbidity as deemed necessary. An example of such a formula employing refined expense factors and incorporating a waiver of premium benefit is[1]:

$$^BG_x = \frac{(1+a)(^BK_{[x]} - {^BK_{65}}) + b \cdot D_{[x]} + c \cdot (N_{[x]} - N_{65})}{(1-n)(N_{[x]} - N_{65}) - m \cdot D_{[x]} - k(N'_{[x]+1} - N'_{x+5}) - (^{B'}K'_{[x]} - {^{B'}K'_{65}})}$$

with terms and symbols defined [as follows]:

a   is the claim administration expense factor

b   is the extra first-year expense (expressed as a factor per unit of coverage according to average policy size)

c   is the constant per policy expense similarly expressed

n   is the expense per premium dollar

m   is the extra expense per first-year premium dollar

k   is the extra expense per second through fifth year premium dollar (implying a step in the renewal commission rate)

B'   identifies the claim cost function valuing waiver of premium, the benefit being related to B of the numerator only if the coverage is disability income and the waiver period is identical with the income period. Since ^BG_x is an annual premium, the term $^{B'}K'_{[x]} - {^{B'}K'_{65}}$ values a benefit of one per year, whereas $^BK_{[x]} - {^BK_{65}}$ may value a different unit of benefit such as $10 monthly, or even a benefit altogether different from disability income.

The formula is for term to age 65 coverage, with level premiums payable over the period of coverage. Use of the term N'_{x+5} rather than $N'_{[x]+5}$ implies that the select period is 5 years or less.

Care should be taken that all elements of the formula are based upon consistent units, whether they be per policy or per unit benefit.

---

[1] Taken from page 131 of Bartleson, E.L., *Health Insurance Provided Through Individual Policies* (Chicago: Society of Actuaries, 1968).

A number of considerations are pertinent in determining whether to use this method to derive gross premiums:
- This method can be less costly to develop, both in time and expense, than the asset-share method.
- Expense and profit contingencies may be less accurate under this method than under the asset-share method.
- Measurement of profit is limited to the percentage of premium method at the interest rate used in the formula.

4.5.3 THE CASH FLOW METHOD

Alternative health-care financing plans, such as Blue Cross, Blue Shield or Health Maintenance Organizations, utilize another method of calculating premiums for individual benefits. Usually, these organizations limit the time horizons of their analyses to relatively short-term periods (such as a year) and project all assumptions only through that period. Implicitly, this assumes that there will be sufficient income in subsequent periods to cover the costs arising from these periods. This assumption is considered reasonable for a number of reasons:

- Such plans are closer in nature to a public corporation than to a private one. They often receive preferential statutory advantages, such as hospital reimbursement differentials and zero premium tax, which help guarantee their ongoing nature.
- Individual policies (and sometimes small group policies) will often be subsidized by the large group policies; this subsidy contributes to their viability.
- Such plans are closely regulated, and regulators view them as being operated in the public interest. The regulators therefore have a stake in their continued financial soundness.
- The geographic concentration of most plans, and the often high penetration in those geographic areas, cause the plan populations to more closely resemble a stationary population than the population represented in a typical block of policies issued by a traditional insurance carrier. This effect is also due to the alternate plan practice of having few policy forms and treating all policy forms as being currently issued (in effect, never creating a closed block of business). Thus there is a steady stream of new entrants replacing those who leave.

Pricing these plans involves only the projection of claims, expenses and amount of in-force business (enrollment). The projected costs are divided by the projected enrollment to arrive at a cost per policy (or "per contract"), and then this result is loaded for expenses using the loss ratio method.

4.6 EXPERIENCE MONITORING AND RENEWAL RATING

For many coverages, and particularly for medical expense insurance, it is recognized at the time of original pricing that there is little possibility the original premium rates will be adequate for more than a few years. In order to monitor the need for such rate actions, it is important that appropriate systems be designed and installed.

4.6.1 MANAGEMENT INFORMATION SYSTEMS

What considerations go into the design of an appropriate management information system for experience monitoring? As usual, there is no single answer. Each system must meet its objectives within the constraints of company resources.

The management information system should be structured to compare the expected and actual financial results of the block of policies. This gives rise to the first important question: What is expected? Ideally, expected results should be consistent with the assumptions used in the original rating. Often, however, company resources may be limited in this aspect of managing the business. For example, policy reserves often are only available on a statutory basis or on a GAAP basis, either of which may not correspond with original assumptions. This can cause substantial distortion in the comparison. Also, the use of the preliminary term reserve method for statutory reporting will cause initial loss ratios to look far better than they would if the reserves arising from original rating assumptions were used.

Profits can emerge from any of the assumptions originally used in rating. This would suggest monitoring profitability according to each of the assumptions used. However, this requires a substantial investment of resources so that it is often necessary to settle for something short of the ideal. For example, many companies will monitor their claims experience on an ongoing block-by-block basis and their expenses on a company-wide basis. Also, persistency may be reviewed only when pricing a new product or when a specific problem develops.

Companies operating under a GAAP system of accounting are much more aware of the incidence of profitability by type of assumption. However GAAP assumptions often will not match pricing assumptions, so that this vehicle is also limited for purposes of experience monitoring.

The most commonly used method is the loss ratio method discussed earlier. In this method, the actual loss ratio, usually on a calendar year, statutory basis, is compared against the expected loss ratio. It is critical when using this method that the two loss ratios be on the same basis in all respects. This means the expected loss ratio should reflect the same mix of business by rating class, reserving basis, and duration as the business on which the actual loss ratio is based. Also, any policy reserves used in the analysis should be on a pricing basis.

A fundamental requirement of any experience monitoring system is that the actuary be satisfied that the model is the best he can develop with the available resources.

An important aspect of a monitoring system is determining the frequency of the reports. At one time many companies examined their experience only occasionally. This was before the phenomenon of double-digit inflation. Most experience analysis now is performed more frequently, with the timing determined by the size of the block of business, the cost of the analysis, and the rating philosophy of the company. The decision must weigh the cost of analysis against the risk of adverse experience.

4.6.2 RENEWAL RATE CALCULATIONS

Once it has been determined that a rate change is necessary, presumably because of adverse experience, the actuary will examine the alternative methods available to determine the change.

One method is to recalculate the asset shares using updated assumptions. This method is not often used, because the block of currently existing policies will likely be substantially different than that originally assumed. Among the differences are:

- the underlying morbidity, lapse, interest, and other asset share model assumptions, which will need to be changed due to changed expectations;
- the mix of cells, which is likely different from that originally assumed; and
- the duration of policies which all started at duration zero in the original calculation, while the existing block is an amalgam of durations.

The loss ratio method is the most common method of determining premium rate changes. In this method the actual loss ratio is compared to the expected loss ratio over a period of time called the experience period and then is projected into the future. The premium rates are then recalculated at a level where the target loss ratio (which may or may not equal the original expected loss ratio) will be met. The target loss ratio may be the overall lifetime loss ratio, or more likely, the future loss ratio at the time of the analysis. Regulators have a substantial amount of input into the choice of target loss ratios. This sometimes includes requiring a higher loss ratio on renewals than on new policies.

When examining actual loss ratios, the denominators (premium) often will initially be based on Annual Statement data. These historical premiums represent premium dollars collected under a number of different rate schedules, the number depending upon how active the company has been in the past in implementing rate changes. It is necessary to adjust those premiums to what would have been collected under a constant schedule in order to have a meaningful basis for projection.

Another consideration is the period of time over which future loss ratios are projected. Regulators will have substantial input here. Normally, only one or two years' inflation are permitted to be recognized in projections.

Regardless of the method used, it is a commonly accepted principle of rating that a policyholder's original rating class should be preserved. Not only does this prohibit transferring individuals from one class to another, but it also prohibits the creation of new classes subsequent to initial introduction of the policy. There have been instances where this has been abridged, but usually only when it is clearly in the interest of all policyholders.

Once the rate increase has been determined, the next step is implementation of the increase. At least one state insurance department has taken the position that its jurisdiction is over rate changes applied to all policies which were *originally* issued to residents of that state, regardless of subsequent residence. That same insurance department requires, for equity reasons, that rate changes be implemented on policy anniversaries rather than on premium due dates. This avoids the situation of insureds who pay monthly premiums, having to pay the increase one month later while annual payers may not start paying the increase for up to eleven months later.

Since approvals from different states come at different times and with different qualifications, it is important to build flexibility into company policy administration and billing systems to handle such differences. In this way rate changes can be implemented at the time and in the manner in which they are approved, minimizing the financial effects of delays.

4.7 OTHER CONSIDERATIONS

Many individual health insurance policies provide that should the insured be disabled, premiums will be waived during the period of disability. As a result, a charge for waiver of premium benefits is incorporated in the premium. When monitoring the experience, insurers may either reduce premiums by the amount of premiums waived under the policy or increase benefits by the identical amount. The approach will usually be based on the company's administrative system as opposed to theoretical considerations. The correct theoretical approach depends on whether the waived premium has commissions and expenses associated with it.

A prorated refund of premium at death is included in some individual health insurance policies. The benefit provides a refund of the prorated portion of the premium upon death prior to the "paid-to" date. The premium charged should reflect this added benefit. However, most insurers do not specifically provide for this feature in the gross premium formula because the charge is small relative to the total premium.

Individual health insurance policies, similar to life insurance policies, provide for a 31-day grace period following the due date of any premium after the first. Because the persistency of health insurance coverages is poorer than that of life insurance, and because a large portion of health insurance is paid for on a monthly premium basis, the cost of this provision is relatively more significant for health than for life insurance. The actuary may want to consider the impact of the grace period on claim costs in evaluating the required premium for coverages that exhibit a high lapse rate or a high proportion of monthly premiums in the modal mix. (If CAST factors are included in the model, this effect will already be implicitly recognized.)

In some blocks of individual health insurance policies, a high proportion of insureds pay premiums on an other than annual basis. The impacts of this are lower investment earnings (because less unearned premium will be held) and poorer persistency. As a result, health insurance modal premium loadings tend to be somewhat higher than they are for life insurance. The principles for calculating the required modal adjustments are identical to those used for life insurance, and include appropriate assumptions as to expense and persistency.

If the insurance company decides to reinsure a portion of the risk under a new policy, it will need to recognize the costs of reinsurance in its premium rates. These costs will be expressed both in the premium per unit that the reinsurer will charge and in the expense allowances that the reinsurer will allow. If the actuary can develop a sophisticated enough model, he can directly incorporate the cost of reinsurance in the calculation of the premium rate structure. Otherwise, analysis of the reinsurance costs in relation to profitability must be performed independently.

Finally, typical disability insurance policy will contain a *recurrent disability* provision. This can be important in evaluating claim costs, since the recurring disability will not have a new elimination period and the maximum length of benefit will be reduced.

4.8 SAMPLE ASSET SHARE CALCULATION

This asset share model is for a disability income policy. Results for one cell are shown. The cell shown is for issue age 45, male, 30-day elimination period, 2-year benefit period and occupation class I.

The major assumptions, not obvious from the table are:

Morbidity: 1982 Disability Table
Interest earned on reserves: 8.00%
Discount rate for percent of premium profitability: 8.50%
Premium mode: 100% Annual, assumed paid uniformly throughout the year.
Policy Reserves: 1964 CDT, 1958 CSO at 4.00%, 2 year preliminary term.

Claim reserves: 1982 Disability Table at 4.50%, linearly interpolated.
Claims assumed in the middle of the year.
Level per policy expenses increase 5% per year.
Average size benefit: $1000 per month.
Test premium: $35.00
Federal Income Tax rate on operating profits: 34%
Tax Reserves: Equal to Statutory

				CLAIMS			EXPENSES			
Pol Yr t (1)	Att Age [x]+t (2)	Lapse Rate (3)	No. of Policies It (4)	Tabular Claim Cost (5)	Selection (and CAST) Factors (6)	Claim Cost (7)	Per Policy (8)	Commissions (%of prem) (9)	Claim Admin. (%of clm) (10)	Other (% of prem) (11)
1	45	0.150	1000.0	10.083	0.65	6.554	200.00	50	7	40
2	46	0.110	850.0	10.753	0.85	9.140	15.00	25	7	25
3	47	0.090	756.5	11.422	0.90	10.280	15.75	15	7	10
4	48	0.080	688.4	12.114	0.95	11.508	16.54	10	7	10
5	49	0.070	633.3	12.806	0.99	12.678	17.36	10	7	10
6	50	0.065	589.0	13.499	1.00	13.499	18.23	10	7	10
7	51	0.060	550.7	14.191	1.01	14.333	19.14	10	7	10
8	52	0.055	517.7	14.883	1.02	15.181	20.10	10	7	10
9	53	0.050	489.2	16.925	1.03	17.432	21.11	10	7	10
10	54	0.045	464.7	18.966	1.04	19.725	22.16	10	7	10
11	55	0.043	443.8	21.008	1.05	22.058	23.27	5	7	10
12	56	0.041	424.7	23.049	1.06	24.432	24.43	5	7	10
13	57	0.040	407.3	25.091	1.07	26.847	25.66	5	7	10
14	58	0.040	391.0	28.049	1.08	30.292	26.94	5	7	10
15	59	0.040	375.4	31.006	1.09	33.797	28.28	5	7	10
16	60	0.040	360.4	33.964	1.10	37.360	29.70	5	7	10
17	61	0.040	346.0	36.921	1.11	40.983	31.18	5	7	10
18	62	0.040	332.1	39.879	1.12	44.664	32.74	5	7	10
19	63	0.040	318.8	42.761	1.13	48.320	34.38	5	7	10
20	64	0.040	306.1	45.643	1.14	52.033	36.10	5	7	10

Pol Yr t (1)	Total Incurred Claims (12)	Total Premium Received (13)	Total Expenses (14)	Clm Res. on t's incurrals (15)	Clm res. on t—1's incurrals (16)	Total Clm Res (17)	Paid Claims (18)	Policy Reserves (19)	Change in Policy Reserves (20)	Unearned Premium Reserve (21)
1	65,541	350,000	519,588	32,528	0	32,528	33,013	0	0	175,000
2	77,688	297,500	166,938	39,371	10,586	49,957	60,258	0	0	148,750
3	77,767	264,775	83,552	40,169	12,844	53,013	74,711	52,955	52,955	132,388
4	79,226	240,945	65,120	40,748	13,121	53,869	78,370	130,799	77,844	120.473
5	80,297	221,670	60,952	41,151	13,435	54,586	79,581	196,336	65,537	110,835
6	79,508	206,153	57,535	40,624	13,683	54,307	79,787	259,163	62,828	103,076
7	78,933	192,753	54,619	40,230	13,612	53,842	79,399	302,897	43,734	96,376
8	78,587	181,188	52,145	39,971	13,574	53,546	78,883	336,491	33,594	90,594
9	85,280	171,222	50,540	44,211	13,574	57,785	81,041	362,013	25,522	85,611
10	91,671	162,661	49,249	48,294	15,125	63,419	86,036	376,455	14,432	81,331
11	97,901	155,341	40,482	52,298	16,600	68,898	92,422	390,573	14,128	77,671
12	103,776	148,662	39,942	56,119	18,030	74,149	98,525	390,768	195	74,331
13	109,358	142,567	39,490	59,789	19,382	79,171	104,336	386,967	(3,801)	71,283
14	118,456	136,864	39,355	65,441	20,669	86,109	111,518	367,578	(19,389)	68,432
15	126,872	131,389	39,208	70,771	22,886	93,657	119,325	341,613	(25,965)	65,695
16	134,640	126,134	39,048	75,788	24,953	100,740	127,556	306,325	(35,287)	63,067
17	141,787	121,088	38,877	80,497	26,875	107,373	135,155	259,475	(46,850)	60,544
18	148,343	116,245	38,696	84,908	28,659	113,568	142,148	199,277	(60,198)	58,122
19	154,066	111,595	38,486	88,952	30,312	119,264	148,369	130,726	(68,551)	55,798
20	159,269	107,131	38,268	92,713	32,294	125,006	153,527	45,913	(84,812)	53,566
21					34,119	34,119	90,887	0	(45,913)	0
22							34,119			

Change in UPR (22)	Earned Premium (23)	Total Statutory Reserves (24)	Change in Total Statutory Reserves (25)
175,000	175,000	207,528	207,528
(26,250)	323,750	198,707	(8,821)
(16,363)	281,138	238,355	39,648
(11,915)	252,860	305,141	66,786
(9,638)	231,307	361,757	56,616
(7,758)	213,911	416,547	54,790
(6,700)	199,453	453,115	36,569
(5,783)	186,970	480,631	27,515
(4,983)	176,205	505,409	24,778
(4,281)	166,942	521,194	15,785
(3,660)	159,001	537,142	15,947
(3,340)	152,002	539,248	2,106
(3,048)	145,614	537,421	(1,827)
(2,851)	139,715	522,119	(15,302)
(2,737)	134,127	500,964	(21,155)
(2,628)	128,762	470,132	(30,832)
(2,523)	123,611	427,392	(42,740)
(2,422)	118,667	370,967	(56,425)
(2,325)	113,920	305,787	(65,180)
(2,232)	109,363	224,485	(81,302)
(53,566)	53,566	34,119	(190,366)
			(34,119)

Pol Yr t (1)	Interest on Reserves (26)	Statutory Pre-tax Profit (27)	Tax (28)	Post-tax Profit (29)	Pres. Val of pre-tax profit (30)	Pres. Val of post-tax profit (31)	Pres. Val of Prem. Received (32)	PV Factor (33)
1	8,301	(401,828)	(136,621)	(265,206)	(401,828)	(265,206)	350,000	1.00000
2	16,249	95,374	32,427	62,947	87,902	58,015	274,194	0.92166
3	17,482	84,346	28,678	55,668	71,648	47,288	224,915	0.84946
4	21,740	52,410	17,820	34,591	41,033	27,081	188,638	0.78291
5	26,676	51,197	17,407	33,790	36,942	24,382	159,951	0.72157
6	31,132	45,1/3	15,359	29,814	30,042	19,828	137,101	0.66505
7	34,786	56,953	19,364	37,589	34,909	23,040	118,147	0.61295
8	37,350	59,994	20,398	39,596	33,892	22,369	102,358	0.56493
9	39,442	54,305	18,464	35,842	28,275	18,662	89,150	0.52067
10	41,064	52,655	17,903	34,752	25,268	16,677	78,058	0.47988
11	42,333	48,823	16,600	32,223	21,594	14,252	68,705	0.44229
12	43,056	51,144	17,389	33,755	20,848	13,760	60,600	0.40764
13	43,067	43,634	14,836	28,798	16,393	10,820	53,563	0.37570
14	42,382	43,675	14,849	28,825	15,123	9,981	47,392	0.34627
15	40,923	34,935	11,878	23,057	11,149	7,359	41,932	0.31914
16	38,844	29,206	9,930	19,276	8,591	5,670	37,101	0.29414
17	35,901	25,698	8,737	16,961	6,967	4,598	32,827	0.27110
18	31,934	23,760	8,078	15,682	5,937	3,918	29,045	0.24986
19	27,070	16,990	5,777	11,214	3,913	2,582	25,699	0.23028
20	21,211	17,849	6,069	11,781	3,788	2,500	22,738	0.21224
21	10,344	109,823	37,340	72,483	21,483	14,179	0	0.19562
22	1,365	1,365	464	901	246	162	0	0.18029
			SUM:	124,116	81,916	2,142,111		

Profit as a % of Premium
 Post-tax (Σ (31) ÷ Σ(32)) = 3.82%
 Pre-tax (Σ (30) ÷ Σ(32)) = 5.79%
ROI = 4.58%
(ROI is an interest rate at which the sum of the present values of (29) equals zero.)

Definitions—Asset Share Calculations

Policy Year
$(1)_t = (1)_{t-1} + 1$, for $t > 1$.
$(1)_1 = 1$

Attained Age
$(2)_t = (2)_{t-1} + 1$, for $t > 1$.
$(2)_1 = 45$

Lapse Rate
$(3)_t$: assumed

Number of Policies
$(4)_t = (4)_{t-1} \times [1 - (3)_{t-1}]$, for $t > 1$.
$(4)_1 = 1,000$

Tabular Claim Cost
$(5)_t$: Values from 1982 Table 3Am for ages 47 52, 57 and 62. Intervening values linearly interpolated.

Selection (and CAST) Factors
$(6)_t$: assumed

Claim Cost
$(7)_t = (5)_t \times (6)_t$

Expenses:

Per Policy
$(8)_t$: assumed

Commissions
$(9)_t$: assumed

Claim Administration
$(10)_t$: assumed

Other % of Premium
$(11)_t$: assumed

Total Incurred Claims
$(12)_t = (7)_t \times (4)_t \times 10$ units

Total Premium Received
$(13)_t = \$35.00 \times (4)_t \times 10$ units

Total Expenses
$(14)_t = (8)_t \times (4)_t$
$\quad + (9)_t \times (13)_t / 100$
$\quad + (10)_t \times (12)_t / 100$
$\quad + (11)_t \times (13)_t / 100$

INDIVIDUAL HEALTH INSURANCE PREMIUMS 87

Claim Reserve on t's incurrals	$(15)_t = (12)_t \times$ A reserve factor calculated to represent the portion of original incurred claim still held at (on average) six months after incurral (See calculation of Disabled Life Reserves Table attached.)
Claim Reserve on t-1's incurrals	$16_t = (12)_{t-1} \times$ A reserve factor calculated to represent the portion of original incurred claims still held at (on average) 18 months after incurral (See calculation of Disabled Life Reserves Table attached.) for $t > 1$. $(16)_1 = 0$
Total Claim Reserve	$(17)_t = (15)_t + (16)_t$
Paid Claims	$(18)_t = (12)_t + (17)_{t-1} - (17)_t$, for $t > 1$
	$(18)_1 = (12)_1 - (17)_1$
Policy Reserves	$(19)_t = 10$ units $\times (4)_t \times$ appropriate policy reserve factor (See values from 1964 CDT Reserve Table attached.)
Change in Policy Reserves	$(20)_t = (19)_t - (19)_{t-1}$, for $t > 1$.
	$(20)_1 = (19)_1$
Unearned Premium Reserves	$(21)_t = (13)_t \times .5$
Change in UPR	$(22)_t = (21)_t - (21)_{t-1}$, for $t > 1$.
	$(22)_1 = (21)_1$
Earned Premium	$(23)_t = (13)_t - (22)_t$
Total Statutory Reserves	$(24)_t = (21)_t + (19)_t + (17)_t$
Change in Total Statutory Reserves	$(25)_t = (24)_t - (24)_{t-1}$, for $t > 1$.
	$(25)_1 = (24)_1$
Interest on Reserves	$(26)_t = 8\% \times [(24)_t + (24)_{t-1}]/2$, for $t > 1$.
	$(26)_1 = 8\% \times (24)_1/2$

Statutory Pre-tax Profit $\quad (27)_t = (23)_t + (26)_t$
$$- [(12)_t + (14)_t + (20)_t]$$

Tax $\quad (28)_t = 34\% \times (27)_t$

Post-tax profit $\quad (29)_t = (27)_t - (28)_t$

Present Value of Pre-tax Profit $\quad (30)_t = (27)_t \times (33)_t$

Present Value of Post-tax Profit $\quad (31)_t = (29)_t \times (33)_t$

Present Value of Premium Received $\quad (32)_t = (13)_t \times (33)_t$

PV Factor $\quad (33)_t = (1.085)^{-t}$

CALCULATION OF MALE DISABLED LIFE RESERVES HELD AT 6 MOS AND 18 MOS 1982 TABLE 8AM

Age (1)	Disabled Life Reserves at				Amount Pd Thru Dur		Proport of Pol's Disabled		Reserve Held at		Res/Incurred	
	4 Mos (2)	6 Mos (3)	9 Mos (4)	18 Mos (5)	6 Mos (6)	18 Mos (7)	6 Mos (8)	18 Mos (9)	6 Mos (10)	18 Mos (11)	6 Mos (12)	18 Mos (13)
42	1041	1095	1175	643	4.9865	8.2107	0.0039	0.0022	4.2317	1.4120	0.4591	0.1467
43	1063	1113	1188	644	5.2419	8.8157	0.0042	0.0025	4.6974	1.5845	0.4726	0.1524
44	1085	1132	1202	645	5.4973	9.4207	0.0046	0.0027	5.1762	1.7576	0.4850	0.1572
45	1108	1151	1215	647	5.7528	10.0257	0.0049	0.0030	5.6683	1.9313	0.4963	0.1615
46	1130	1169	1229	648	6.0082	10.6307	0.0053	0.0033	6.1735	2.1056	0.5068	0.1653
47	1152	1188	1242	649	6.2636	11.2357	0.0056	0.0035	6.6920	2.2806	0.5165	0.1687
48	1156	1194	1252	652	6.6834	11.9367	0.0059	0.0037	7.0775	2.4376	0.5143	0.1696
49	1159	1200	1262	654	7.1031	12.6377	0.0062	0.0040	7.4667	2.5959	0.5125	0.1704
50	1163	1206	1272	657	7.5229	13.3386	0.0065	0.0042	7.8595	2.7553	0.5109	0.1712
51	1166	1213	1282	659	7.9426	14.0396	0.0068	0.0044	8.2559	2.9159	0.5097	0.1720
52	1170	1219	1292	662	8.3624	14.7406	0.0071	0.0046	8.6559	3.0776	0.5086	0.1727
53	1188	1233	1300	663	9.2525	16.6017	0.0081	0.0054	9.9603	3.5793	0.5184	0.1774
54	1206	1247	1309	664	10.1426	18.4628	0.0091	0.0061	11.2924	4.0827	0.5268	0.1811
55	1224	1261	1317	666	11.0326	20.3239	0.0100	0.0069	12.6522	4.5880	0.5342	0.1842
56	1242	1275	1326	667	11.9227	22.1850	0.0110	0.0076	14.0395	5.0950	0.5408	0.1868
57	1260	1290	1334	668	12.8128	24.0461	0.0120	0.0084	15.4546	5.6039	0.5467	0.1890
58	1286	1311	1349	669	14.0751	26.7421	0.0133	0.0096	17.3739	6.4039	0.5524	0.1932
59	1312	1333	1363	671	15.3373	29.4380	0.0145	0.0107	19.3479	7.2072	0.5578	0.1967
60	1339	1354	1378	672	16.5996	32.1340	0.0158	0.0119	21.3765	8.0138	0.5629	0.1996
61	1365	1376	1392	674	17.8618	34.8299	0.0171	0.0131	23.4597	8.8238	0.5677	0.2021
62	1391	1397	1407	675	19.1241	37.5259	0.0183	0.0143	25.5976	9.6370	0.5724	0.2043
63	1415	1416	1417	676	20.2097	40.0800	0.0195	0.0157	27.6089	10.6292	0.5774	0.2096
64	1439	1435	1427	676	21.2953	42.6342	0.0207	0.0172	29.6641	11.6232	0.5821	0.2142
65	1464	1453	1438	677	22.3808	45.1883	0.0219	0.0186	31.7632	12.6189	0.5866	0.2183
66	1488	1472	1448	677	23.4664	47.7425	0.0230	0.0201	33.9062	13.6164	0.5910	0.2219
67	1512	1490	1458	678	24.5520	50.2966	0.0242	0.0216	36.0930	14.6156	0.5952	0.2252

Definitions- Calculation of Male Disabled Life Reserves Held at 6 Mos and 18 Mos - 1982 Table 8AM

Age	$(1)_t = 41 + t$
Disabled Life Reserves at 4, 6, 9, 18 Month	$(2)_t$, $(4)_t$ and $(5)_t$ Values from 1982 Table 8Am at ages 42, 47,....67. Intervening values linearly interpolated.
	$(3)_t = .6 \times (2)_t + .4 \times (4)_t$
	(This approximation is very rough and not recommended for real use.)
Amount Paid Through Duration of 6 and 18 months	$(6)_t$: Total values through 6 months from 1982 Table A2m for ages 42, 47,....67. Intervening values linearly interpolated.
	$(7)_t$: Total of values through 18 monthes from 1982 Table A2m for ages 42, 47,... 67. Intervening values linearly interpolated.
	(Number disabled at the end of each month used as an approximation for payments in that month.)
Proportion of Policies Disabled at 6 months	$(8)_t$: Values at 6 months from 1982 Table A2m for ages 42, 47,... 67. Intervening values linearly interpolated.
Proportion of Policies Disabled at 18 months	$(9)_t$: Values at 18 months from 1982 Table A2m for ages 42, 47,....67. Intervening values linearly interpolated.
Reserve Held at 6 and 18 months	$(10)_t = (8)_t \times (3)_t$
	$(11)_t = (9)_t \times (5)_t$
Reserve/Incurred at 6 and 18 months	$(12)_t = (10)_t / [(10)_t + (6)_t]$
	$(13)_t = (11)_t / [(11)_t + (7)_t]$

VALUES FROM 1964 CDT RESERVE TABLES AT 4%
POLICY RESERVE CALCULATIONS
MID-TERMINAL

ATT AGE (1)	ACC (2)	SICK (3)	TOTAL (4)
45	0	0	0
46	0	0	0
47	1	6	7
48	2	17	19
49	3	28	31
50	5	39	44
51	6	49	55
52	7	58	65
53	8	66	74
54	8	73	81
55	9	79	88
56	9	83	92
57	10	85	95
58	10	84	94
59	9	82	91
60	9	76	85
61	8	67	75
62	6	54	60
63	4	37	41
64	2	13	15
65	0	0	0

Definitions — Values from 1964 CDT Reserve Tables at 4%

Attained Age	$(1)_t = 44 + t$
Accident/Sickness	$(2)_t$ and $(3)_t$: From published reserve tables, 1964 CDT at 4%.
Total	$(4)_t = (2)_t + (3)_t$

Chapter 5

RESERVES AND LIABILITIES FOR INDIVIDUAL HEALTH INSURANCE

by Robert Shapland, F.S.A.

Various types of accounting reserves/liabilities are applicable to individual health insurance. The discussion here first covers the general theory and purpose of these accounts. Then the accounts are described in greater detail within the five general categories of

1. premium adjustments,
2. policy reserves,
3. adjustments related to claims,
4. adjustments related to rate credits and dividends, and
5. contingency reserves.

As the reader will discern, many of these categories are interrelated.

The later sections include expansions of the theoretical foundations as well as provide information regarding legal requirements for statutory accounting statements. While treatment of these items under GAAP is not covered, the theoretical information presented should provide a strong foundation for such accounting.

Because reserving principles for health insurance are being reexamined at the time of this writing, regulations and practices in some areas may change in the near future. This chapter attempts to explain reserving principles to the extent that the reader can understand the rationale for change and possibly participate in it. It also assumes that the reader has some knowledge of life insurance accounting procedures and an understanding of policy reserve principles for life insurance.

5.1 THE ESSENTIALS OF ACCRUAL ACCOUNTING

As with other businesses, there is not an exact timing match in the cash flow of an insurer's revenues and expenditures. Therefore, in order to properly measure profit and loss within an accounting period, and simultaneously net worth, accounting procedures must recognize prepaid and unpaid revenues and expenditures. Under NAIC insurance accounting rules, these items are labeled "reserves" or "liabilities." Items related to future periods of insurance coverage or to the continuation of past claims are usually designated as *reserve items* while items related to past periods of coverage or claims already payable are usually designated as *liabilities*.

A simple example of recognizing prepaid or unpaid revenues and expenditures would involve recording the receipt of an annual premium from an insured on a "per cause" major medical policy on its December 1st policy anniversary date. Then, when measuring yearly profit and loss on December 31st, proper accounting must either defer some of this premium revenue to the subsequent annual accounting period as unearned premium or recognize the future expenditures that will arise after December 31st from the remaining insurance coverage as reserves/liabilities. Another example would arise if this insured become hospitalized December 28th for ten days and the claim payment related thereto is paid on January 15th. On December 31st, the unpaid benefit amount related to covered hospital treatment through December 31st (the first four days of hospitalization) would be reflected in claim liabilities while the continuing benefits related to hospital treatment after December 31st (the last six days of hospitalization) would be reflected in claim reserves.

The procedures followed in making accounting adjustments depend on perceptions as to the time periods to which the various insurance revenues and expenditures belong, which in turn are based on historical practice, rating principles, general accounting principles, and rules set forth by laws and regulations. Some of these procedures also reflect the purpose or recipient of the resulting accounting statements.

Because perceptions are involved, even a short-term insurance policy can involve different viewpoints as to the time allocation of its various revenues and expenditures. Accounting for long-term renewable contracts is therefore much more complicated in this respect. Where renewal is uncertain, premium schedules are subject to change, expenses are variable and unpredictable, or future claims are subject to inflation or other uncertainties, time allocation of revenues and expenditures can be complex.

Special problems arise when the long-term claim stream is not expected to move in unison with the long-term premium stream. For example, claims might be expected to increase each year because of policyholder aging, the wearing off of initial health underwriting selection, antiselection against the company via good risks lapsing and poor risks renewing, inflation, enhancements in medical care and so on. Simultaneously, the insurer may intend to use a long-term premium structure, which levels out the charges for one or more of these claim trend factors.

The historical NAIC approach to recognizing prepaid and unpaid revenues and expenses has been based on

- using a limited list of revenue and expenditure adjustments to cash transactions to reflect incurred transactions related to insurance coverage periods prior to the accounting statement date, and
- recognizing certain elements of the prospective revenue shortfall related to the use of a long-term leveling premium structure.

The limited nature of NAIC adjustments stems from the desire to interject conservatism into the measurement of solvency and, possibly, from past practices developed in a simpler environment. Changes in the environment, including those affecting both experience and rating practices, have placed accounting tenets in a state of change and have given rise to a number of actuarial papers and proposals regarding new reserve approaches and standards.[1] At the time of the development of this chapter, the different viewpoints expressed in these papers and reports have not been resolved by new NAIC valuation standards. Readers interested in furthering their knowledge of accrual accounting principles related to individual health insurance are

---

1 References include:

Proposed "NAIC Reserve Standards for Individual and Group Health Insurance Contracts" submitted by the American Academy of Actuaries Subcommittee on Liaison with the NAIC Accident and Health (B) Committee. Subcommittee members include William J. Bugg, Jr., William A. J. Bremer, G. Scott Bucher, Michael Kazakoff, James Olsen, Frank Rubino, Peter M. Thexton, John P. Wagner, and E. Paul Barnhart, Chairperson. Three discussion drafts were exposed by the American Academy of Actuaries (December 1985, July 1986, and March 1987). A total of over 50 letters were received in response to these discussion drafts and copies are available from the American Academy of Actuaries.

Spencer Koppel, Francis T. O'Grady, Gary N. See, and Robert B. Shapland, "Reserve Principles for Health Insurance," Society of Actuaries *Transactions* 1985, Volume XXXVII, pp. 201-234. Discussion letters regarding this paper follow on pp. 235-240.

E. Paul Barnhart, "A New Approach to Premium, Policy, and Claim Reserves for Health Insurance," Society of Actuaries *Transactions* 1985, Volume XXXVII, pp. 13-41. Discussion letters regarding this paper follow on pp. 43-95.

Peter A. Gerritson and Walter B. Lowrie, "Policy Reserves in Group Insurance," Society of Actuaries *Transactions* 1983, Volume XXXV, pp. 689-716.

"Report of the Health Subcommittee of the Standing Technical Advisory Group to the NAIC Life, Health and Accident Standing Technical Actuarial Task Force on Structure for Consideration of Health Coverage Valuation Standards," April 29, 1985. Health Subcommittee members submitting this report include John M. Bragg, Anthony J. Houghton, James Olsen, Charles Habeck, Willis W. Burgess, and W. H. Odell, Chairperson.

encouraged to read these reports along with the various discussion papers and letters related thereto. Such reading would broaden one's knowledge of the wide range of viewpoints that exist regarding statutory accounting principles and practices.

5.2 PREMIUM RESERVES

This section covers the treatment of accounting adjustments for premiums received which produce insuring periods extending beyond the ending accounting date and premiums owed to cover insuring periods beginning before the ending accounting date.

5.2.1 UNEARNED PREMIUM RESERVE

The collection of a premium providing coverage for a period extending beyond the current accounting period is a common operating practice. A calendar year accounting period is assumed to be in use throughout this chapter. For example, a semiannual premium due and collected November 1 would provide coverage for 2 months in the accounting year in which it is collected and for 4 months in the subsequent accounting year. When such a premium is received, the entire amount is immediately recorded as "collected premiums." On December 31, two-thirds of the collected premium is deferred via its recognition in the "unearned premium" reserve account, Exhibit 9, Part A, line 1 in the Annual Statement. In practice, some insurers estimate unearned premiums as one-half of the modal premiums on polices in force on the valuation date under the assumption that premium due dates on various policies are evenly distributed throughout the year.

A general examination of unearned premiums raises a question as to whether those should be calculated on a pro rata gross premium basis or on some other basis. The answer depends on the treatment of related expense items, whether or not morbidity costs are incurred on a pro rata basis, and on objectives regarding conservatism. For example, if commissions or other expenses have already been paid on the entire premium and a prepaid expense account is not set up, then logically less than the pro rata gross premium could be considered. Similarly, if claim costs are not constant over the premium period, a pro rata basis may be inappropriate. From a prospective viewpoint, the minimum unearned premium reserve would be equal to the present value of the claims and expenses expected to be incurred over the remaining premium period. A greater reserve would defer the recognition of some or all of the entire premium period profit or even produce more conservative financial statements.

Under level premium life insurance, only the unearned mortality "net" valuation premium is recognized under NAIC accounting rules. This takes place in the calculation of mean policy reserves. However, if there will be administrative or other expenses incurred subsequent to the accounting date related to the remaining premium period, then logically more than the net unearned mortality premium should be set up in order to also cover these expenses (unless a liability for these expenses is set up in a separate account).

For reasons of conservatism, health insurers have been required to set up gross unearned premium reserves (under statutory accounting) without being able to recognize offsetting prepaid expenses. An exception to the gross basis can occur where level premium policy reserves are involved. Here, the insurer must set up the greater of the policy reserves or the gross unearned premiums. Where insurers use mean policy reserves reflecting unearned net premiums as under life insurance, net unearned premiums would be in use unless the gross unearned premium reserve is greater than the mean policy reserve. However, many insurers choose to set up midterminal policy reserves plus gross unearned premiums. For policies not requiring policy reserves, gross unearned premiums are required.

Actually, when policy reserves are used, the answer to the question of whether unearned premiums are recognized on a gross or lesser basis becomes more complex. This is because NAIC health insurance policy reserve standards allow the use of modified reserves up to the two-year preliminary term basis. The purpose of such modifications is to allow amortization of prepaid initial expenses, or recognition of lower renewal expenses, to the extent of the difference between net level policy reserves and the modified policy reserves. This difference could be viewed as a reduction from gross unearned premiums.

Because the conservatism resulting from setting up unearned premium reserves on a gross basis may place an undue hardship on some insurers and because this practice is inconsistent with requirements under life insurance, some consideration has been given to reducing this reserve requirement. One proposal would set NAIC minimum unearned premium reserves at [L.R. + .25(1 - L.R.)] times the pro rata unearned gross premium. Here, "L.R." represents the loss ratio used to calculate premium rates. For example, if an insurer operated on a 60 percent loss ratio, the minimum unearned premium reserve would be 70 percent of the unearned gross, that is, 60 percent for claims and 10 percent for unpaid expenses.

5.2.2 ADVANCE PREMIUMS

A special separate NAIC liability account has been adopted for collected premiums providing for a period of coverage beginning after the accounting date. This liability is called "advance premiums" and has historically been set up on a gross basis even when collection expenses, commissions and other expenses have been paid and booked. This liability is shown in the Annual Statement in Exhibit 1, Part 1 lines 4 and 14; in Schedule H Part 2, line A2, and on page 3, Liabilities, Surplus and Other Funds line 9.

5.2.3 UNCOLLECTED PREMIUMS

This account recognizes due and unpaid premiums as an asset. The portion of such premiums providing coverage beyond the statement date would be included as unearned premiums. On individual health insurance policies NAIC accounting rules allow recognition of premiums that are overdue for payment by 90 days or less, but only the first modal premium payment that is past due. Due and unpaid premiums are shown on page 2, Assets, line 18 and on page 7, Exhibit 3, Part 1, lines 1 and 11.

Because of the dubious collectibility of such premiums under individual policies, many insurers recognize this asset only under group and credit policies. It might be noted that NAIC rules do not call for the recognition of commission and other unpaid expenses related to recorded uncollected premiums.

5.2.4 DEFERRED PREMIUMS

Deferred premiums arise when mean policy reserves are used. Mean policy reserves assume that a full annual premium has been collected and thus this reserve is overstated when this is not the case. Therefore, insurers are allowed to recognize the uncollected portion of the annual net premium as an offsetting asset when mean policy reserves are used. This asset is shown in the Annual Statement on page 2, Assets, line 17 (with amended title to indicate health insurance is included) as well as in Exhibit 1, Part 1, lines 2 and 12. As under life insurance, recognition of the "cost of collection in excess of loading" on deferred premiums is recognized in the Annual Statement on page 3, Liabilities, Surplus and Other Funds, line 16. Since most insurers use midterminal policy reserves as opposed to mean policy reserves for health insurance, the use of deferred premiums under health insurance is rare.

5.3 POLICY RESERVES

In principle, policy reserves are the result of the adoption of a long-term "levelizing" rating system. When claim costs increase by policy duration, insurers often adopt rating plans wherein a portion of the early gross premiums is meant to help cover the higher costs arising later on.[2] A simple example here would be the adoption of a pricing strategy under which premiums are intended to remain level for a period of years, to age 65 for instance, while claim costs are expected to increase over that period because of aging.

Theoretically, when measuring solvency under such a rating system, policy reserves represent the shortfall of the present value of all future

---

[2] The opposite situation can arise when claim costs decrease each year as under maternity coverage or reducing benefit policies.

revenues in meeting the present value of all future expenditures related to in-force policies.

Historically, legally promulgated minimum policy reserve tables for health insurance have been limited to recognizing interest, the aging component of long-term claim costs under a level premium system, and mortality tables to measure the impact of policy termination. Other cost components included in long-term rating plan have not been reflected in these tables with the exception of preliminary term reserve modifications reflecting amortization of higher than average initial expenses, and loadings for conservatism in the claim cost assumptions to cover experience fluctuations. However, these loadings could also be viewed as covering other durational changes in costs.

Mathematically, promulgated policy reserves can be viewed either as the accumulated value of retrospective net premiums collected in excess of retrospective tabular claim costs, or as the present value shortfall of prospective net premiums in meeting prospective tabular claim costs.

Broad policy reserve standards for individual health insurance have been adopted by the NAIC, with amendments made in 1986. The full text of these standards is shown in the Appendix 1. In these standards, policies are defined as falling into four classes as follows:

1. Noncancelable
2. Guaranteed Renewable
3. Policies that are nonrenewable for reasons other than deterioration of health, including collectively renewable policies, where premiums are based on the level premium principle.
4. All other individual policies.

For policies of type 1, 2, or 3, the minimum policy reserve standards are based on the following:

- Interest: The greater of (i) the maximum rate permitted by law in the valuation of currently issued life insurance or (ii) the maximum rate permitted by law in the value of life insurance issues on the same date as the health insurance
- Mortality: The mortality used for life insurance issued on the same date as the health insurance
- Morbidity:

    Total Disability Benefits

    > 1965 to 1985 issues: 1964 Commissioners Disability Table
    > 1987 and later issues: 1985 Commissioners Individual Disability Table A or B

1986 issues: Optional use of either the 1964 Table or either of the 1985 Tables

Hospital, Surgical and Maternity Benefits

1955 to 1981 issues: 1956 Intercompany Hospital-Surgical Tables
1982 and later issues: 1974 Medical Expense Tables

Accidental Death Benefits

1965 and later issues: 1959 Accidental Death Benefits Table

Cancer Expense Benefits

1986 and later issues: 1985 NAIC Cancer Claim Cost Tables

All Other Benefits, including major medical
standards that place a sound value on the liabilities

- Negative Reserves: May be used to offset positive reserves in the same policy, but the mean reserve on any policy should never be less than one-half the valuation net premium
- Reserve Modification: The 2-year preliminary term modification is the maximum modification from net level reserves
- Reserve Method: Mean reserves reduced by appropriate valuation net deferred premiums is the minimum; the aggregate reserve for all policies valued on this basis should not be less than the aggregate gross pro rata unearned premiums
- Alternative Valuation Procedures and Assumptions: May be used provided the result is not less than that produced by the above

It should be noted that deficiency reserves are not required for health insurance under current NAIC standards. Deficiency reserves have limited meaning if net valuation premiums are based on assumptions not closely related to anticipated experience. Because of the changes taking place in health insurance claim experience because of inflation, utilization trends, the impact of duration and underwriting standards, and the use of mortality rates to depict lapsation, minimum valuation standards may not produce relevant net premiums in many situations although the reserves may be realistic.

Laws and regulations as well as actuarial standards of practice require that larger reserves be adopted when the minimum standards are not adequate. For example, the NAIC model regulation for Reserve Standards For Individual Health Insurance states that "... adequate reserves be established by the insurer in any case where experience indicates that these minimum standards do not place a sound value on the liabilities under the policy." However, guidelines defining "adequate reserves" or "sound values" are not provided. For example, in undertaking a policy reserve valuation in this context, should the actuary recognize all future costs or only claim costs? Should he recognize all the factors impacting on those costs including durational morbidity, inflation, persistency and antiselection? Or, should he recognize only the impact of aging, interest and death as recognized in the minimum standards? Can he recognize expense loading margins in renewal premiums that are not allowed in the minimum standards? And, to what degree can he recognize probable future increases in premiums and the resulting lapsation of policies? Since, at the time of this writing, standards for answering these questions have not been adopted by either the NAIC, the regulators or actuarial associations, the requirement for recognizing greater than promulgated minimum policy reserve standards has limited practical meaning.

Current NAIC minimum policy reserve standards have not kept pace with the impact of inflation on benefit costs under some coverages nor do they recognize the impact of factors other than aging on policy duration claim costs. They also ignore voluntary lapsation and apply only to level premium policies. Thus, there recently has been considerable discussion about changing these standards. This discussion has elicited a wide range of viewpoints. For example, some actuaries feel that all factors affecting costs should be recognized either explicitly or implicitly in valuation standards. They have provided examples demonstrating significant impacts on reserves of such unrecognized factors as policy lapsation, policy durational, differences in morbidity, and inflation.

Especially perplexing problems exist in addressing valuation standards for policies subject to periodic rate increases. Treatment of the impact of inflation on benefit costs is one problem area. Another is the determination of reserves for certain step-rated plans with "leveling" premium structures intended to incorporate the impacts of health underwriting selection on initial morbidity experience and the wearing off of that selection as compounded by antiselection. To the extent that an insurer anticipates increasing annual claim costs in the adopted rating plan for such step-related policies, a "leveling" premium system is in place. The extent of "leveling" is indicated by the difference between initial loss ratios and the anticipated lifetime[3] loss ratio. This has supported a suggested approach to policy reserves labeled benefit ratio reserves wherein reserves are initially based on the retrospective difference between actual loss ratios and the anticipated lifetime loss ratio. More specifically, policy reserves would be equal to the excess of the present value of past premiums times the lifetime anticipated loss ratio over the present value of past claims (before any preliminary term adjustment in recognition of the recoverability of initial expenses). Mathematically, this retrospective calculation is seen to be equivalent to the more traditional prospective calculation:

---

3   "Lifetime" as used here includes shorter periods over which premiums are based, such as "to age 65."

Anticipated Loss Ratio (ALR) =

$$\frac{\text{Present Value of Past and Future Claims}}{\text{Present Value of Past and Future Premiums}}$$

Therefore,

(1): Present Value of Past Premiums x ALR − Present Value of Past Claims (that is, retrospective morbidity fund)

= (2): Present Value of Future Claims − Present Value of Future Premiums x ALR (that is, prospective morbidity shortfall)

Further support for this retrospective approach to policy reserves is provided by the current NAIC Model Rate Filing Guidelines. These guidelines limit the approval of premium increases to those which will produce lifetime loss ratios which meet minimum loss ratio standards. To the extent that past loss ratios have been less than the lifetime anticipated loss ratio, an insurer is obligated to incur future loss ratios higher than the lifetime anticipated loss ratio before rate increase relief will be approved. This creates a prospective morbidity revenue shortfall, (2) above, equal to the retrospective morbidity find, (1) above, if future premium increases are ever needed. This shortfall would be reduced to the extent that renewal premium expense margins are recognized (that is, by preliminary term adjustments).

If future premium increases are not needed or if the insurer changes the anticipated loss ratio used to determine its renewal premiums, then the policy reserves needed to cover future morbidity revenue shortfalls would differ from the retrospective calculations.

Various methods have been proposed for releasing retrospectively calculated reserves either when it becomes clear that premium increases will not be needed (that is, the anticipated lifetime loss ratio will not be attained) or to recognize amortization of initial expenses. More importantly, different viewpoints exist regarding whether policy reserve adequacy should be tested on a prospective net premium or gross premium valuation basis. Under the net premium basis only the present value of the morbidity portion of future gross premiums and future claims are considered in the valuation.

Even greater diversity of opinion exists regarding the extent to which the benefit ratio reserve concept should be applied. Some actuaries feel that it should be applied to most contracts, including many currently subject to tabular reserve tables. Some feel it should be applied only to policies not subject to tabular reserve standards. Some would limit application to policies which are priced under "leveling" premium systems. Here, "leveling" premium systems are defined as those recognizing actual early loss ratio margins in setting renewal premium rates. Still others oppose benefit ratio reserves altogether since they oppose the rating concept contained in the NAIC Model Rate Filing Guidelines. These guidelines involve returning initial loss ratio shortfalls to policyholders via future premium inadequacies without corollary recoverability of initial loss ratio overages.

Policy reserves are shown in Exhibit 9, Part A, line 2 of the Annual Statement.

5.4 CLAIM RESERVES AND LIABILITIES

Claim reserves/liabilities represent the present value of future claim payments on claims incurred prior to the valuation date. In establishing claim reserves/liabilities, several considerations come into play. These include

- the basic accounting principle of proper matching of revenues and expenditures,
- the measurement of solvency, which requires the recognition of outstanding liabilities independently of whether or not future revenue will be sufficient to cover them,
- the proper categorization of future claim payments to claim reserves versus policy reserves, and
- conservatism.

These somewhat conflicting considerations have led various actuaries to support different recommendations regarding statutory claim reserves/liabilities standards.

For example, some actuaries have felt that the primary purpose of establishing claim reserves/liabilities is the proper matching of revenues with expenditures. They have therefore recommended that one should look primarily to rating principles in establishing claim reserves/liabilities. By rating principles, they mean the rules or understandings that establish which premiums are to be used to meet each claim payment.

By historical statutory accounting practice, premium revenues are allocated to various accounting periods based on the coverage period to which they apply (except for "levelized" premium policies where a portion is transferred to a different period via policy reserves). Under this approach it follows that specific claim payments meant to be covered by premium revenues allocated to past accounting periods would be recognized as claim reserves/liabilities if not paid by the end of the last accounting period. Further, this approach implies that claim reserves/liabilities differ from policy reserves in that claim reserves/liabilities are intended to cover specific claim payments allocable to past premium revenues while policy reserves reflect the excess of future claims (and other general expenditures) over future premiums (and other general revenues) stemming from the use of a "levelizing" premium system.

A shortcoming of this approach is that the determination of which premiums are meant to cover which claims is not always clear cut. This is because laws, regulations, and policy provisions often do not establish these relationships. However, certain concepts regarding these relationships may be widely applicable based on historical practice. For example, if an insurer becomes liable, at the time of an accident or sickness, for continuing medical expenses or for disability income related thereto, it is common practice to ascribe all related claim payments to the accounting period in which the accident or sickness commenced. Theoretically, however, insurers may not always be legally bound to this rating practice and could rely on future premiums to help pay for such claims. It might be noted that this occurs when negative policy reserves are present (such as under maternity benefits).

Some policies, such as Medicare supplement and major medical forms, often cover continuing medical expense stemming from past accidents or sickness only if the policy stays in force. Here, it is less clear whether an ongoing claim is meant to be covered by premiums allocated to the period during which the accident or sickness commenced, or by ongoing premiums.

As another example, some actuaries feel that policy provisions should be used to determine when each claim payment becomes incurred, and thus becomes a statutory liability. They feel that a chaotic condition would exist if claim reserves were based on nebulous rating practices. For example, they feel that a provision requiring a policy to remain in force in order to provide coverage for a continuing course of treatment establishes the "date of treatment" as the "incurred date" for each treatment claim. In other words, in this situation, they recommend that claim reserves/liabilities represent only the claims that will be paid after the valuation date if the policies were not in force after the valuation date. Any other future claim payments related to past accident and sickness would be recognized in policy reserves.

Another suggested approach would ignore rating principles and policy provisions under such contracts and require statutory claim reserves/liabilities to recognize all future claim payments stemming from ongoing claims commencing prior to the valuation date. This approach is based on the potential danger in allowing insurers to rely on future revenues to pay for such ongoing claims. This approach would take into account the projected probability of paying ongoing claims as impacted by policy provisions limiting an insurer's liability to pay such claims.

Once one determines the premium date to which each claim payment is allocable, it is common practice to assign this as the incurred date for that payment. This incurred date is the foundation for determining claim reserves/liabilities (that is, future claim payments which will have an incurred date prior to the valuation date). Current NAIC accounting procedures call for separating the recognition of these future claim payments chargeable to the past into two categories, namely, "claim liabilities" and "claim reserves." Claim liabilities represent those benefits which have already accrued as of the accounting date, for example, benefits related to medical treatment or to periods of disability prior to the valuation date. On the other hand, claim reserves represent claims which have not yet been accrued as of the policy date since they arise from continuing medical care or from periods disability after the accounting date. These claims are not a certainty as of the accounting date since they are contingent on future medical treatment or disability and on meeting various policy requirements.

The NAIC has also chosen to split these two categories into subcategories. The paragraphs below provide a brief description of these subcategories.

Claim liabilities appear in Exhibit 11 of the Annual Statement, in the following subcategories:

1. Due and Unpaid: These are benefits for which all processing requirements have been completed except for actual payment. Insurers often do not allocate any of their liabilities to this subcategory as they immediately pay all such benefits.
2. In Course of Settlement: these are accrued benefits where processing has commenced, but is not completed to the point where the amount of liability has been fully determined. This category has further subcategories of "resisted" and "other." " Resisted" claims are those that have been denied and are subject to currently pending litigation, or threatened litigation, as of the accounting date.
3. Incurred But Unreported: These are accrued benefits for which the insurer has not yet received initial notice as of the accounting date.

Claim reserves appear in Exhibit 9 of the Annual Statement, in the following subcategories:

1. Present Value of Amounts Not Yet Due on Claims: This reserve equals the present value of claim payments related to medical treatment, periods of disability and so on after the valuation date on claims incurred prior to the valuation date. This reserve is shown in Part B on line 1. Here, "present value" refers to the allowed use of interest discounts to reflect the time difference between the valuation date and the payment dates. This reserve includes claim payments to be made under unreported claims as well as underreported claims.
2. Reserve for Future Contingent Benefits (Deferred Maternity and Other Similar Benefits): This reserve is shown in Exhibit 9 of the Annual Statement in either Part A on line 3, or in Part B on line 2. It relates to extended maternity and other extended benefits remaining in effect after normal policy termination. For example, maternity benefits may be payable after contract termination if the pregnancy commenced while the policy was in force.

As another example, policy provisions might call for benefits for continuing medical care to cease on policy termination except when the claimant is disabled at the time of termination, in which case benefits continue for up to 6 months while disabled.

NAIC rules call for these future contingent benefit reserves to be set up on the basis that all policies terminate on the accounting date. Thus, it is assumed that deferred benefits must be prefunded at all times, independently of the probability of policy termination and rating practices.

Some actuaries feel that the important question here is about the rating practices used to determine which premiums should be charged for these future benefits. For example, are maternity claims paid on in-force policies meant to be charged against premiums earned at the time of birth or at the time of conception? Similarly, does a disability continuation provision change the premiums intended to pay medical expense claims on disabled lives under policies remaining in force? The answers to these questions would determine whether these claims are covered in claim or policy reserves.

On the other hand, other actuaries feel these reserves should be determined under the assumption that all policies terminate as of the valuation date. This approach allocates all claims becoming payable after the valuation date to claim reserves if they are payable independently of in-force status after the valuation date. This would call for assigning incurred dates for maternity and medical expense claims on disabled lives based on the date of conception and date of disablement, respectively, under policies with these deferred benefit provisions.

5.5 CALCULATION OF CLAIM RESERVES AND LIABILITIES

The amount of claim payments that will be made after the accounting period, recognized under claim reserves/liabilities, is unknown when the financial statement is being prepared. Therefore, this figure must be estimated, and as with other actuarial quantities, this estimate is based on past experience to the extent appropriate.

The approach to claim reserves/liabilities estimation can take many forms including the use of claim run-out data, average size claims, tabular reserves, ratio formulas, individual claim estimation and loss ratio estimation. Often, a combination of these methods is used in determining the claim reserves/liabilities for each of the subcategories described in Section 5.4.

5.5.1 CLAIM RUN-OUT METHOD

The foundation of this method is the assumption that past claim run-out patterns can be used to predict future ones. This method involves the use of claim payment charts that tabulate claim payments by incurred period and by payment period. Here, the periods used can be years, quarters or months. For example, the claims paid each month could be summarized by the month of incurral. These tabulations would be contained in the following type of run-out chart for claims incurred and paid in 1985:

Table 5.1

Month Incurred	Month Paid				
	Jan 1985	Feb 1985	March 1985 ...	Nov 1985	Dec 1985
Jan 1985	****	****	****	****	****
Feb 1985		****	****	****	****
March 1985			****	****	****
•					
•					
•					
Nov 1985				****	****
Dec 1985					****

Actually, the chart would be maintained for many years of incurred and paid claims in order to be able to examine the complete pay-out pattern of the block of business being examined. For example, if all claims are settled within 36 months of incurral, one might examine the claim run-out tabulations for claims incurred for the last 5 or 6 years.

There are several methods of using claim run-out charts. One involves calculating the percent of ultimate claims that are paid after 1 month, 2 months and so on following the incurral month. These calculations could produce results such as the following:

Table 5.2
Claim Completion Percentages

Month Incurred	Completed Months from Month of Incurral							
	1	2	3	4	...	34	35	36
Jan 1981	5	25	35	42	...	99	100	100
Feb 1981	4	23	34	41	...	100	100	100
March 1981	5	24	36	42	...	99	99	100
•								
•								
•								
•								
•								
Dec 1982	6	26	36	43	...	99	100	100

For estimating claim reserves/liabilities as of December 31, 1985, one would make assumptions as to the completion percentages experienced through that date relative to the ultimate payment on claims incurred

January 1983 through December 1985 (since these claims would not yet be paid in full). For example, if one estimated that after 1 month, 2 months, 3 months and so on from incurral month, the payments to date represent 5 percent, 24 percent, 35 percent and so on, of the ultimate pay-out, then the claim reserves/liabilities on December 31, 1985 for claims incurred in December 1985 would be 95/5 times the December 1985 payments to date; for claims incurred November 1985, 76/24 times November 1985 payments to date; for claims incurred October 1985, 65/35 times October 1985 payments to date; and so on. Stated another way, the claims incurred in November 1985 paid through December 1985 represent 24 percent of the total incurred claims for November 1985. Therefore, the incurred claims are the amount paid through December divided by .24. Since 24 percent of the incurred claims have already been paid, the claim reserves/liabilities are the remaining 76 percent. Thus, the factor is 76/24.

In determining the assumed completion percentages, one must be aware of seasonal cycles or patterns, the impact of changes in claim paying practices, changes in health care practice, changes in inflation and so on that should be taken into account in utilizing past patterns to predict future patterns. For example, an increase in the backlog of claims in process of payment would change the run-out pattern, claims incurred in winter months might have a different run-out pattern than claims incurred in summer months, and an increase in the rate of inflation would increase future run-out dollars relative to past run-out dollars.

Because of different run-out patterns by type of health insurance (long-term disability, short-term disability, hospital indemnity, major medical, medicare supplements), run-out charts are normally tabulated separately by policy form or groups of forms having similar run-out characteristics.

Run-out patterns also are affected by the length of time the policies have been in force, especially if annual, as opposed to quarterly or monthly, run-out charts are in use. For example, under an annual period system, if there was a normal 2 month delay between incurred date and first payment date, a policy form first sold after November 1 would have no claims paid by December 31 (and have a completion ratio of zero) while a form first sold several years ago would have experienced considerable claim completion by December 31 for claims incurred in the current year. Thus, it is often important to develop completion factors that vary by year or quarter of issue.

Another approach to using claim run-out charts is the development of continuance probabilities. For example, under a quarterly tabulation system, one would develop the ratio of claims paid through the nth quarter following the incurral quarter to those paid through the $(n - 1)$ quarter. These ratios would then be used to calculate estimated remaining claim payments for each incurred quarter.

Yet another approach uses the paid loss ratios for each incurred period, developed cumulatively over time. For example, under a quarterly tabulation system, the numerators in the loss ratio calculations for a given incurred quarter are the sums of the cumulative claims paid through the various subsequent quarters. The denominators are the premiums earned in the incurred quarter. The developing loss ratio patterns are used to estimate the ultimate loss ratio that will materialize for each incurred quarter. The claim reserve is then calculated by subtracting claims paid through the accounting date from the final claim accumulation that produces the estimated ultimate loss ratios.

For example, the resulting loss ratio development chart might look as follows:

Table 5.3

Quarter Incurred	Loss Ratios Paid-to-Date Through This Quarter							
	1/83	2/83	3/83	4/83	1/84	2/84	3/84	4/84
1/83	.08	.20	.30	.38	.40	.40	.40	.40
2/83		.09	.21	.31	.39	.41	.41	.41
3/83			.19	.22	.32	.40	.42	.42
4/83				.10	.22	.32	.40	.42
1/84					.09	.22	.31	.39
2/84						.10	.23	.33
3/84							.10	.23
4/84								.10

Thus, if one projected, from the pattern in table 5.3 that the ultimate loss ratio for the third quarter of 1984 would be 43 percent, then the claim reserves/liabilities, for the December 31, 1984 valuation would be 43 percent minus 23 percent, or 20 percent, of the earned premiums for the third quarter of 1984.

The run-out or completion method presents problems where the claim payment patterns involve a long pay-out period with considerable fluctuations, such as under long-term disability insurance. In such cases, the actuary often supplements the paid-to-date data with estimates of remaining pay-out based on the characteristics of each remaining open claim, for instance, claim annuity reserves for disabled lives. This procedure is usually limited to those incurred periods where remaining open claims are identifiable such as under long-term disability policies for claims incurred more than 12 months prior to the accounting date. The historic completion percentages, utilizing this remaining pay-out estimate, would be used to establish estimates of future pay-out for incurred periods where all remaining claimants are not yet identifiable. Thus, where long pay-out patterns are involved (long-term disability or major medical), accuracy may call for limiting the use of the claim run-out method to recent incurred periods, such as those falling in the last 12 months, and using individual claim estimates for claims incurred in prior periods.

5.5.2 AVERAGE SIZE CLAIM METHOD

Under this method, part of the claim reserve/liability is estimated by applying an average size claim assumption to a count of open claims in a given category. For example, for claims reported but unpaid, the reserve would be derived by multiplying the claim count by an assumed average size claim. Similarly, regarding claims for which some payments have been made but are still open, an assumed remaining average claim would be applied to the claim count. The average claim assumption would be based on studies of the history of the average developed under similar claims. As with the claim run-out method, the user must be careful to differentiate between coverages with different averages, recognize secular patterns, the impact of inflation and so on. This method can not be used to set the total claim reserve directly since a count of unreported claims is unavailable. For such claims, other methods must be used, such as including a percentage increase over the reserve otherwise calculated.

5.5.3 TABULAR METHOD

This method applies tabular factors to individual claims to estimate the remaining claim payments. Usually, this method is used for long-term disability claims where regulatory standards have established minimum reserves for claims incurred more than two years prior to the valuation date. Under such disability claims, claim annuities representing the present value of remaining claim payments can be calculated by several methods: by using tables of annuity values, by calculating annuities from disability continuance probabilities, or by commutation function tables. The minimum standard in many states is based on the disabled life annuities under the 1964 and 1985 Commissioners Disability Tables with an interest discount at the maximum interest rate allowed for life insurance issued on the date the claim is incurred. An insurer may use its own experience on claims incurred less than 2 years prior to the accounting date, based on the use of run-out or other methods. Disabled life annuity valuation is usually limited to the periods of disability after the accounting date, with claim liabilities for unpaid periods of disability prior to the accounting date calculated on an exact basis under the conservative assumption that all open claims will remain in disability status through the accounting date. For example, if disability payments are $500 a month and the last payment covered disability through December 15th, the accrued liability on December 31st would be $250 while the unaccrued liability would be based on a disabled life annuity table. It might be noted that disabled life annuity values usually depend on age at disablement, length of disability at time of valuation, and the remaining benefit period at that time.

5.5.4 FORMULA METHOD

The formula method is similar to the average claim size method except that policies in force, annualized premiums in force, past claim counts, pending claim counts, or past claim payments are used instead of that date, to one of these bases are examined for trends and an estimated current ratio is established.

The validity of this method depends on the inherent stability of the particular ratio. Therefore, economic conditions, claim paying practices and other factors impacting on a ratio's stability need to be examined when considering this method.

An advantage of this method over the average claim size method is that it can include the amount for unreported claims.

5.5.5 INDIVIDUAL CLAIM ESTIMATES

In some instances, claim department personnel are asked to estimate the remaining claim payments on certain claims, based on their judgment taking into consideration the characteristics of each claim. They may use data tabulated from past claims, which indicates the impact on ultimate claim liability of some claim characteristics such as cause of disability. This method is also used to estimate the liability that will arise from claims subject to pending lawsuit or otherwise rejected by the insurer. Here, legal department personnel might make the estimates.

5.5.6 LOSS RATIO METHOD

For relatively new forms, where historical claim information is either not available or not credible, actuaries sometimes make an assumption as to what the loss ratio will be and calculate claim reserves/liabilities accordingly. For example, if earned premiums are $ 100,000 and the assumed loss ratio is 55 percent, then incurred claims will be $55,000. If the insurer has already paid $8,000 as of the valuation date, the estimated claim reserves/liabilities would be the remaining $47,000. In estimating the loss ratio for this purpose, it may be appropriate for the actuary to take into account the appropriate loss ratio assumed in the underlying premium calculations, loss ratio development under similar policies and so on.

5.6 ALLOCATION OF CLAIM RESERVES AND LIABILITIES TO ANNUAL STATEMENT CATEGORIES

As mentioned earlier, NAIC accounting standards for the Annual Statement call for splitting claim reserves/liabilities into several categories and subcategories. This split often requires additional tabulations and analysis since the calculation method used may not lend itself to these splits.

For example, if using the claim run-out method, the calculation result would represent the total reserves/liabilities and this amount must be broken down via some allocation method. Here, many insurers allocate none of the reserve to "due and unpaid" since they immediately pay all claims as soon as their liability is fully established. For the unreported and the pending portions, they may look to the historical distribution of past years' claim payments between those on claims opened versus unreported at the end of the year of incurral, based on whether the claim number was assigned before or after the end of the year. Within these splits the calculation of the present value of the amount not yet due might be based on studies of the average time lag between the date of medical treatment, or period of disability, and payment of the benefit related thereto. If this period was 1 month, then the portion of the future claim payments in excess of those paid in the following month would represent the present value of amounts not yet due on claims.

5.7 CLAIM RESERVE TESTING

Frequent testing of claim reserves is extremely important in order to validate the methodology used, to check on the average claims assumed (including the disabled life annuity table used) and to discover trends not previously recognized in the established reserve system. This means that insurers should compare previous reserve estimates against the subsequent claims actually paid together with the remaining estimated liability as of the date of the test, with appropriate adjustments for interest reflecting the time value of money.

This type of testing (excluding interest adjustments) is required in the Annual Statement, since in Schedule H the previous year's claim reserve is tested against the related claim payments and remaining reserve for the current year. Also, in Schedule O, this claim run-out testing is extended for 5 years, but is limited to policies that are noncancelable, guaranteed renewable and nonrenewable for stated reasons only.

The accuracy of these tests depends on the accuracy of the incurred dates contained in the claim payment records tabulated for this purpose. If claim payments are not properly matched against the proper premiums via assignment of correct incurred dates, both reserve calculations and subsequent testing will be invalid.

Claim run-out testing on long-term disability benefits should also be approached cautiously. This is because both the original claim reserves and the subsequent tests use the same disabled life annuity table. For example, the initial claim reserve might be $1,000,000 while the following year's claim payments and remaining reserve might be $200,000 and $900,000 respectively. Ignoring the impact of interest, this does not necessarily mean that the initial reserve was inadequate by only $100,000. For example, if the claim annuity factors were only 50 percent of the sufficient amounts, the full initial shortage would not show up because the $900,000 remaining reserve would also be deficient. A sufficient reserve table in this case would have produced an initial reserve of $2,000,000 and a 1-year test of $200,000 in payments and $1,800,000 in remaining reserve. It is therefore important to test these reserves on a longer run-out basis so that any possible insufficiency in the remaining disabled life annuities would not have a material impact on the test.

An alternative test that avoids the necessity of waiting several years to ascertain accuracy would be an annual comparison of actual termination experience with that assumed in the table.

5.8 RESERVES FOR WAIVER OF PREMIUM BENEFITS

Currently, no standards are in place for either policy reserves or claim reserves related to waiver of premium benefits. It might be noted here that waiver of premium benefits are typical under disability income policies but are also possible on other types of coverage, for instance, hospital indemnity and nursing home benefit policies.

Proposals regarding revisions in regulatory standards for health insurance reserves in general have generated some discussion of this subject. Here, the discussion has centered on waiver of premium reserves for persons currently on waiver. There has been little discussion of policy reserves related to waiver of premium benefits although conceptually one can visualize level premium funding of such benefits.

Several viewpoints have surfaced regarding reserves for those currently on waiver. One view looks to benefit provisions and assumes that a claim liability exists equal to the present value of future waived premiums for all persons under this benefit. Here, recognition of waived premiums could be viewed on a gross basis or net of expense loading margins over renewal expenses. Another view sees a liability related to the waived tabular policy reserve net premiums. This view is somewhat dependent on whether or not the tabular reserve claim costs were developed for active lives only or for active and disabled lives combined (and similarly on whether tabular reserves are maintained on active lives only or on total lives). Yet another view looks to the rating methodology used to calculate gross premiums. Under this view, if gross premiums were calculated assuming that premiums and claims stem only from active lives, then no additional claim liability is seen to arise for policyholders under waiver. This is because the waiver of premium provision is not viewed as an additional benefit creating a loss of premium revenue, but is viewed merely as an explanation of the gross premium assumptions. This situation might arise, for example, under step-rated disability income insurance.

5.9 ESTIMATED EXPENSES OF INVESTIGATION AND SETTLEMENT OF POLICY CLAIMS

It is logical that accounting practices would call for the cost of investigating and settling claims to be charged against the same premiums as the claims themselves. Therefore, a liability must be recognized for the expenses incurred in paying the claims covered under claim reserves/liabilities.

This claim expense can be estimated by many methods, but is usually based on the ratio of this expense to the claim payments. This ratio can be tabulated by type of benefit and level of health underwriting (if these factors affect relative claim investigation expense), as well as by claim status such as unreported, continuing, and so on (if this materially increases the accuracy of this liability). To the degree the claim reserves include interest discounting, the expense ratio method automatically applies similar interest discounting.

Other methods for estimating this liability would include applying functional cost factors based on expense analysis. In other words, costs of establishing a claim file, paying continuing claims, and so on could be applied. This could require estimating claim reserve counts as well as amounts. This liability amount is reported on Page 3, line 14 of the Annual Statement.

5.10 CONTINGENCY RESERVES

Since health insurers are subject to the risk of loss, it is prudent to establish contingency reserves as the portion of surplus, considered as needed to protect the rights of policyholders to realize the benefits promised in their policies. This amount is recorded on Page 3, line 29A of the Annual Statement.

Achieving reasonable allocation of surplus funds for this purpose is a difficult task since the probabilities and amounts of future losses are not subject to exact calculations. Fluctuations in claim frequency and severity are subject to unpredictable forces including inflation, unemployment, medical care practices and epidemics.

Some indication of the severity of these fluctuations can be determined by examining past experience. Unfortunately, the future may be far different from the past. Another indication of the needed level of contingency funds can be derived by calculating the impact of various levels of unfavorable experience.

Naturally, the extent of possible future losses is limited in part by the right to increase premiums or to refuse to renew policies. The right to increase premiums limits an insurer's potential loss to the extent that it is exercised and an effective experience monitoring system is in use. However, any antiselection induced by rate increases reduces its effectiveness in limiting future losses. Given the complexities of calculating the needed level of contingent funds, many insurers defer to using a simple method such as some percentage of 1-year's premiums. This percentage might vary by type of coverage, based on the perceived level that future loss ratios could exceed the break-even point and the number of years this could continue.

5.11 PROVISION FOR POLICYHOLDERS' DIVIDENDS PAYABLE IN THE FOLLOWING CALENDAR YEAR

Participating health insurance policies will usually have, at any valuation date, dividends already declared which are payable in the following year. Theoretically, the portion of these dividends chargeable to past earned premiums as of that date should be recognized as a liability. Proper matching of revenues with disbursements also calls for recognizing estimated undeclared dividends chargeable to past earned premiums.

Rules adopted by the NAIC call for recognizing all unpaid dividends declared by the valuation date independently of whether or not the experience period to which they apply extends beyond the valuation date. This liability is broken down between dividends already due and unpaid as of the valuation date (even though contingent on collection of premiums due) and dividends payable in the following calendar year. This liability is shown in Exhibit 7 and on Page 3, lines 6 and 7, of the Annual Statement.

Chapter 6

UNDERWRITING INDIVIDUAL HEALTH INSURANCE

by John W. Hadley, F.S.A.

The primary function of the individual health insurance underwriter is the same as that of the individual life or group or even property and casualty underwriter—the evaluation of risks. The basic differences among the various lines are the methods of evaluation and the variety of tools available in making the evaluation, and in assigning the applicant to an appropriate risk class. Throughout this chapter the term "underwriter" is used only to refer to those responsible for evaluating the risk and deciding whether or not a policy is to be issued. In other contexts, salespeople are often referred to as field underwriters, but that usage is avoided here. The term "agent" will be used to refer to the agent, broker, or other person or organization doing the actual individual sales.

The assignment of an individual to his appropriate rating category involves a myriad of considerations, not all of which are accounted for in formal methods or objective tools. Since the subjective judgment of the underwriter is a crucial element in proper risk management, a goal of this chapter is to acquaint the reader with differing circumstances where such judgment has substantial impact on final decisions.

6.1 THE BASICS

It is the underwriter who decides whether the requested coverage should be offered as applied for, offered on some other basis, perhaps at a higher premium level, or rejected. Proper underwriting is critical to the financial success of the product. The experience under the product will vary greatly according to the degree (and efficiency) of underwriting, so that the pricing and underwriting processes are inextricably linked. This is perhaps more true for health insurance than for any other personal line. One piece of evidence to support this is the fact that with fully underwritten individual insurance, many insurers will issue up to 90 percent of life insurance applications as applied for, while the figure is probably closer to 80 percent for health insurance.

6.1.1 FIELD UNDERWRITING

The underwriting process normally begins with the agent or broker. The types of health insurance often sold via direct response or other mass-marketing techniques, such as travel accident or hospital income policies, almost always involve little or no underwriting. Here the concentration will be only on coverage that is underwritten to a significant extent.

The agent generally meets with the client, completes the application and perhaps arranges for a medical exam or other special tests required by the insurer's underwriting rules. This primary contact is crucial. In effect the agent is prescreening applicants through the decision of whether or not to approach them, what products to offer and so on. Thus the agent plays a critical role in the success of the product, a factor that will be discussed further in Sections 6.4. and 6.7.6.

6.1.2 PRELIMINARY SCREENING

Before the completed application is given to the underwriter for evaluation, many insurers will have much of the information keyed into a computer. This serves several purposes:

- The application can be prescreened by the data entry personnel or a computer program to ensure that it has been properly completed. Missing or inconsistent information can be corrected, and the applicant may be given a preliminary evaluation, before the underwriter is involved.
- Speed of underwriting, percentages of applications that are never issued or that are never paid for, and other useful statistics can be easily monitored.
- If the underwriter accepts the application, the policy record can be more rapidly entered into the policy administration system, speeding up the issue process. This rapid service will improve the agent's chances for ultimately placing the policy.

Once the prescreening process is complete, it is the underwriter's responsibility to classify the applicant by occupation and evaluate the risk. A common method in use for both health and life insurance is the *debit system*. Here each application starts from a base of 100 debits, and a certain number of additional debits (or, less often, credits) is assigned for any significant unusual conditions such as avocations or medical history that affect the probable future claims level. The total will then be used to determine whether the case should be issued or declined according to the ranges of debits/credits the insurer uses to make these distinctions, or whether some other action should be taken. For example, one insurer may decide that the standard rating class should range from 100-160 debits, so that an application assigned 30 debits for elevated blood pressure and no other debits/credits would be a standard risk. The range of debits allowed for standard risks will vary by insurer, and will affect the level of claim costs assumed in pricing the product.

The acronym NIAAF stands for Not Issued As Applied For, encompassing all possible actions other than accepting or rejecting the application outright. The term used for this category may vary by insurer, but NIAAF will be used throughout this chapter.

6.1.3 MEDICAL/NONMEDICAL UNDERWRITING

There are three basic types of underwriting, as defined by the level of medical information required by the company for the evaluation process. *Nonmedical underwriting* involves the completion by the applicant of a questionnaire regarding medical history (both self and family) and current physical condition. This would normally be a part of the basic health insurance application, although it could instead be a separate form submitted with the application. The term "nonmedical" derives from the absence of a medical exam. Although the underwriter reserves the right to require a medical exam as conditions warrant it on an individual basis, there is no routine requirement for one.

The other two types, *medical* and *paramedical* underwriting, involve an examination performed by either a physician or a paramedic. In addition to a physical exam, the doctor or paramedic would ask questions similar to, but often more detailed than, those contained in the nonmedical questionnaire. In such situations, the applicant would not complete that portion of the application.

Which of the three levels of underwriting is appropriate will vary according to the level of benefits, the occupation class of the applicant, and the age of the applicant. In addition, the extent of the medical exam may vary by other factors; for example, an insurer may require an electrocardiogram on all applicants older than age 50. The insurer will almost always have published guidelines specifying when each level is required, although the underwriter may be allowed to waive certain requirements if conditions warrant it.

The health insurance underwriting process is complicated by the great diversity of medical coverage. Within the major medical category, coverage can vary by benefit period, coinsurance factor, deductible, presence or absence of inside limits, calendar year versus aggregate benefits and so on. While for the most part few of these variations will be found within any one insurer's major medical product line, an insurer generally will offer products with more than one level of benefits. The underwriter must be familiar with the impact of benefit variations on the risk inherent in each product. Also, care must be exercised in any attempt to compare several companies' underwriting procedures, since the details of the products offered may be a factor in differing practices.

Underwriting procedures must likewise be in harmony with pricing assumptions. One insurer may sell a high volume, low benefit, low expense product, while another may sell a smaller volume of high benefit products for which the larger financial impact justifies more extensive underwriting. Even different procedures for different products within one insurer's portfolio will occur, as many of the features of the coverages will change over time due to factors such as competitive pressure, experimentation and attempts to correct past deficiencies.

6.1.4 CONDITIONAL RECEIPT

The agent often collects the first premium with the application, giving the applicant a conditional receipt in return. This receipt provides the applicant with the coverage applied for, effective on the date the receipt is given, conditional on the application being approved as applied for. If the application is subsequently rejected, the insurer returns the premium and no coverage was effective. On the other hand, if the application is accepted as applied for, the insured has two advantages: if there is a change in insuring age in the meanwhile, premiums will be based on the younger age; and should the insured suffer a claim in the interim, it is covered. The insurer also has the advantage of a more effective commitment on the part of the applicant, generally reducing the early lapse rate.

Conditional receipts are common in health insurance and the advantages to the applicant are particularly important in medical coverage, where claims are frequent. Thus a 1980s trend in court interpretations is particularly disturbing to health insurers. The courts of several states, including California, have interpreted conditional receipts as indiscriminately binding. These rulings have held that the insurance is unconditionally in effect until the application is accepted or rejected, and if rejected, often in effect until the premium is returned to the applicant. Because of this trend, many insurers are limiting the situations or states in which they will allow a conditional receipt, or even eliminating the use of such receipts. Where an insurer continues to use such receipts, the agent becomes an even more important element of the process; the agent's prescreening will often determine the level of risk inherent in the receipt.

6.2 HEALTH INSURANCE UNDERWRITING CONTRASTED TO LIFE INSURANCE UNDERWRITING

There are many aspects of individual health insurance that make its underwriting more complex than that for life insurance. One example is the possibility (virtual certainty, for most forms of medical coverage) of multiple claims from various causes. Thus the underwriting process often is an attempt to gauge an expected claims level rather than the likelihood of an earlier than usual claim.

Another difference is the higher claim incidence rate. Insureds are much more likely to be disabled at some point during their working lifetimes than to die. Health insurance policies with short elimination periods or small deductibles have even higher probabilities of claims. For medical insurance, each insured is likely to submit several claims, especially where family coverage is provided. In addition, the benefit amounts cannot be predicted in advance. For example, the total hospital benefit payments for a claim will depend on the length of confinement. Similarly, disability income benefits depend on the duration of disability.

Differences in the control of benefits have a direct influence on the underwriting process. The most important of these is the difference in incentives. Health insurance benefits are paid directly to, or on behalf of, the insured, whereas a third party, the beneficiary, receives the benefits to be paid under life insurance.

The presence of disability insurance affects both the probability of claim and the average duration of claims. While few people want to be unhealthy, once they are, their outlook may change. The person who is forced to stay home a few days may find it a relief from the hectic pace of the work place, and might therefore stay out longer than necessary.

The subjective nature of a disability also presents problems rarely present in life insurance. Except for the most serious disability, there is no absolute standard for the determination of when one is or isn't disabled. Thus the individual circumstances or psychology of the insured can enter into the determination.

A problem for medical coverage is the elective nature of certain charges. Many surgical procedures, such as tonsillectomy, are desirable but do not necessarily correct a life-threatening situation. Also, many conditions can be treated by alternative procedures, sometimes at widely different costs. For instance, minor operations can often be performed in an outpatient clinic or even a doctor's office as an alternative to an overnight hospital visit.

A complication with disability coverage is the need to study business earnings, even where strictly personal coverage is applied for. Here the event insured against (income loss during disability) is highly dependent on the stability of both employment and earnings. These will directly affect the ratio of potential benefits to income, and thus the incentive to return to work once disabled.

Additionally, the health underwriter has fewer relevant statistical studies to help evaluate the significance of many conditions. This is due to many factors, including

- the variety of products and the variety within products. To the extent that these affect the claims experience, separate studies are required, but may not be feasible due to cost and limited amounts of data.

- the need to study not just claim incidence, but also claim duration and aggregate costs.
- geographic variation in claims experience.
- the frequent changes in methods of treatment (and costs thereof) for various conditions.

6.3 ACTIONS AVAILABLE TO THE UNDERWRITER

The health underwriter has three basic alternatives: issue the policy as applied for, issue other than as applied for, or decline the application. The NIAAF option is an important and frequently used one, and the health underwriter has many choices in this regard.

A health underwriter can issue a policy subject to a flat extra premium, either temporary or permanent, or subject to a percentage extra premium. A health underwriter can also make a counter offer of coverage different than applied for.

Optional benefits are an important element of disability income insurance. Where residual disability income protection is offered as an option, many applicants will request it. Clearly this availability of options gives the underwriter many choices for variations in coverage. The underwriter could also offer a shorter benefit period (5 years instead of to age 65), a longer elimination period (90 days instead of 30), a smaller amount ($1,000 per month benefits instead of $1,500), or even combinations thereof.

Medical coverage does not involve optional benefits to nearly the same extent, although there are often alternative surgical schedules or hospital daily benefit limits. The underwriter can also change other aspects of the coverage such as the deductible, or, under a family policy, decline a particular member and accept the rest.

Perhaps the most important tool available to the underwriter is the exclusion rider. An exclusion rider, also referred to as a waiver, eliminates coverage for disability or medical charges resulting from a specified condition. These are analogous to the general exclusions that prevent payment in case of war, suicide or other events that the company considers uninsurable. An exclusion rider is quite effective where the specified condition is relatively isolated and unlikely to increase the risk of a claim from other causes, such as is the case with an ulcer.

The exclusion rider has a major disadvantage. It removes a portion of the policy's coverage, often in the area where the insured most needs it. Thus it reduces the value of the policy to the insured. However, an exclusion rider often allows an otherwise uninsurable applicant to receive coverage at standard rates, or may be an alternative to an unaffordable extra premium. This extra tool forces the health underwriter, in most NIAAF situations, to evaluate the risk from more than one point of view; that is, with and without the exclusion. The underwriter must also carefully evaluate whether or not an exclusion rider is appropriate for the particular condition. On the other hand, one reason the exclusion rider is so important is that extra premiums are less effective for health insurance and are difficult to determine. This is because

- many health policies contain a disability waiver of premium provision. Thus the extra premium will be collected only until the insured is sick or injured long enough to satisfy the elimination period.
- even in the absence of a waiver of premium provision, the insured could lapse the policy after a large claim commenced, and the insurer would still, in most cases, be liable for that claim during the remainder of the benefit period.
- the insured's high degree of control over claim costs and incidence, as well as the incentives discussed earlier, creates the potential for a high level of antiselection.

One action often taken in life insurance is to back date policies prior to the date the application is written. This is generally done to preserve a younger insurance age. The insured pays a premium for a period of time during which no coverage was provided, in exchange for lower payments throughout the remainder of the policy. This is rarely allowed in the health insurance business. Perhaps the most important reason is the difficulty of determining in advance that no claim commenced during that earlier period.

6.4 SOURCES OF INFORMATION AVAILABLE TO THE UNDERWRITER

The basic application form, plus any supplemental questionnaires that may be required, is the most important source of information. It provides billing information, details concerning the coverage applied for, personal information about the applicant such as occupation and earnings, medical history and current health condition, and data on other insurance coverages. The level of detail requested in the application is a function of the product. It will vary according to the degree of underwriting contemplated, as well as the level of risk inherent in the product.

An inspection report may be ordered by the underwriter. It is an independent evaluation of the applicant's risk profile. The report can be broad or limited in scope, covering any or all of finances, health, general reputation, driving record, habits and so on. The information is usually generated through the applicant's family, friends, and business associates or through evaluation of tax returns, driving records or available public information. The inspector can be a third party, independent of the insurer, or an employee of the insurer.

Medical examinations can range from a simple examination to a detailed medical evaluation including an electrocardiogram, blood and urine analysis and other tests. An exam will sometimes be requested by the underwriter in connection with a nonmedical application. For example, where a serious condition such as a history of high blood pressure or diabetes exists and the applicant has not seen a doctor recently, a current medical evaluation is usually needed.

An attending physician's statement (APS) is a written statement by the applicant's personal physician regarding a specific examination or operation. For instance, the application may indicate that the applicant was treated for a mild heart attack two years earlier. An APS will give much more detail, including the doctor's evaluation of the condition at the time, enabling the underwriter to assess its significance in evaluating the current application. The APS can be more useful than a medical exam, as the personal physician will have a better knowledge of the applicant's medical history, and normally will have better clinical records than any other source.

A financial questionnaire is often required in connection with disability income applications involving large amounts of coverage. The applicant is asked for detailed information on net worth, earned and unearned income, business and personal income, pension contributions and so on. Increasingly, insurers have attempted to incorporate these questions into the basic application, requiring a separate, more detailed questionnaire only for the largest amounts. The insurer may also permit the underwriter to use alternatives to the questionnaire such as tax returns or detailed financial statements from the applicant's accountant.

Two reasons for such a variety of financial requirements are the difficulty of verifying an applicant's financial situation, especially where the applicant is self-employed, and the aversion many applicants have to what they may perceive as an intrusion into their personal finances. Tax returns tend to be the best source, and with the applicant's permission, can be obtained for a fee directly from the Internal Revenue Service (IRS). The time required to obtain them from the IRS will, however, delay the underwriting process.

The Medical Impairment Bureau (MIB) is a nonprofit organization that maintains records regarding conditions of underwriting significance on policyholders and applicants, as furnished to it by member companies. MIB will provide to a member company on request any information in its files on a specific individual. However, information from the MIB can only be used as a guide to identify areas about which the underwriter may need additional information. It cannot be used as the basis for a final underwriting decision.

Most insurers have a physician either assigned to the underwriting unit, or available to consult with underwriters. The underwriter will confer with the physician on specific cases where the diagnosis or prognosis presented in an APS or medical examination is unclear, or when the underwriter doesn't have sufficient medical expertise to evaluate a particular condition.

It is important that the insurer have an adequate internal mechanism to identify whether or not an applicant has previously applied for coverage, or is currently insured. Applications and other underwriting or claim information developed on a previous occasion, even if developed in connection with an unrelated product, will immediately direct attention to particular areas of concern, and may show inconsistencies worth investigating between prior and current admitted information. A prior report may render unnecessary APSs or medical exams, particularly if the information was recently developed. Checking internal files can be of particular importance because courts have sometimes prevented the recision of a policy in a situation where it was shown that the insurer had knowledge of a condition in its files.

Finally, underwriting the agent as well as the applicant can be vital to the financial success of a health insurance program. Obviously, it is important that agents bring in broad cross-sections of insurable risks, rather than just those who are looking for health insurance because of suspected future medical problems. Underwriters often have access to regular reports by agent or agency on production, persistency, claim indices, or other measures of the quality of the agent's business. This allows them to underwrite the producer as well as the applicant.

6.5 EFFECT OF PRODUCT ON UNDERWRITING

Product affects underwriting in many ways. Naturally, the scope and detail of the application and other information requested will vary according to the kind and extent of insurance offered and the renewal guarantee included. In other words, the risk level of the product is one determinant of the level of underwriting. Underwriting long-term noncancelable disability income coverage requires more care than does the underwriting of accident only coverage with limited renewal rights.

Economics is also a factor. The expected average premium level, and the allowance for underwriting expense therein, must directly affect the level of underwriting. This is also a consideration in different applications for the same product; it is not practical to spend as much time and money underwriting a $500 per month disability income case as one for a $5,000 per month indemnity. This is one reason that limits for such requirements as medical versus paramedical versus nonmedical underwriting, financial questionnaires and inspections generally vary according to the size of the case.

Another determinant of the level of underwriting is the marketing strategy. The nature of the market may require certain underwriting concessions; for example, an association may endorse a product only if every member who applies is guaranteed coverage. Similarly, direct response applications dictate relatively simple underwriting procedures: few of the 1 or 2 percent who would normally respond to a mail offer would bother if it required the completion of an involved application form.

6.5.1 MEDICAL EXPENSE INSURANCE

Medical expense coverage is a very popular form of insurance. Everyone is aware of the rapidly increasing costs of medical care, and most adults have some form of coverage to protect themselves. Medical expense policies require less selling effort than other coverages, as most people are already convinced of the need. With much greater frequency than for life or disability income insurance, the applicant may have initially contacted the agent to secure medical coverage or, once contacted by an agent regarding other insurance, may have steered the discussion to medical coverage. In addition, a person may be much more likely to want medical coverage after a medical problem develops, or after some other event highlights the need. Thus antiselection can be a serious problem.

A complicating factor in dealing with these problems is the wide array of products that are or have been sold. What should the underwriter do if the applicant has a 10-year-old $100 deductible major medical policy with a $20,000 benefit limit, and is applying for a $10,000 variable deductible policy with a $1,000,000 benefit limit to supplement it? Depending on company policy, he might

1. issue as applied for, leaving open the possibility of future allegations of overselling, since the latter policy would pay only if bills exceeded $20,000.
2. refuse to issue, despite the fact that the applicant may understand the duplication of coverage perfectly well, and simply wants the peace of mind afforded by essentially unlimited coverage.
3. refuse to issue unless the applicant drops the existing coverage, even though the smallest deductible under the newer policy is $500, so that the applicant would be forced to pay an additional $400 of each claim submitted.
4. issue as applied for, but require that the applicant sign a statement that he understands the duplication of coverage.

Rapid medical advances and changes in technology (often bringing with them quantum leaps in costs in return for breakthroughs in the ability to prolong the patient's life) are a fact of life. These require constant surveillance, not just for use in pricing and policy construction, but also to keep the guidelines used to evaluate the various conditions in line with reality. Any advance that has a significant impact on the prognosis for a particular condition, especially one frequently encountered on applications, such as cardiovascular ailments, should affect underwriting standards. Reinsurance activity can be a solution to this mammoth undertaking, by providing a second organization's input to difficult cases. Reinsurers tend to keep a close watch on underwriting standards, and have seen and presumably evaluated a number of insurers' underwriting guidelines in developing their own. Paradoxically, a medical advance that significantly improves an insured's expected lifetime, and consequently would lead to more liberal life insurance underwriting, may require more conservative health underwriting. This is because it may indicate either or both a strong possibility of extended and costly care, and a greatly extended lifetime of medical care.

The need for medical coverage increases with age, as it does for disability income insurance. However, since disability income insurance replaces earned income, it is appropriate only for claims occurring during a person's working lifetime, while medical costs can be a concern throughout an individual's lifetime. However, Medicare is available for older people, and thus few medical policies are written on a lifetime renewable basis. Those that are would normally be limited benefit policies such as hospital indemnity, or plans providing for conversion to a Medicare Supplement plan at age 65. In any case, the medical underwriter is likely to see a great many more applications at advanced ages than is the disability income insurance underwriter.

The most significant factors in the disability income insurance underwriting process, income and occupation, are of a different level of concern for medical business. Unlike disability income insurance, the need for medical coverage is unrelated to employment status. However, the amount charged to a patient may be affected by the patient's income. The underwriter must still consider such items as whether the insured can afford the premium payments. If the applicant is unemployed at time of application, the underwriter might wonder if there was a medical reason that the applicant was willing to use his savings to pay for the policy.

Careful scrutiny is required where significant maternity benefits are included in the policy. Pregnancy or the contemplation thereof is a significant event that often will cause a family to consider updating their medical expense coverage.

Medical insurance brings in the complication of family coverage. It may be necessary to expand the application to ask questions about the spouse and children. Caution must be exercised where there is a possibility of handicapped children, as many policies (as a consequence of various state requirements) provide guaranteed lifetime coverage for such children.

6.5.2 DISABILITY INCOME INSURANCE

Long-term noncancelable and guaranteed renewable disability income plans require the most comprehensive underwriting of any health insurance product. This is not surprising since many insurers will frequently issue $10,000 or more of monthly tax-free benefits on plans providing lifetime benefits for certain disabilities, and will even add a COL adjustment rider to such a plan. While the probability of a jumbo claim is very small, it would only take one or two more than expected to cause the line of business serious financial difficulty.

Business overhead expense (BOE) underwriting requires an extensive review of business finances. An example of a particularly thorny problem here is how to consider business depreciation. One school of thought says that since this is not a "real" expense, but rather a bookkeeping entry and subject to a high degree of control by the insured, it should not properly be included in the issue amount. Not only is it subject to manipulation, but where the depreciation involves a large capital expenditure, such as a new x-ray machine for a doctor's office, there will usually be a business loan, which may very well already be protected by disability credit insurance. However, because the item being depreciated is generally integral to maintaining the office, competitive pressures have led most major insurers to cover depreciation under BOE policies.

Even more extensive knowledge of the business expenses is necessary where buy/sell disability income insurance is involved. Here the situation will involve multiple owners, and one of the more difficult problems is to determine the portion of the business that is attributable to the individual insured. The same problem exists, perhaps to an even greater extent, when BOE is issued to a person who is not a sole proprietor.

Whereas BOE underwriting requires evaluation of the ongoing expenses needed to run the business, buy/sell requires a valuation of the business itself. This is complicated by the variety of accounting methods in use, and honest differences of opinion regarding which is the best. In addition, the absence of one of the owners because of disability may very well lower the value of the business, at least where that owner is an active participant.

It may be necessary to have issue limits, just as with individual disability income, but based on the assessed value of the firm. Most insurers are willing to write 75 percent or more of that value.

For large cases, the insurer should carefully review the firm's buy/sell agreement. For smaller cases or firms without a formal agreement, the insurer may want to have a standard one available for their use. It is vital that the buy/sell agreement and the intended buy/sell disability income insurance policy be consistent. For instance, the definition of disability for purposes of the buy-out should be the same in both; ideally the agreement should defer to the policy for such things. The underwriter must also ensure that the indemnity amount in the policy isn't greater than the voluntary buy-out amount in the firm's agreement. Otherwise there would be an incentive to claim disability rather than undertake a voluntary buy-out, if one partner wanted out.

The underwriter would expect all partners to take out buy/sell disability income insurance and should investigate if this is not the case. The reason may simply be that the other partners are too old or in too poor health for the product to be affordable. On the other hand, the partner applying for coverage may be hoping to capitalize on it. The same question applies on BOE applications, but since BOE is more widely sold, a common answer will be that the other partners already have such coverage.

Key-man disability income insurance involves underwriting considerations similar to those for regular individual disability income insurance. An additional complication is the need to evaluate the key man's worth to the business. Salary is usually taken as a guide to this. It is practical to underwrite such coverage somewhat liberally, as it generally provides only short-term benefits.

Accident-only disability income insurance rarely involves extensive underwriting, primarily because of the low premium. Any underwriting would focus on whether the applicant is involved in any dangerous activities (such as hang gliding) or has any medical problems (such as epilepsy) that might create an abnormal accident risk.

6.5.3 MEDICARE SUPPLEMENT INSURANCE

Most states have enacted legislation to make it easier for senior citizens to obtain medical care coverage, and have adopted regulations governing acceptable forms of such coverage, so that there is little underwriting involved.

The one aspect of such underwriting that comes up continually is double (or triple) coverage. Frequently senior citizens are so frightened by the prospect of astronomical medical bills that they will apply for additional coverage even when their current insurance package is complete. In some cases this will be because an agent has convinced them that they do need extra coverage; in other cases he may have tried to replace a hodge-podge of policies with one comprehensive policy. The underwriter may be asked to assume the role of a public relations officer, explaining to applicants exactly what they do have in hopes of convincing them not to retain or purchase unnecessary coverages.

6.6 EFFECT OF RENEWABILITY ON UNDERWRITING

The renewal provision in the policy will determine the insurer's right to reevaluate the risk or the class of risk at some point after policy issue. Thus one would expect a noncancelable policy to be underwritten more conservatively than a guaranteed renewable policy, and a guaranteed renewable policy to be underwritten more conservatively than a conditionally renewable or a cancelable policy. This tends to be the case. Renewal rights are closely related to the type of product and the marketing technique. For example, because of the steady increase in medical costs, major medical coverage on a noncancelable basis is no longer written and for direct response marketing, underwriting is likely to be quite limited, no matter what the renewal clause is.

6.7 SPECIFIC UNDERWRITING FACTORS

In this section the specific characteristics of the risks reviewed in the underwriting process are discussed in detail.

6.7.1 OCCUPATION

While occupation is of little concern to the medical insurance underwriter, except to the extent that there is an occupational accident or sickness hazard, it is one of the most important factors in evaluating a disability income insurance application.

Most insurers will separate occupations into several occupational classes according to both the specific occupations and the types of job duties involved. For example, attorneys, accountants and doctors generally fall into the top class, irrespective of specific duties, whereas other occupations such as nursing or veterinary medicine normally require some job description to determine the appropriate classification. The top class is usually confined to professional occupations characterized by a high degree of specialization and training, and to executives of such a high level of earnings that a similarly high level of motivation to work is involved.

Many insurers have a second professional occupation classification for applicants who don't quite make the top class. Such applicants might include accountants who don't yet have their professional designation, or potential executives who haven't yet reached the high earnings level.

In addition, there are usually one or more nonprofessional classifications. The most liberal would generally be one for office employees and non-office workers whose duties involve clerical work or light manual work with little or no occupational hazard. Classification beyond that would vary according to the level of manual duties performed, as was discussed in Chapter 3.

Disability income insurance is not meant to insure against inability to find or hold a job, nor against general economic events that result in layoffs. However, since these factors do influence claim rates, their probabilities must be considered. A back problem that didn't prevent the applicant from working before may suddenly become disabling once the applicant is faced with unemployment. Such a situation may be to all intents and purposes legitimate, with the applicant having been so strongly motivated to work that he forced himself to overcome the disability as long as he had a job to go to.

Applicants will sometimes have multiple occupations. In such cases one must evaluate the extent to which the applicant is involved in each. Where the occupations fall into different occupational classes, it is almost always necessary to classify the applicant in the higher risk group. The insured will be more predisposed to disablement at all times when engaging in two occupations than when engaging in one occupation. This is particularly true if one occupation is stressful. In addition, there is the possibility that when the insured is prevented by disability from performing one job, he may be able to shift his energies to the other, and possibly earn substantially more from the alternative occupation than was the case previously.

In many cases, it will be necessary for the underwriter to require an application amendment signed by the applicant to clarify the job duties. This can reassure the insured as to the exact nature of the coverage, and can avoid questions or litigation at time of claim. It is particularly important where own occ coverage is involved. For instance, if an applicant stated that he is a trial attorney, but a large portion of his job duties were not related to trial work, an amendment to say that he is an attorney (rather than a trial attorney) would be in order. Lacking this, should the attorney suffer a stroke that impairs his speech and renders him unable to perform his trial duties, he would expect full benefits under an own occ definition even though he returned to office duty. A court would be likely to agree with him on the basis that the insurer knew what his actual duties were, and had agreed that he was specifically a trial attorney by accepting the application as written.

6.7.2 INCOME

At least as important to the disability income insurance underwriter as occupation is income. Not just salary must be considered, but also bonuses, company-provided pension contributions, commissions, unearned income and potential income (net worth). It will be the underwriter's assessment of the level of earnings that determines the total amount of coverage in which the insurer will be willing to participate.

The underwriter must evaluate both the level of earnings and earning stability. Naturally it would not be prudent to insure a person at his current income level of $75,000 if $25,000 of that was an exceptionally large bonus unlikely to be repeated. There are certain occupations, commodities brokers are an example, where income tends to fluctuate quite a bit. In some cases, insurers will treat such occupations as uninsurable, or as insurable only on limited benefit plans.

The underwriter must evaluate all income sources that would be available if the applicant becomes disabled. To the extent that an applicant has large amounts of unearned income or potential income, these sources of support during disability must be treated the same as though they were provided by other disability coverage. Furthermore, to the extent that income is diverted into investments, the need for disability protection is less, since such investments can be foregone during a disability without downgrading the applicant's standard of living.

Therefore, in evaluating applications for large amounts of disability income coverage, the applicant's net worth and unearned income must be considered. This is true regardless of occupation or income level, as they are potential sources of funds to help maintain the applicant's normal standard of living during any period of disability. A prime consideration is the liquidity of any such net worth and earnings; naturally the applicant cannot rely on them if they are not easily accessible. Should an applicant have a large source of liquid funds available during an extended period of disability, the need for disability income coverage is reduced.

The personal residence is normally excluded in any evaluation of net worth. However, what should be done when the applicant has a summer home and a cottage in the mountains as well, or has a very large house and grown children? A long-term disability might influence the family to sell a vacation home, since the disabled member is unlikely to use it much, or to move into a smaller house. It is impossible to take into account all of the situations that might occur, but this points out another reason it is unwise to insure too large a percentage of a person's net income.

As was discussed in Chapter 3, only after-tax income is insurable, and disability income insurance benefits are not taxable if the individual pays the premium. Therefore, insurers generally increase their issue limits for coverage paid for by the employer. It is undesirable to insure more than about 80 percent of after-tax earnings (after deduction for projected OASDI benefits), because of two factors: some expenses disappear during disability, such as commuting expenses and other business related expenses, and a financial incentive to return to work must be maintained.

6.7.3 AVOCATIONS

The implications of avocations can be serious. Race drivers, scuba divers, balloonists and so on are exposed to abnormal accident risks. Depending on the frequency of the activities, it may be necessary to add an extra premium, reject, or add an exclusion rider eliminating coverage for disabilities arising from these particular activities.

6.7.4 MEDICAL HISTORY

This is probably the most important factor for all applicants over age 35 or 40. It is also the factor most similar to life underwriting. Chronic conditions are very serious, while acute conditions are serious only if they are likely to recur or cause residual problems. Certain conditions such as overweight, diabetes and nervous disorders may delay recovery from a disability, as well as increasing the risk of the disability occurring.

In evaluating medical history and medical conditions, it is necessary to be aware of regulatory requirements. Many states now have regulations or laws to prevent insurers from declining or rating policies because of blindness or other physical handicaps. As long as these do not bring an increased risk of disability or a decreased recovery rate, such regulations do not pose much problem. Issuing a policy to such a person is often possible only if a rider is added to clarify, for instance, the operation of the lifetime-loss-of-use benefit in case of blindness.

6.7.5 OTHER INSURANCE

Other benefits payable to the applicant in the event of disability are a vital concern in the determination of the appropriate issue amount. Naturally, if it is determined that the appropriate amount of coverage on a particular applicant is $5,000 per month, and he already has $3,500 in force, he should not be issued more than $1,500 on the current application. However, it is not always easy to determine the appropriate offset. In doing so, one must be conscious of taxation of benefits, length of benefit period, and the elimination period of the coverage applied for. For instance, suppose an executive applies for $3,000 of coverage, and the most he should be allowed in total is $4,500. Suppose that his company will provide salary continuance in the amount of $6,000 for 3 months, followed by $4,000 for the next two years. How much additional coverage should be offered?

The first question to come to mind is whether the coverage applied for contains an elimination period close to 2 years. If so, there is no need to take into account the company-provided benefits at all, and the full $3,000 should be allowed. (However, the underwriter might want to find out why the applicant hasn't requested the full $4,500; maybe he has other insurance.) The definition of "close to" will vary among insurers. Those who allow a 2-year elimination period will generally require it. Others may allow full coverage with a 1-year elimination period.

Suppose the executive insists on a 90-day elimination period. Now he should be issued

$$\$4,500 - \$4,000 = \$500$$

of additional coverage, right? Wrong! Since the $4,000 of benefits he already has are paid for by his employer, they will be taxable to him. Thus when determining the amount of tax-free benefits he can purchase, he should receive credit for the amount of employer-paid benefits he will lose in taxes. If we assume a 20 percent credit, he could be issued

$$\$500 + .20 \times \$4,000 = \$1,300.$$

Similar considerations apply to medical coverage, except that taxation of benefits is rarely a consideration; medical benefits are nearly always non-taxable. Here instead of the elimination period, the deductible would integrate two insurance packages. For instance, there should be no concern in issuing a $10,000 deductible major medical policy on top of a medical care package with an aggregate benefit limit of $10,000 or less. Many current major medical policies have variable deductibles under which the deductible is the greater of a specified amount or the amount of benefits provided by other coverage. This allows a great deal of flexibility in coordinating with other plans. Still, it would not be desirable to issue such a policy with a $500 deductible to someone who has another plan providing benefits up to $10,000. While this could be done, there would likely be misunderstandings.

The insured is paying a large premium under both plans to receive coverage in the $500-$10,000 range, even though only one will pay benefits. A deductible as near $10,000 as possible should be used.

Another concern is government-provided benefits. For medical insurance, Medicare eligibility must be considered for older applicants, as was discussed earlier. For almost everyone applying for disability income insurance, eligibility for OASDI or other government programs must be considered. Generally, insurers take this into account in the development of their issue and participation limits, reducing the amount of long-term benefits otherwise available by the amount of assumed government benefits. However, with widespread publicity concerning the strict eligibility rules for OASDI disability benefits, there has been much concern that those benefits will not materialize. Many insurers offer some form of social insurance rider to eliminate this risk. This would pay extra benefits if the insured is disabled under the terms of the individual contract, but is unable to collect from OASDI or other government sources.

Where employer-provided benefits are available, one must also consider whether these are integrated with government benefits. If they are, the approximate amount of government benefits should be deducted from the group benefits before offsetting against the amount of long-term coverage to be offered.

Likewise to be considered are extended sick leave benefits for which an applicant may be eligible through his employer, although these would rarely cause any concern unless an extremely short elimination period was requested. On the other hand, cash-sickness benefits, mandated in some states, are a concern. Since these typically have a maximum benefit period of 26 weeks, most insurers ignore them for coordination of basic disability income insurance benefits. However, for short-term (1 or 2 years) supplemental benefits and social insurance riders, the maximum issue limits will generally be reduced, or the applicant will be required to take at least a 6-month elimination period, if the contract is to be issued in one of those states.

6.7.6 OTHER FACTORS

There are many other factors to consider in evaluating the risk, especially where long term disability coverage is concerned. One factor which received more attention in the past is morals. Here the concern is primarily with the person's ethics. Is the applicant one who is likely to attempt to cheat the insurer? While it would be difficult to make "poor morals" stand up in court as a reason to decline an application, if there is evidence of questionable ethical standards, it would be prudent to investigate all aspects of the case very carefully in case there have been factors of significance not fully disclosed on the application.

Another important factor is habits. Certain lifestyles are more likely to lead to venereal diseases, lung cancer, heart disease, alcoholism, stress-related problems, and so on.

Foreign travel often involves extra risks, especially if the travel is to an area of political unrest. The risks involved are not just in actual claims, but in the difficulties (and expense) inherent in verifying and settling any claims that take place overseas.

For BOE coverage, working from one's residence presents a problem. It is nearly impossible to distinguish many personal expenses from business expenses unless the office is a separate building, or at least has a separate entrance, and no direct access to the house. Some insurers will not consider applicants working from their residence.

The agent is always an important consideration. The agent who sells few health policies may unintentionally misrepresent policy provisions, just from lack of familiarity. In addition, his business may involve a significant degree of antiselection, because often it will have been the client who initially asked the agent about health insurance instead of the other way around. The tendency is increasingly towards monitoring the agent's block of business, and being more or less liberal in terms of which requirements are necessary and whether or not to take the application at face value according to the agent's past performance. In addition, a good rapport with the agent can save the underwriter time and effort; the agent will be more willing to help get needed information and will often supply it with the application. The extra trust the agent may have in the underwriter's judgment will also reduce appeals or complaints from the field.

Optional benefits often require special considerations based on the coverage they offer. For instance, a social insurance option should not be allowed if the applicant would not suffer a loss from not receiving social insurance benefits. This could be the case if the applicant already has group coverage fully integrated with OASDI benefits; if he has already has such an option in an in-force policy in the full amount of potential benefits; or if he is ineligible for social insurance benefits to begin with. In this last situation, the applicant should instead purchase additional basic long-term coverage; the premium for the social insurance option would be insufficient, given that his coverage would be essentially identical to basic coverage.

Guaranteed insurability options allow the insured to avoid the underwriting process on future limited purchases. Thus it is appropriate to underwrite the original application more thoroughly than otherwise. One way insurers do this is to add some portion (perhaps all) of the potential future purchases to the current amount to determine what underwriting requirements are necessary. For instance, if special tests and x-rays are required on all applications above $5,000 of monthly income, and if the applicant is applying for $4,500 with an option that guarantees the purchase of up to $1,200 more, the underwriter would require those tests. In other words, the request for a guaranteed insurability option would cause the application to receive a higher level of scrutiny.

It is difficult to set specific guidelines for an underwriter to follow in underwriting optional benefits. There are many common sense strictures such as not allowing a salaried employee to buy residual or partial benefits because a salaried employee will generally return to work at full salary or not at all. Thus the only guidelines in common use, other than those mentioned above, are to

- disallow certain options such as COL adjustments for higher risk occupation classes.
- allow only more limited versions of the options for higher risk occupation classes. For instance, offer a more limited residual disability benefit such as one that requires a preceding total disability for benefit eligibility, to nonprofessional classes.
- disallow certain options such as guaranteed insurability with substandard premium classes.
- disallow options involving liability for accidental injury (such as accidental death and dismemberment) to applicants with above average risks of such injury (such as private pilots).

6.8 ISSUE AND PARTICIPATION LIMITS

An underwriter has an element of control against overinsurance through prescribed issue and participation limits. The *issue limit* is the total amount of coverage an insurer is willing to issue to an individual applicant, while the *participation limit* is the total amount of an individual's coverage from all benefit sources in which the insurer is willing to participate. These can be, and often are, the same amount. An insurer will generally have both a schedule of limits that varies by income and an absolute upper and lower limit independent of income. Limits will generally vary by occupation class, and there will often be separate limits for social insurance riders, and separate (higher) limits that apply to situations where the employer pays the premium.

A schedule of issue limits by income level is developed by estimating the amount of after-tax income an individual would lose while disabled. In doing so, one must account for the probable amount of OASDI or other social insurance benefits the disabled insured will receive, as well as his tax bracket and tax rate. The schedule of issue limits will also take into account an appropriate level of income replacement. It is unwise to replace the total after-tax income, as the disabled person would not be financially motivated to return to work. Most insurers would insure about 80 percent of after-tax earnings for lower incomes, and would reduce the percentage substantially as income rises.

To determine the credit for having the insured's employer pay the premium, one could make a similar calculation and develop a complete scale by income. However, this is a fairly complex calculation and not always easy to explain to the agent or insured who feels they should be entitled to more. Most companies apply a fairly simple factor to the basic issue limit such as by raising the limits 20 percent where premiums are paid by the employer.

Absolute lower issue limits are generally around $400—$500 in monthly income. The limit is generally dictated by the expenses of underwriting and issuing a policy, and will usually be reduced for additional coverage written on an existing client. Absolute upper issue limits, on the other hand, vary dramatically from company to company. The limit is set to control the risk the company must bear on any one life, and tends to be higher in larger companies with large amounts of surplus available. There are insurers who will not write more than $2,000 or $3,000 of monthly income on one life, while there are several with issue limits in excess of $15,000 of monthly income. Maximum issue limits are usually quite a bit lower on the higher risk occupation classes.

Low maximum issue limits can lead to morale problems among the field force, or at least among those who tend to be the better producers and who work in the larger income, professional market. To combat this problem, most smaller insurers will set an absolute upper issue limit substantially higher than their retention limit, then arrange for a reinsurer to absorb the risk above the lower limit, or will sometimes set a substantially higher participation limit.

Setting a higher participation limit can help assuage the agent by assuring him that his company will at least participate in any large case he is involved in, even though it will not issue the full amount of coverage the client is seeking. This can be a very important agent incentive considering the prevalence of commission bonuses and other benefits based on the level of production. This action also, in effect, serves as a low cost form of reinsurance, enabling the insurer to participate in a larger risk than would otherwise be undertaken, but without the costs of a formal reinsurance agreement. However, this route could lead to losing the sale completely, if the agent does not want to have the applicant go through the underwriting process with multiple insurers. It can also lead the insurer into overinsurance problems–a larger than anticipated percentage of its portfolio may end up at the retention limit.

One area where the use of participation limits higher than issue limits has become quite common is with disability coverage for applicants at the older issue ages, past 50 or 55 for instance, since insurers will often have a lower maximum issue limit at these older ages. Lower issue limits are set for these older ages because disability is more likely, the approaching retirement age reduces incentives to return to work, if disabled, and effective underwriting is more difficult. Also since most disability income insurance policies expire between ages 65 and 70 and retirement brings almost certain lapse, the profit outlook for policies written at advanced ages is not good. Thus companies are often unwilling to issue new policies in large amounts to persons over age 55, but will allow additions to existing coverage, and will participate in such cases if shared with other carriers.

One other complication could be presented by a large amount case with a guaranteed insurability benefit. Since the exercise of an option typically requires that the insured qualify for additional coverage under the insurer's then current issue and participation limits, a benefit should not be purchased that cannot be fully exercised according to the limits in effect. For example, if the maximum issue limit is $10,000, a guaranteed insurability benefit on a $9,000 policy is effectively limited to a $1,000 increase. If the applicant pays for a policy that provides options of up to $2,000 of increases in coverage, misunderstandings are likely to develop when he tries to exercise those options. This problem might never develop if the insurer happens to raise its issue limits in the meanwhile, but the more prudent course is to issue a smaller guaranteed insurability benefit.

6.9 RENEWALS/POLICY CHANGES/ REINSTATEMENTS/RATE REVISIONS/ UPDATES

Very few individual health insurance policies allow for renewal underwriting. Even policies that are renewable only at the option of the insurer generally provide for cancellation or rate increases strictly on an underwriting class basis. However, a few situations do involve a form of renewal underwriting.

When an insured requests a change to his policy involving an increase in the insurer's liability, the insurer will need to reevaluate the risk. Such changes could include requesting a shorter elimination period, a longer benefit period or additional optional benefits under a disability income insurance contract or a lower deductible or higher benefit schedule under a medical care policy. The amount of underwriting will depend on the significance of the change. However, because only a small amount of additional premium and liability is involved relative to that under the original policy, the underwriting will usually be quite limited, perhaps restricted to having the insured fill out an abbreviated nonmedical application form. The decision is usually to allow or disallow the change; exclusion riders or extra premiums are rarely an option.

Frequently an insured will apply for reinstatement of a lapsed policy. When a reinstatement application is made, the underwriter has at his disposal all of the same tools as he had at the time of the original policy issue. Unless the policy has been lapsed for some time (3 months for instance), it would be practical to have the applicant complete the nonmedical application form. If it has been 6 months or more since lapse, the underwriter should underwrite it as if it were a new case, and may even want to require application for a new policy (at the new insurance age and premium level). It is important to verify that the facts disclosed on the reinstatement application match those on the application taken for the original policy. The underwriter must be careful not to delay too long in completing the process. Most states require a provision that if the reinstatement application is not rejected within 45 days, the policy is deemed to be reinstated.

Since the insurer is not allowed to add exclusion riders or extra premiums to a policy after issue, it would seem sensible that the insurers would not be expected to drop riders or extra premiums after issue because of improvement in the insured's health. However, it is often necessary to do so to conserve the policy. The underwriter must carefully evaluate the situation, especially since it is unlikely that someone judged substandard at issue will have no residual elements that continue to adversely affect the situation.

Replacement of an in force policy (with the same insurer) is a form of renewal underwriting. Often this will occur when a newer, more liberal policy form has been introduced for sale. Because the underwriter will have access to all of the information developed at the time of the original application, his focus of attention will be on any change in the applicant's health or financial status. Should the application be rejected, he will still have the in force policy, so that some weight should be given to the magnitude of the change in coverage in determining the final outcome.

An insurer may make special offers to existing insureds to update their policies by adding new optional benefits or by converting to a newer policy series. In such cases, there will generally be a limited period of time (such as 30 days) during which such updates are guaranteed or subject to simplified underwriting.

6.10 SPECIAL UNDERWRITING SITUATIONS

Quite often, especially when dealing with large groups such as associations, the insurer will make certain underwriting concessions. These often involve higher nonmedical limits, waiving certain special medical tests, reduced income verification requirements and so on. The most significant underwriting concession, used primarily for direct response marketing or very large groups, involve offers of guaranteed issue.

Guaranteed issue offers mean that the insurer agrees to accept the risk as applied for, as long as certain requirements are met. Usually these include restrictions on the amount of coverage or on the plan of insurance available, and a minimum participation level among members of the group to reduce the antiselection risk. This is a liberal guarantee that, in essence, removes the underwriter from the picture, except when certain applicants want more coverage or a more favorable plan than is guaranteed. In those cases, the underwriter can at most decline the excess over the guaranteed amount or plan.

A more limited variation of the guaranteed issue concession is referred to as a guarantee-to-issue. Here the insurer guarantees that everyone who applies will be issued a policy, but reserves the right to rate up or waiver the policy, and to issue a less favorable plan than requested. This means that the guarantee is significant only for those people who otherwise would be uninsurable. Because this is a very limited risk, this form of guarantee will often be allowed on relatively small groups; some insurers allow this with 25 lives or even smaller groups. Since each application is reviewed, the underwriter's work is impacted only very minimally by such a guarantee.

Often insurers will offer a more liberal form of the guarantee-to-issue contract, perhaps agreeing not to rate any policies, but only to add waiver riders. They might agree that the least favorable plan they will issue will be something significantly more favorable than their least attractive plan. In such situations, they will usually make qualification for the program more restrictive, possibly through minimum participation requirements or by restricting the guarantees to certain classes of employees or members within the group. Such concessions are a necessity with large groups or associations where it is required that all members be offered coverage.

As has been discussed, the basic underwriting process for health and life insurance is quite similar. However the health insurance underwriter has more tools at hand, such as the exclusion rider, to allow policies to be issued to substandard risks. Despite this, a significantly higher percentage of health insurance applications are declined. Possibly the most important reason is that the insured's higher degree of control over claim incidence and costs, combined with the differing incentives due to payment of benefits to the insured rather than to a beneficiary, brings the potential for a much higher level of antiselection. This additional potential for antiselection makes substandard business that much more risky. Thus substandard issues are not allowed as high a debit count as for life insurance.

Chapter 7

INDIVIDUAL HEALTH INSURANCE CLAIMS ADMINISTRATION

by John W. Hadley, F.S.A.

After a claim is submitted, the claim examiner's job is to determine

1. whether there are grounds for rescission or reformation (if the policy is contestable),
2. whether the submitted claim meets the criteria for payment required by the policy, and
3. how much should be paid.

With medical insurance, claims will be incurred during the contestable period on a large percentage of policies. Thus the first question frequently arises. The second and third questions require careful analysis because of variations in benefit formulas by type of claim, provider of services, state (due to mandated benefits and other state variations in coverage), the particular policy series involved and so on.

Disability income insurance policies with elimination periods of 30 days or more are characterized by infrequent claims. However, these will usually have a higher claims incidence during the contestable period than will life insurance policies. In addition, disability income insurance customers are often offered opportunities to upgrade their coverage through conversion to a newer, more liberal policy series or by adding new or improved optional benefits. To the extent that these options are underwritten, the contestable period will usually be reestablished.

The second question is also a critical one for disability income insurance. The determination of whether or not the claimant is in fact disabled can require a great deal of judgment and expertise.

The third question is rarely difficult to answer for disability income insurance. However, the claim examiner is in the unique position of often being able, through careful claims management, to affect the total payments made over the duration of the claim.

These questions will be explored in detail in this chapter. A simple approach would be to characterize the normal mode of the life insurance versus medical expense versus disability income claims operations as claim payment versus claims processing versus claims management, respectively.

7.1 THE CLAIMS EVALUATION PROCESS

In the claims evaluation process, the data needed to evaluate the claim are developed, then the legitimacy of the claim is validated.

7.1.1 THE BASICS

The basic steps in the claims evaluation process are the following:

1. The insurer receives notice of claim and, soon after, the completed claim form.

   Notice of claim for reimbursement benefits will usually be received soon after a claim is incurred, as the insured will want any bills paid quickly. The main exception is for claims of small amounts. The insured may often allow such claims to accumulate, and then submit several bills for reimbursement at one time.

   For disability income insurance policies, notice will often be substantially delayed, particularly if a long elimination period is involved.

2. APS's, hospital and other medical records or bills are requested.
3. The original application file and any other company records are assembled.
4. A determination is made as to what benefits are being claimed.

   The benefits claimed will usually be obvious from the claim form. However, it is quite possible that the request for payment may be different from the intent of the policy. This could happen because of poor policy construction, misunderstanding of the coverage provided, wishful thinking on the part of the claimant, or an attempt to get something to which the claimant knows he is not entitled.

   It is often necessary to contact the claimant during the claims process. Thus the claim examiner may also serve as a public relations officer for the insurer. The examiner is one of the few company people other than the agent who is in regular contact with insureds.

5. The policy status at the time of claim is determined to verify that the claim occurred while the policy was in force.

   The examiner checks for the possibility that a preexisting condition is involved, and verifies that the policy has not lapsed before the claim occurred.

6. The extent of liability is determined. The examiner must determine whether the claim is actually covered, whether the policy should be contested, and the appropriate benefit payment.

The examiner must be particularly careful if the policy under which the claim is being made is not currently sold, as more recent versions of the same provisions may be administered differently. The claim examiner should always have available (and carefully analyze) a copy of the actual policy form under which the claim has been submitted, and must consider any exclusions or amending riders. There also may have been policy updates that extended liberalized benefits retroactively to existing policies, and the examiner must be familiar with these.

The details of the claims evaluation process continually evolve due to

- revisions to policy wording,
- new or revised policy benefits,
- court decisions,
- revisions to underwriting guidelines,
- advances in medical technology,
- competitive pressures, and
- changes in the average claimant profile due to revised marketing or pricing emphasis on different market segments.

7.1.2 CONTESTABILITY AND RESCISSION

The determination of whether all or part of a policy is contestable cannot wait until adequate proof of loss is received. This is because the contestable period usually runs for a fixed time period from the date of issue, change or reinstatement, and proof of loss can require a substantial amount of time to develop.

Upon notice of claim, the examiner verifies whether or not the policy is in the contestable period. If so, and there was not a prior claim for which contestability was already reviewed, an investigation is initiated to determine whether or not there were any misrepresentations on the application. Throughout this chapter, the term "application" will refer to the original health insurance application and any supplemental questionnaires or other evidence of insurability submitted by the insured in support of a request to upgrade or reinstate the policy. Almost without exception, representations on these may be used in the contest of a policy only if legible copies were attached to it.

If there have been misrepresentations, the examiner must determine materiality. The general rule is that a misrepresentation is material if

1. it was knowingly false,
2. it was material to acceptance of the risk and

3. it was relied upon in issue of the policy.

In other words, the underwriter, if properly informed, would not have issued the same policy. This can mean that the application would have been declined, or simply that an exclusion rider or extra premium would have been added. It could also mean that a particular optional benefit would not have been allowed, in which case there would be grounds to retroactively delete the benefit from the policy. Grounds for rescission may also include errors of omission, such as an admission of only one of several hospitalizations.

It is not always necessary to prove that a misrepresentation was material. Some courts have considered that certain types of questions (particularly those related to hospitalization) are automatically material, or even that every question on the application is material. However, the norm is that the insurer must prove materiality. In doing so, it may be useful to point to industry practices with regard to the particular underwriting information. Naturally the insurer will have a stronger case if able to point to an industry practice than if taking an unusual underwriting stance.

To determine materiality, the claim examiner would generally discuss the case with an underwriter and a company medical director. The examiner would then review the evidence and applicable state laws to see if rescission or some alternative course of action is appropriate. A final step for large or unusual claims might be for the examiner to present a recommendation to a committee that includes personnel from various disciplines within the health insurance area. If the decision is to rescind, a check would be sent out, normally via certified mail, for a refund of premiums.

There is normally no need to show that the situation misrepresented relates in any way to the current claim, although some states have enacted legislation to require this. A likely scenario might be that an insured submits a claim for disability due to an auto accident. The claim examiner, in investigating the claim, discovers that the insured materially misrepresented his income on the application, and the policy is rescinded on that basis.

When a claim is submitted, it results in payment of benefits or notification that a certain amount of the deductible has been met, unless the claim is unfounded or the policy is contested. However, it is often necessary to pay the claim prior to completion of the investigation. Undue delay in claims payment after receipt of proof of loss may be considered an unfair claims practice. If the policy is later contested, the rescission may include a demand that benefits be repaid.

7.1.3 CLAIM VALIDITY

Assuming that no contest is to take place, the next step is to determine the validity of the claim. The first stage is to determine whether the policy was in force when the claim was incurred. This is simple for life insurance where there is a readily determinable date of death. For health insurance, the operative date is that on which the claim commenced. Determination of an exact date is not always easy.

The next step is to determine whether or not the condition causing the claim preexisted the policy. For example, there may be grounds for denying reimbursement for treatment of high blood pressure if the insured had high blood pressure before applying for the policy. The examiner must consider whether the exclusion rider on the policy, if any, relates to the claim. Also to be considered is whether the claim meets the policy definitions. For medical care insurance, this would include answering the following questions:

- Was all treatment performed in an eligible facility?

  In addition to hospitals, this may include nursing homes, hospices, and extended care or convalescent homes.

- Were all services provided by eligible practitioners?

  In addition to physicians, these may include chiropractors, optometrists, acupuncturists, practical nurses, therapists, and so on.

- Were services performed within the time frames required by the policy?

  For instance, many policies require that extended care services commence within a specified time after a hospital stay.

Company practice may allow for exceptions to policy definitions. For example, as an alternative to costly long-term hospital confinement, the examiner may allow a less expensive extended care facility not provided for by the policy provisions.

Disability income insurance policies may have differences in benefit period or other aspects of the coverage according to whether disability was the result of accident or sickness, so that this determination will be important. There may also be optional benefits, such as a social insurance rider, that complicate the determination of benefit eligibility. And most important is the determination of whether the insured is in fact disabled under the terms of the contract. Here the examiner must consider

- the definition of disability, that is, own occ versus any occupation and so on,
- the duties of the occupation and the degree to which their performance is affected by the disability, and
- the diagnosis of the condition causing disability.

The examiner will need at least the following information:

- the nature and cause of the disability,
- the history of the disability,
- the type of work done by the insured (particularly, the specific duties involved and the percentage of time spent on each),

- when the insured last worked,
- whether or not the disability is job related, and
- a statement from a physician regarding the diagnosis, the degree of disability (as related to the specific duties of the job), the history, progress and prognosis for the disabling condition.

7.2 CLAIM PAYMENT

The last step in the claims process is to determine the amount and make the payment. The basic benefit amount is determined by the indemnity amounts, reimbursement schedules or benefit formulas specified in the policy. It may be necessary to partially or fully offset the amount of benefits provided by other insurance, workers compensation, OASDI or other social insurance sources, depending on policy provisions and applicable laws, which will vary by state. A statement should accompany the payment as to how the amount paid was determined. The statement should show any assignment of benefits, which occurs often with medical coverage where the insured prefers to have payment made directly to the provider.

Under per illness medical coverage, once the deductible has been met, expenses related to that specific illness will continue to be reimbursed without a new deductible until the end of the benefit period. Depending on the policy, this may be a few months, a year, a few years, or even the lifetime of the insured. Thus with each new claim for benefits, the examiner must verify whether it represents a new or a continuing claim in order to properly apply the benefit formula. The same is true of all cause coverage, but there is usually less question as to whether a specific charge is part of the current claim.

The examiner will also have situations where the exact amount to be reimbursed is not specified in the policy. Surgical schedules, for instance, delineate the benefit amounts for only the most common procedures. The examiner must compare the surgery performed to similar types listed in the schedule, or refer to published relative value schedules, in order to determine an appropriate payment. The examiner must be alert to multiple procedures performed during one operation, particularly for per illness coverage or where part of the surgery is of an essentially elective nature.

For disability income insurance policies, the payment takes the form of a monthly annuity that continues for the lesser of the benefit period or until the insured recovers or dies. Thus the examiner must initiate the annuity along with appropriate controls established to ensure that

1. continued disability is verified before each payment is made, with a periodic in-depth review of the case,
2. payments do not continue past the end of the benefit period, and
3. the case is completely reevaluated at the time the definition of disability changes under the terms of the policy.

The disability income insurance benefit may not always involve level payments. As discussed in Chapter 3, inflation protection benefits have become quite popular. These provide for automatic increases in benefits, with the increases linked to the CPI or some other index of cost of living. This provision requires periodic redetermination of the benefit amount. Adjustments are also required for residual disability benefits. Here the benefit amount is not tied to a published index. but rather to the ratio of the claimant's current earnings to his predisability earnings.

7.3 SOURCES OF INFORMATION AVAILABLE TO THE CLAIM EXAMINER

The sources of information used include

1. claimant's statement: The claimant will be asked to complete an insurer-provided claim form. This will detail information sufficient to identify the specific policy under which the claim is being made, and it will furnish the claimant's description of the basis for the claim.
2. APS: For medical insurance, the claim form will usually contain a section for the attending physician to complete to indicate the course of and reason for treatment; with disability income insurance a separate statement from the attending physician would usually be required.
3. itemized bills (for medical insurance): These will be needed by the examiner in determining the extent to which the services provided are covered under the policy. This information is vital when the coverage provides for different coinsurance percentages or deductibles or benefit limits for various types of services. Unfortunately, the detail available on bills will vary dramatically according to whether services are provided in a large hospital, an outpatient clinic or a doctor's office, and according to which hospital, clinic or doctor provided the service.
4. underwriting file: The information developed at time of policy issue can be quite revealing, and can facilitate the examiner's investigative work.
5. inspections: Reports prepared by independent inspection agencies, or by the insurer's investigation department, may be used not only in potential rescissions, but also to analyze questionable claims.
6. Disability Income Record (DIR): This is a source of information similar to that maintained by the MIB providing disability claim information to member companies.
7. medical examinations: Since medical insurance generally provides retrospective reimbursement coverage, independent medical examinations usually are not ordered. They are ordered, however, for disability income insurance claims, particularly in situations where the claimant has not been seeing a doctor regularly, or where there appear to be suspicious circumstances surrounding the disability. Almost all disability

income insurance policies provide the insurer with the right to require that the claimant be examined by a physician approved by the insurer at least annually throughout the disability. The examiner may waive this requirement when the nature of the disability is obvious.

8. agent information: The agent will often know the claimant well, and if so, has likely seen or talked to the claimant since the claim commenced. However, this very relationship may create a reluctance upon the agent's part to reveal anything that might affect the outcome of the claim. While it may be possible for the medical claim examiner to get to know an agent's block of business and establish some rapport, this may be difficult for the disability income insurance examiner. This is because the claims rate is so low that the examiner will see few claims from any particular agent.

7.4 EFFECT OF PRODUCT ON CLAIMS ADMINISTRATION

The higher the deductible or longer the elimination period, the lower the claim frequency, claim payments and claim administration costs. This is due to two factors: benefit payments saved on the initial portion of large claims and the entire amount of small claims; and administrative cost savings from the elimination of the smaller, more frequent claims. Thus a higher percentage of claims department expenditures will be actual claims payments. There will be a practical limit to this effect, though, as the larger the claim, the greater the scrutiny required, so that a higher deductible, or elimination period, often brings with it more extensive claims handling per claim.

Although the elimination period can make a substantial difference in administrative costs by eliminating short duration claims, it may be waived in certain situations. For instance, it is common for policies with elimination periods of a week or less for sickness disabilities to provide for no elimination period in case of accident. Similarly, presumptive disability clauses generally waive the elimination period.

A similar approach is sometimes found in medical care coverages, where the deductible is lowered or eliminated, or the coinsurance percentage is raised, for certain types of claims. This is most often used to encourage services that may help to reduce overall claims costs, such as a second surgical opinion.

In general, the differences in underwriting by product will also be reflected in differences in claims management. This is because the underwriting information developed at policy issue will form the basis for any rescissions at claim time. One exception of interest is renewability. Although the renewal clause will influence the level of underwriting, it will have no appreciable effect on the claims process. This is because once a legitimate claim has been incurred, the insurer is liable for the duration of the claim.

Several product-line-related variations in the claim examiner's job have already been discussed. One of the most fundamental is in the effect the examiner has on the loss ratio.

The medical claim examiner typically reviews claims for services that have already been provided, that is, the examiner looks at the claims retrospectively. Thus there is little room, except on continuing claims, for the examiner to affect the level of benefits paid.

The disability income insurance claim examiner, however, looks at claims prospectively, assessing not just the benefits currently owed, but the future outlook for the claim. At some insurance companies it may even be the examiner's responsibility to set reserve values for certain claims based on an evaluation of the probable ultimate benefit level, and to negotiate lump sum sentiments on long-term claims. Through judicious use of insurer-paid rehabilitative programs or encouragement of alternate courses of treatment, the examiner has the opportunity to improve recovery rates. In addition, the substantially subjective nature of disability determination requires a maximum of expertise on the part of the claim examiner. Thus the knowledge and judgment of the examiners can be crucial to the profitability of the disability income insurance line.

7.4.1 MEDICAL CARE COVERAGE

The principal task the claim examiner faces with regard to most medical coverages is to determine whether the specific claim is covered and the amount of benefits to be paid. This is because of the substantial variability in coverage due to product variations, inside limits and other variables in coverage according to the specifics of the claim. Even when the specific benefit formula is known, the calculation of the benefit amount may require analysis, as many reimbursement coverages provide some relationship to reasonable and customary charges. This will often require that the examiner study the individual bills in relation to prevailing costs.

Another major task is to determine whether payments are available from other sources. Many contracts have some form of coordination of benefits clause in an attempt to ensure that the claimant doesn't receive reimbursement in excess of 100 percent, so that information as to other sources of payment is vital. There may be situations in which the insured is not actually liable for any costs, such as where services are provided as a professional courtesy, or where a veteran is treated in a Veterans Administration hospital. In such cases, the provider, if aware that the person is insured, may bill the insurer at normal rates, even though they would otherwise waive or reduce the charges.

Rescissions are less complex for medical coverages than for disability income insurance. Usually only medical information is germane to the underwriting action for medical insurance, whereas disability income insurance involves factors such as income (for eligibility and amount), other insurance (for amount), and occupation (for occupation class). Thus almost all medical rescissions are based on medical information, while this may account for only a narrow majority of disability income insurance rescissions.

The medical claims area will, much more often than for disability income insurance, attempt to reform the policy rather than rescind it. Thus, for misrepresentations of facts that would not have brought outright declination, there will often be an attempt to amend the policy to put the insurer in the same position as if fully informed at policy issue. This is rarely done in the disability income insurance line, because the integrity of the insured is critical to the profitability of the business. The presence or degree of disability can be subjective and subject to manipulation by the insured.

The most labor-intensive medical coverage from a claims viewpoint is Medicare supplement insurance. The benefit formulas are complex and change frequently, because of the need to integrate with Medicare benefits. There may be multiple coverages to deal with in addition to those provided by Medicare. Most importantly, the claimants are elderly, hence subject to high claim rates; they are often confused about their coverage, as well as concerned about medical costs, and thus require a great deal of attention.

7.4.2 DISABILITY INCOME COVERAGE

As discussed earlier, disability income insurance requires a very high degree of judgment from the claim examiner because of the subjective nature of disabilities. This is the most important aspect of the disability income insurance claim examiner's job, and overshadows any differences by type of disability income insurance product.

To the extent that only short-term coverage is provided, a claim will be accorded less attention. It is not cost effective for the examiner to expend as much effort on a claim that can last at most 6 months as on one that could continue for the claimant's lifetime. On the other hand, more effort will be required if the policy provides benefits that increase over time, such as through an inflation protection benefit.

There is one type of disability income insurance product that involves substantially different concerns--income replacement coverage. This is because such policies provide that, once the disabled status has been determined, continuation of benefits is based on continued income loss rather than on continued disability. The determination of the initial disabled status will not differ from that for other types of disability income insurance coverage, but thereafter the focus is on earnings. Thus the examiner must monitor closely the claimant's income, and the concern with possible malingering, emphasis on rehabilitation and so on, will all be related primarily to effects on the claimant's future earnings rather than on continuance of disability.

7.5 TOOLS AVAILABLE TO CHALLENGE QUESTIONABLE CLAIMS

A number of tools are available to the claim examiner to challenge questionable claims.

7.5.1 INCONTESTABLE CLAUSE

The standard incontestability provision prevents almost any defense or avoidance of the policy after the expiration of the contestable period. This prevention normally applies even if fraud was used to obtain the contract. It is possible to specifically except fraud from incontestability, thereby allowing that as a defense for the life of the contract. However, several states won't allow such an exception. There are other defenses that can occasionally be used after the expiry of the contestable period, such as the assertion that there was never the "meeting of the minds" necessary to valid formation of a contract. This could occur, for instance, if the policy was obtained by someone impersonating the applicant. In addition, it is always possible to assert that the event insured against has not occurred, that the insured really is not disabled under the terms of the policy, or that the contract was already fully performed.

In order to make full use of contestability, the application must be designed so as to be as objective as possible. Subjective questions such as "Do you intend to travel outside of the United States during the next six months?" are of little value in the contest of a policy.

In life insurance, it is common to find the phrase "during the insured's lifetime" as a modifier to the standard 2-year contestable period. This is used to extend the period indefinitely if the insured dies while the policy is still contestable. An additional modifier added to some disability income insurance policies is "excluding any period of disability." Since those people who seriously misrepresent their health at policy issue are likely to incur disabilities during the early years of the policy, this improves the defenses available to the insurer. This also prevents the claimant near the end of the contestable period from avoiding an investigation that might lead to rescission by simply neglecting to report the claim until the contestable period has expired.

There are no absolute legal standards about how incontestability works for reinstatements, policy changes and replacements as there have been conflicting court decisions on the subject. The prevailing opinion is that the normal incontestability provision applies equally to changes and replacements, so that such actions are contestable to the extent of the change in coverage for the normal contestable period, measured from the date of the change.

If a changed or reinstated policy is rescinded, this usually means the original policy remains in force as it existed immediately prior to the change or reinstatement. Thus a disability income insurance policy issued for $2,000 of monthly income that was upgraded to $5,000, if rescinded, could result in a complete rescission of coverage, or rescission of only the additional $3,000 of liability, depending on the status of contestability of the original $2,000 policy. If the $2,000 policy has been continuously in force to the date the new policy was rescinded, and if that period were still less than the contestable period, then the $2,000 policy could be contested. Such considerations will be important in determining whether or not to attempt rescission — obviously it is less worthwhile to contest a policy on which only the residual disability rider is still contestable than if the entire coverage can be rescinded.

7.5.2 PREEXISTING CONDITIONS EXCLUSION

A preexisting conditions exclusion provides that if a claim is incurred within a specified period after policy issue, and is the result of a condition not fully disclosed on the application, the insurer may exclude that claim from coverage. The insured must have been aware of the condition, either because of a medical diagnosis or symptoms that should reasonably have caused the insured to have sought medical advice. The clause can be viewed as a broad exclusion rider that operates for a limited period of time.

The usual period after policy issue specified in the exclusion is 2 years (as with contestability), although for Medicare supplement insurance most states limit it to 6 months. In addition, there is usually a requirement that the condition have manifested itself within a certain period of time prior to the time the application is taken.

This clause is of little importance to the disability income insurance examiner, who would generally prefer to rescind the policy. However, it can be useful if the investigation has not generated conclusive grounds for rescission, and is frequently used by the medical claim examiner.

Many conditions tend to recur and can generate long duration claims, so that they involve a high risk exposure. It is especially important to check for preexistence of heart disease, lung disease, mental illness, cancer, digestive or kidney diseases where a preexisting conditions exclusion is still effective.

7.5.3 GOOD HEALTH CLAUSE

Another tool used by some carriers is a good health clause. This provides that the policy does not become effective unless delivered and the first premium paid during the good health of the insured. This would generally be taken to mean that there has been no deterioration in the insured's health since the application was taken, and thus helps protect the insurer against conditions commencing or deteriorating during the underwriting process. It can also provide some protection against health problems not disclosed because the applicant was not yet aware of them, although courts have been divided on this question, particularly if the insurer required a medical exam. As with contestability, for the good health clause to be applied the problem must be material to insurability. Courts will generally tie the good health clause into the contestability period, so that once the policy is incontestable, the good health clause can no longer be invoked.

7.5.4 OTHER EXCLUSIONS

Most risks that expose the insurer to the possibility of catastrophic losses can be minimized through appropriate underwriting guidelines designed to assure a spread of risks. Some risks over which the insurer exercises little control are excluded from coverage, hence the war and military service exclusions as discussed in Chapter 2.

Suicide, intentionally self-inflicted injury and felony exclusions are not of much significance to the level of claims costs. These are designed primarily to conform to public policy. In fact, the injury exclusion need not be in the policy for it to be used in defense of a claim denial, since a self-inflicted injury is neither an accident nor a sickness. However, the legal stance is stronger with the exclusion spelled out in the policy.

As mentioned in Chapter 3, benefits due to pregnancy were once routinely excluded from disability income insurance coverage, and medical policies carefully limited the extent to which maternity benefits were payable. Most jurisdictions require that complications of pregnancy be covered to the same extent as any other sickness, and some have mandated maternity benefits for medical policies. This has created some concern, especially for disability income insurance coverage, because of the extent to which pregnancy is a voluntary event, and hence not insurable in the usual sense, and the distinction between normal pregnancy and complications thereof is sometimes not clearly determinable.

The misstatement of age provision, while not strictly an exclusion, can be used to void a policy if the issue age is such that, if known at time of issue, no coverage would have been issued. If instead a lower amount would have been issued, the provision can be invoked to reduce the amount to that which would have been purchased by the actual premium paid at the actual age at issue.

7.6 OTHER FACTORS AFFECTING CLAIMS ADMINISTRATION

Many factors affect the way claims are administered. Some of these involve recognition of the nature of the disability and whether rehabilitation is possible. Other factors involve adjustments for the claimant's employment and income tax status. Unfair claim practice regulations vary by state and must be incorporated into the claims administration process. Also, a company's system for monitoring loss ratios, its past experience with interpreting policy provisions and its claims department organization are internal factors that affect administration.

Most health insurance policies have a provision addressing recurrent disabilities. This is important, as it determines when a new elimination period, deductible or benefit period will apply to a claim. In a policy containing a small deductible or elimination period and short benefit period, it is beneficial to the insurer to have a liberal definition of recurrences. If the deductible or elimination period is large and the benefit period long, the reverse is true. Such provisions vary from insurer to insurer; a common form provides for a claim to be considered a recurrence if it is due to the same or a related cause as a prior claim, and is incurred within 6 months of the end of that claim.

Rehabilitation benefits are becoming increasingly common under disability income insurance policies. These vary from guarantees that engaging in a job under a rehabilitative program will not be considered recovery from disability to agreement to pay for an insurer-approved rehabilitative program. Insurers can gain by encouraging rehabilitative programs, at least where there is expectation of a return to work by the claimant. Even insurers without rehabilitative benefit provisions in their policies are often willing to provide rehabilitation for promising claimants.

Examiners must be alert to the possibility of rehabilitation when the claim is first submitted. Effective rehabilitation requires that the disabled person begin rehabilitation as soon as possible after the disability commences. It is also necessary to consider rehabilitation in light of the specific definition of disability. There is no advantage to the insurer, except in public relations, from funding vocational rehabilitation for a claimant with an own occ definition; here rehabilitative efforts should concentrate on a return to the claimant's own occupation.

Protection against partial disabilities is a popular optional benefit with disability income insurance policies. This benefit provides partial benefits for disabilities that either prevent the insured from engaging in some duties of the occupation, or from working full time. These provisions originated as "residual" coverage, allowing insureds partial benefits when they first returned to work after total disability, but now often provide such benefits even if there was no period of total disability.

There has been much discussion as to whether these benefits ultimately increase or reduce claim costs. On the one hand, partial benefits are incurred where there might otherwise be no liability. On the other hand, the availability of partial benefits may encourage a quicker return to work, at least on a part-time basis. One aspect is certain, though. The need to track earnings during disability and to establish the predisability earnings level in order to calculate benefits complicate claim administration.

As discussed in Chapter 3, presumptive total disability clauses are common in disability income insurance policies. They provide that an insured who has suffered a severe loss, generally two limbs, sight or hearing, will be presumed to have suffered a total disability. Thus the usual requirement that the claimant be under a doctor's care, and any further evidence of inability to engage in one's occupation, are waived. In addition, benefits would usually be deemed payable for the full benefit period, regardless of earning power. One complication these benefits present the claims examiner is the potential for a nondisabling condition to later result in a presumptive disability, such as with degenerative eye disease.

What does the disability income insurance examiner do if the claimant is unemployed or retired at the time of claim? Should the definition of disability depend on the duties of the most recent job held? If the insured is unemployed because of layoffs or having been fired, it may be difficult to establish when he is able to return to work, so that determination of the end of disability will be complicated. Also, if there is no job to return to, recovery will result in a financial loss for the claimant, creating a poor climate for a speedy return to good health.

Federal Law PL97-123, enacted in 1983, was designed primarily to restore minimum benefits for certain OASDI beneficiaries. However, it also included a requirement for the withholding of FICA and railroad retirement (RRTA) taxes for those disability income benefits considered to be "sick pay." These were defined to be those paid for in whole or in part by the employer. Exempt are certain benefits not considered to be sick pay (such as overhead expense and additional rider benefits such as for hospital confinement or accidental death) and benefits payable more than 6 months after the employee ceased working for the employer. Thus benefits under a policy with a 6 month or longer elimination period would not seem to be affected. However, since a residual disability claimant must be working, presumably such benefits would be subject to withholding throughout disability. Not only must the insurer withhold taxes, but the insurer must also notify the employer of the amounts being withheld, and under certain circumstances could be required to withhold the employer's portion as well.

There have also been attempts to require that insurers allow the claimant to have state taxes withheld from disability income benefits. Few claimants are likely to take advantage of such a vehicle, but to the extent they would, claims administration would be further complicated.

The model NAIC Unfair Claims Practices Bill, as adopted in most states, provides standards for what is considered unfair claims practices, and may encourage punitive damage claims if the insurer violates those standards. In most jurisdictions this requires evidence of repeated violations, but courts have sometimes held otherwise. To protect itself, an insurer should have detailed guidelines regarding such items as length of time

- for claims payment,
- to delay payment if a claim investigation has not been completed,

- to send out claims forms,
- required to acknowledge communications from claimants, and
- from receipt of proof of loss to the final acceptance/rejection.

The key people in risk selection, and therefore the key people in maintaining the loss ratio at an acceptable level are the agent, the medical or paramedical examiner, the inspector or phone verifier, and, of course, the underwriter. In addition, there is the claim examiner. To the extent possible, it is useful to measure loss ratios by each of these people.

Unlike medical claims where experience accumulates quickly, it takes a long time for credible experience to develop under disability income insurance coverage, by which time the results are of limited applicability. For this reason, many insurers have instituted some form of "Good Business Index" that can provide an early warning sign of the quality of a certain block of disability income insurance business. This index will be based on an analysis of the characteristics of the business sold—items such as volume of business sold per agent, average policy size, average issue age, and persistency. To encourage a larger volume of business sold in the highest quality areas, many insurers award additional compensation for such business.

The *loss ratio*, the percentage of premium revenue paid out on claims, is a simple tool for measuring the overall claims level. The traditional disability income insurance loss ratio widely used and accepted by both insurers and insurance departments can be deficient as a tool to monitor the progress of the business and the efficacy of the claims operation. This is because it is easily distorted by

- the reserve method used,
- interest rate assumptions,
- the exclusion of lapse rate assumptions, and
- the difference between expected morbidity and that assumed in claims cost calculations.

The normal pattern on a closed block is a steady increase due to aging and erosion of underwriting selection. It is helpful to restate the loss ratios in terms of more realistic assumptions, taking account of variations by type of product or benefit, so that a relatively level loss ratio is expected. Changes in loss ratios are then easily interpreted.

An alternate method used by many insurers is to study the ratio of actual to expected claims by as detailed a breakdown as is statistically significant. This helps to point out such problems as

- underwriting practices more liberal than warranted,
- unrealistic pricing assumptions, and
- the need for additional training for claim examiners or underwriters.

While medical loss ratios suffer from some of the same defects, and a similar study could be beneficial, this is not usually done. This is because of the large number of categories into which benefits fall, and the consequent problems with designing statistically significant cells. Also, since claims are submitted with much more frequency than for disability income insurance, the loss ratio tends to follow a more predictable pattern, making it a more usable tool.

Input from the claims area is integral to good policy and benefit drafting. The claims area will have had first-hand exposure to how the provisions are administered in submission of claims, and to where there may be problems in their interpretation (especially where the wording doesn't quite match up with the insurer's intent). They will also have insight as to which provisions may be expensive to administer, and how to redesign them to minimize the expense. Naturally, though, since the claim examiner is exposed almost exclusively to those insureds who have submitted claims, there is a tendency for them to see negatives more than positives, so such input must be taken with a grain of salt.

Claims operations are variations on two themes. The first, which is the norm for small insurers' is to have one department handle claims for all product lines. The second is to establish separate departments for distinct product lines. This usually improves operations through increased expertise on the part of the examiners, once there is a large enough volume of business to spread expenses appropriately. Some of the largest insurers have gone as far as to regionalize their claims operations. Unless there is an extremely large block of business that justifies highly compensated managers for each of the regional claims operations, this is not usually cost effective for health insurance. These products require a higher degree of expertise than any other claims operations, so that without careful management it is easy to lose control of the business.

Chapter 8

SELLING INDIVIDUAL HEALTH INSURANCE
by Noel J. Abkemeier, F.S.A.

The selling of individual health insurance coverages has many variations by type of product, type of market, marketing channel and method of compensation. It is also subject to government regulations and, perhaps most importantly, to the agent's ability to offer products that meet a customer's needs. Because both individual life and health products are often sold by the same agents, selling techniques for individual life insurance will be described where necessary to aid in the explanation of the methods used for individual health insurance.

The discussion in this chapter is focused on acquainting the reader with those aspects of the selling process that provide information for insurance plan design and pricing decisions.

8.1 MARKETS AND PRODUCTS

The two broad consumer markets for individual health insurance are persons and businesses and the two broad product markets are disability benefits and medical expense coverage. An agent may operate in all combinations of these markets or concentrate his efforts in one or more segments. While these products can be sold independently, his range of markets for individual health insurance is typically determined by the needs of customers who buy other insurance products as well.

Personal health insurance selling, particularly of disability income products, is an integral part of meeting financial requirements identified by a needs analysis. Thus benefits are often sold in conjunction with life insurance products in a program based on financial need.

Whether or not a needs analysis is performed, sales material can effectively integrate common life and health insurance product combinations. Issuing the health insurance, particularly disability income, as a rider on a life insurance policy can aid in maintaining good policy persistency. In a similar fashion, combined billing can support better persistency. Likewise, business health insurance coverage satisfying the needs of a proprietorship, partnership or corporation is often sold along with business life insurance.

A combined life and health marketing approach can also stimulate multiple-line sales while simplifying application completion and the collection of underwriting information.

Agents who sell personal property and casualty insurance such as automobile or homeowners' often find personal health insurance, particularly medical expense coverage, to be a logical additional product for their clientele. Also, individual health insurance may be sold to businesses in conjunction with property and casualty commercial insurance.

Disability income insurance sold as personal insurance may either satisfy the basic needs of income protection or supplement benefits provided through previously purchased group or individual disability income coverage.

A customer for basic individual protection would be a self-employed person or someone working for a company that does not provide disability income as an employee benefit. The financial goal might be an amount which, when added to benefits available from social insurance programs, provides an appropriate, from an underwriting perspective, percent of predisability after-tax income. Those social insurance programs would include OASDI and state cash sickness programs.

Supplementary disability income coverage may be needed by an individual who has only limited benefits through his employment or whose previously purchased individual policy has become inadequate due to an increased earnings level. Other supplementary disability income insurance may be sold to satisfy a specific need such as covering the amount of monthly payments for a home mortgage or a credit purchase. In this case, an attempt is usually made to sell the policy in tandem with a life insurance policy that will pay off the outstanding balance of the financial obligation.

Just as is the case with disability income coverage, personal medical expense insurance is sold both to provide basic protection and to supplement other individual or group programs.

The basic individual medical expense market consists of persons who are self-employed or who are not provided similar coverage as an employee benefit. A full agent's portfolio would include both long-term products designed to provide coverage for many years and short-term products intended to provide interim coverage before the insured becomes eligible for coverage under an employee benefit program.

Long-term products include hospitalization, major medical and comprehensive policies. Hospitalization policies are designed for customers who have limited funds available both for premiums and for major cost sharing in the event of hospitalization. The major medical product is designed for customers who desire coverage for extremely expensive medical costs at a low premium although they can afford considerable cost sharing when medical expenses are incurred. Such a product can be adapted to a customer's need by setting the deductible to a small enough amount to be affordable, but large enough to also make the premium affordable. The comprehensive product is designed for purchasers who wish to avoid almost all of the risk of high medical expenses and who are able and willing to pay a high annual premium to accomplish that.

Short-term medical expense policies are primarily marketed to newly graduated students seeking their first jobs and to other individuals who are either between jobs or satisfying a waiting period before eligibility for employee medical expense benefits. A typical short-term policy will provide coverage for 60 to 180 days. The benefits may be as broad as provided by long-term products, or may be limited to hospitalization benefits in recognition of the reduced amount of underwriting the insurer can afford to conduct for the small premium.

Supplementary medical expense products may complement a limited medical expense coverage provided by another plan, provide benefits for a specific need or fill a general need irrespective of other medical expense coverage.

A product complementing an existing plan could be designed to provide benefits before expenses were large enough to qualify for reimbursement under the other plan, to provide benefits after the other plan's benefits were exhausted or to provide simultaneous benefits. Thus a low-benefit hospitalization plan could supplement an existing major medical plan or a high-deductible major medical plan could supplement an existing hospitalization plan. Such products are generally not a good fit unless specifically designed to supplement policies issued in prior years. A supplemental hospital indemnity plan could fill the gap between current hospital room costs and the benefit limits in an old plan. A Medicare supplement plan is a precise and specialized product, although the customer has some choice of extent of coverage.

Products designed for a specific need assume the customer has limited medical expense benefits and would be well served to have coverage for a particular event with above average probability of occurrence and/or that would create large expenses. Examples include travel accident and travel sickness insurance, sports accident insurance and cancer insurance.

Some supplemental insurance is designed to provide additional cash in the event of illness regardless of actual expenses incurred and regardless of the adequacy of any existing medical expense coverage. Hospital indemnity policies are often structured to provide additional cash benefits to help pay for extraordinary expenses such as transportation and meals incurred by family members during a long hospitalization. Its sales appeal results from its low cost.

Some of the personal insurance products described above could be viewed as business insurance to the extent that they provide self-employed persons with benefits normally provided as employee benefits by corporations. However, two types of disability benefit policies are designed solely for business purposes.

The business overhead expense policy is intended to cover the need of independently practicing professional or business people for reimbursement of continuing overhead expenses while disabled. This type of policy should be sold as a companion to a personal disability income policy.

A disability buy-out policy is designed for partnership arrangements to provide able partners with a lump-sum payment or installments to buy out the business interests of a disabled partner. This creates opportunity for multiple sales as coverage should be purchased on each life and should be upgraded periodically to recognize changing percentages of interest within the partnership and the changing value of the partnership.

8.2 MARKETING CHANNELS

The insurance agent and customer in a one-on-one setting is the most common method of selling individual health insurance. The agent can be affiliated with an insurance company in several different ways: as a full-time employee, as a representative of a general agency, or as a broker. Some agents may sell one company's life insurance products and another company's health insurance line in order to have the desired product mix. Some supplemental health insurance is sold to employees in group plans on a payroll deduction basis. Usually such sales result from a thorough canvassing of the employees, accomplished by agents or special solicitors.

Direct marketing sales have become substantial and are expected to continue to increase. The most common direct marketing method is mass mailing of sales literature to members of recognized associations and customers of identified companies with the goal of receiving a certain percentage of insurance applications in the return mail. An important ingredient in such selling is the sponsoring organization's endorsement of the insurance product, although in some cases member or customer lists are purchased and it is not possible to use a third-party endorsement. Another direct marketing technique is newspaper advertising. A customer might purchase a policy by mailing in a coupon or calling a toll-free telephone number, or may request more complete sales literature by coupon or telephone. The latter approach may be followed up by telephone solicitation by the insurer. Direct telephone selling, or telemarketing, is an approach whereby the initial customer contact is made by telephone. The objective of the initial call may be an immediate sale or it may be to send out literature, the latter to be followed by a second sales call. Other methods of direct marketing are expected to develop with the maturing of electronic communication technologies.

Because of the lack of face-to-face contact between buyer and seller and the consequent difficulty of delivering subtle sales arguments, direct marketing products are limited to simple, low premium, supplementary coverages, often ones with high benefit levels and low frequencies of occurrence.

Some very simple, single premium, short-term coverages such as travel accident and sickness insurance are sold to individuals through travel agents and in booths and vending machines at airports.

Through arrangements with employers, group plan participants losing their coverage due to termination of employment may purchase individual conversion policies. These policies often have very limited benefits and high premiums since many purchasers of conversions are uninsurable, that is, unable to buy adequate short-term coverage elsewhere. These policies have extremely poor persistency because many insureds eventually become eligible for group coverage elsewhere, find an individual insurer who will provide coverage or go without insurance if they consider the cost excessive in relation to the benefits provided.

8.3 COMPENSATION

Compensation for selling individual health insurance varies with the objectives of the insurer and the nature of the sales force as well as by policy year, type of policy and type of sales person.

The pattern of compensation is primarily influenced by the emphasis an insurer places on its individual health insurance line. If the primary business of the insurer is life products, high initial (first-year) commissions or other attractive total compensation packages are common. Property/casualty insurers tend to offer low and flat compensation on the sale of health insurance products. The extreme compensation pattern is a level fee, such as 10 to 15 percent in all years, generally as a sign that a company has de-emphasized the products.

A compensation structure of large, early-year commissions is more common for disability income insurance than for medical expense insurance. This reflects the fact that the disability income sale is often made in conjunction with a life insurance sale, and thus merits equal attractiveness to the agent. Also since this product has been profitable on a predictable basis, life insurers consider it to be deserving of sales emphasis. Often the disability income policy compensation pattern is the same as that for the life insurance product, for example, a first-year compensation of 55 percent and renewal compensation of 5 percent. Some companies pay a reduced first-year commission, 35 percent, for instance, and increase the renewal compensation commensurately. Medical expense insurance commonly has lower initial and higher renewal compensation percentages because the premium is generally larger and policy persistency is poorer. This payment pattern accomplishes the dual objectives of making the first-year compensation sufficiently large to stimulate sales and sufficiently small that it is possible to amortize the expense over future premiums despite poor persistency.

It is not uncommon that an insurer will have various levels of compensation for individual health insurance policies — high first-year commissions for disability income and some medical indemnity products, intermediate first-year commissions for moderate premium medical expense coverages, and low first-year commissions for high premium medical expense policies. Medicare supplement insurance may generate lower compensation than other insurance plans with comparable premiums because the product bears a legally mandated higher loss ratio.

Some insurers may pay the same sales compensation on single premium products, such as short-term medical expense, as they pay on the first year of an annual premium medical expense insurance, if the rate is not too high, so there is no financial incentive in the agent's selection of the appropriate product for the customer. Other insurers may pay a lower compensation and control product selection through strict underwriting rules.

Sales through employee payroll deductions and telemarketing are usually made by salaried personnel, but could be made by agents compensated on a percentage basis.

The degree to which an agent is vested in renewal compensation upon termination of service differs by insurance company. Vesting may be greater if the agent sold for a company but was not an employee, as in the case of a broker, but it is limited if the agent was financed by the company at the beginning of his career. It is common in the latter case that the number of vested renewal commissions will vary in proportion to the agent's length of service with the insurer. Often full vesting is granted as a form of employee benefit in the case of death or disability of the agent.

Amounts of premium increases on products such as attained-age-rated medical expense insurance or policies with built-in rate increases often are treated as renewal premiums for compensation purposes. This is because the increases are generated by forces outside the sales process and are foreseeable at the time of sale. Increases in benefit limits, initiated by the agent, usually receive first-year compensation on the premium increase.

Persistency bonuses are sometimes paid to encourage more careful selection of customers and better customer servicing by the agent. These incentives are more important for medical expense insurance than for life or disability income insurance because lapse rates are often higher than those for life insurance. Volume bonuses are offered by some companies on individual disability income insurance business with the commission percentage grading up as the volume of business sold by the agent increases. Another incentive for persistent business is to pay higher first-year compensation on contracts with less frequent premium payment periods, in recognition of the persistency inherent in the premium mode. Also, some companies pay no compensation if the policy lapses within the first three months.

Replacement policies from the same insurer usually generate first-year compensation only on the increase in premium, as a disincentive to unnecessary switching. On the other hand, an insurance company might pay full compensation on a replacement if it feels replacement should be encouraged, either because it is in the customer's interest or the company wishes to promote a better series of products.

Renewal compensation is a combination of service fees and deferred commission and varies by company. During an agent's employment, he is expected to provide all necessary service to the customer. Upon an agent's termination of employment, his nonvested business may be given to another agent. Subsequent compensation for the new agent could be the full renewal compensation, in recognition of the servicing responsibilities, or reduced renewal compensation, reflecting elimination of the deferred commission component. An insurer might pay these amounts immediately upon assigning the business to the new agent, or the agent might be required to upgrade the coverage in a specified manner.

Group conversion policies are ordinarily placed through the joint efforts of the employer and the insurer's service department, thus no sales compensation is paid. The agent to whom the conversion policy is assigned may receive a service fee. If the agent successfully sells a fully underwritten individual insurance policy in lieu of the group conversion, full sales compensation is paid.

8.4 SPECIAL SALES CHARACTERISTICS

Many state laws and regulations require that the customer be provided an *outline of coverage* for fair disclosure of the important benefits and limitations of the policy. These outlines are prepared by the insurer, approved by the state insurance department (in certain jurisdictions) and provided to the customer by the agent at the time an application is taken or the policy is delivered. On direct marketing business, the outline may be included with the sales material or may be delivered with the policy.

Many states have replacement regulations requiring disclosure to the customer that he may incur certain risks if he lapses an old policy and purchases a new one, particularly with a different insurer. Areas of warning include preexisting conditions limitations, restarted "Time Limit on Certain Defenses" or "Incontestable" provisions, new probationary or waiting periods and loss of equity in level premium policies. The company must develop and receive approval of the appropriate form and then monitor its proper usage.

Many states have regulations specifying the content of advertising material. Benefits must be reasonably described and exclusions and limitations must be fully disclosed. In some states the advertising material must be approved prior to use, but generally it is simply necessary that the material be in compliance with laws and regulations.

A few states mandate that certain options or coverages be made available to an applicant at the time of sale. The insurer must monitor the offer and maintain proper records to demonstrate that the laws have been complied with.

Direct response selling has uniquely adapted advertising and disclosure laws and regulations. Other regulations control telephone sales techniques and the supervision of telephone sales personnel.

8.5 SUMMARY OF AGENT SALES AND SERVICE STEPS

An agent must perform a number of tasks in the course of selling individual health insurance. These include the following:

1. Qualify the customer to avoid overinsurance on disability income.
2. Analyze insurance needs in relation to existing benefits, which are not necessarily homogeneous.
3. Convince the customer of the need to supplement existing coverage.
4. Explain to the customer, to the extent necessary, the differences among noncancelable, guaranteed renewable, non-renewable for stated reasons only, and optionally renewable policy guarantees.
5. Deliver an outline of coverage in a fashion compatible with the sales process and forward a customer receipt to the insurer.
6. Administer a replacement questionnaire and deliver a replacement disclosure, if necessary.
7. Explain multiple variables in the policy including benefit period, waiting period, elimination period, deductible, coinsurance, inside limits and out-of-pocket limits.
8. Compete with dissimilar products. Products are not standardized among insurers and often defy comparison. Reimbursement products compete with indemnity products. Similarly designed benefits may have dissimilar pricing structures.
9. Offer internal replacement upgrade policies. It is not uncommon for a new product line to render obsolete a prior product with limited benefits.
10. Offer optional coverages, whether by insurer request or legislative mandate.
11. Perform strong field underwriting to compensate for the high potential of antiselection.

12. Utilize and explain the appropriate conditional or binding receipt clauses.
13. Sell a high cost product and compete in a market characterized by price shopping.

At the time the agent delivers the policy, two actions are of great importance:

1. Explain the company's underwriting actions. For example, the agent must convince the customer of the appropriateness of the insurer's action to eliminate coverage for specified conditions.
2. Review the policy benefits in order to minimize the characteristically high first-year policy lapse rate.

After a policy is in force, a number of circumstances can arise that require the agent to reaffirm the policy sale or to sell additional coverage. Examples are the following:

1. Rising costs of medical expenses and, consequently, premiums can cause policies to become nearly unaffordable for some customers and undesirable to others.
2. Changing financial circumstances of an insured can change the benefit structure needed in a medical expense policy.
3. The company introduces a new, upgraded product series.

Chapter 9

ANNUAL STATEMENT REPORTING OF INDIVIDUAL HEALTH INSURANCE

by **Anthony B. Richter, F.S.A.**

Insurance companies, like other business enterprises, prepare reports of their financial results and conditions. The Annual Statement, which serves this purpose, is the primary financial report required by state insurance departments. The Annual Statement is also the vehicle through which insurance departments, working with the NAIC, have achieved almost uniform reporting among all companies and states.

The Annual Statement has evolved over a period of decades and can be a formidable document to those who are unacquainted with its history and language. This chapter is intended to acquaint the reader with the format of this report, specifically with those aspects related to individual health insurance products.

9.1 BACKGROUND

Annual Statements are prepared on standard forms, collectively known either as the *Association Blank* or *Convention Blank,* and the NAIC has provided detailed instructions as to their completion. A company must file, in each state in which it is licensed, a statement for each calendar year by March 1 of the following year. (Insurance company fiscal years always coincide with calendar years.) Because of differences in the nature of their businesses, separate blanks are provided for life and accident and health companies, fire and casualty companies, and fraternal associations. Individual health insurance is written by some casualty companies, and it has been argued that it has more in common with casualty insurance than with life insurance. For example, individual health insurance insures against economic loss rather than loss of life, and claim experience is relatively more sensitive to prevailing economic conditions. In fact, prior to 1947, life insurance companies reported individual health insurance results in the Miscellaneous Blank of the Annual Statement, which was also used for any property and casualty business the company might have.

In 1947, the format of the life insurance company Annual Statement was changed to give more explicit recognition to health insurance as a separate and distinct line of business. Individual health insurance data were no longer included in the Miscellaneous Blank, but were included instead with the Life Insurance Blank. Since 1950, insurance companies other than life companies have reported health insurance in the Fire and Casualty Blank. The remainder of this chapter will be primarily concerned with the reporting of health insurance sold through life companies. In 1947, the Life Insurance Blank was amended to include Schedule H and Exhibit 9, which are specifically designed for health insurance, and a special individual health insurance column was added to other exhibits showing results by line of business. These changes reflected the emergence of health insurance as a major line of business in many life insurance companies.

Schedule H and Exhibit 9, as introduced in 1947, included the following categories of individual health policies: "Accident Only," "Accident and Health," "Non-Cancellable Accident and Health" and "Hospital and Medical Expense." These categories caused confusion because they were not mutually exclusive. In 1967, they were replaced by the following categories based on renewal provision: "Non-Cancellable" (on which premiums may not be increased), "Guaranteed Renewable" (on which premiums may be increased, but only on a class basis), "Non-Renewable for Stated Reasons Only," "Other Accident Only," and "All Other" (mainly commercial policies and single premium short-term medical expense policies).

In 1979, further changes were made to Schedule H, titled the "Accident and Health Exhibit." As described by the NAIC Subcommittee on Blanks, these changes were made mainly to achieve complete consistency in this schedule among life and health companies, fire and casualty companies, and fraternals; to provide more relevant data; and to present that data in a more logical format. The reconciliation of premiums in force from the prior version was removed, and more detailed information about premium, policy and claim reserves and reinsurance assumed and ceded was added.

As of the time of this writing, no significant changes in the treatment of individual health insurance in the Annual Statement have been made since 1979. However, changes in the format of the Annual Statement are often discussed and any such changes might affect individual health insurance reporting requirements.

9.2 STATUTORY AND GAAP ACCOUNTING PRINCIPLES

The accounting principles that have evolved to satisfy state insurance department requirements are known as *statutory accounting principles*. The specifics of these principles are included in the insurance laws, regulations and administrative rulings of the various states, and in the instructions and footnotes to the Annual Statement. Statutory accounting principles are conservative in many respects, in recognition of the primary responsibility of the states to ensure insurance company solvency.

Businesses not subject to the statutory accounting requirements affecting insurers use Generally Accepted Accounting Principles (GAAP), which are based on a "going concern" concept, rather than on solvency alone. In general, statutory accounting principles emphasize financial soundness, while GAAP is more oriented to profitability. In particular, under GAAP, certain acquisition expenses, which are charged to earnings in the year of issue under statutory accounting, are amortized over the life of the policies. As it applies to insurance companies, GAAP involves matching related income and expense in the same accounting period, and the computation of such items as policy reserves on assumptions such as "realistic as possible." Reserves so calculated then become more like the "natural reserves" described in actuarial literature.

Certain insurance companies reporting to the Securities and Exchange Commission or those that have their stockholder reports certified by an independent accountant are required to use GAAP in addition to statutory accounting principles. The remainder of this chapter will be solely devoted to statutory accounting requirements.

9.3 MOST IMPORTANT ANNUAL STATEMENT SECTIONS FOR INDIVIDUAL HEALTH INSURANCE

In brief, the Annual Statement consists of a schedule of assets (page 2), a schedule of liabilities and surplus (page 3), a Summary of Operations, which is the income statement on page 4, Cash Flow (page 4A), an Analysis of Operations by Line of Business (page 5), plus numerous other supporting exhibits and schedules. From the standpoint of the individual health line of business, the most relevant portions of the Annual Statement are considered by many to be the following:

1. Analysis of Operations by Lines of Business (page 5)
2. Schedule H, Accident and Health Exhibit
3. Exhibit 9, Aggregate Reserve for Accident and Health Policies.

Samples of these documents for a hypothetical life insurance company appear at the end of this chapter.

9.3.1 ANALYSIS OF OPERATIONS BY LINES OF BUSINESS

Statutory accounting places heavy emphasis on the balance sheet, comprised of the assets on page 2 and the liabilities and surplus on page 3. However, neither of these pages includes a breakdown by line of business, even though the company must internally maintain such a breakdown to properly allocate such items as investment income and federal income tax. Over the years, increased attention has been paid to the income statement, which is broken down by line of business in the analysis of operations on page 5. Results for the individual health line are shown in column 11, "Accident and Health—Other."

The analysis of operations on page 5 is a formidable document drafted to apply to all lines of business, but it is possible for purposes of analysis to simplify the format somewhat by extracting those entries of primary significance to the individual health line, as follows:

Line No.

1 — Premiums and annuity considerations.

4 — Net investment income.

11 — Disability benefits and benefits under accident and health contracts.

13 — Group conversions.

17 — Increase in aggregate reserves for life and accident and health contracts.

21 — Commissions on premiums and annuity considerations.

22 — General insurance expenses.

23 — Insurance taxes, licenses and fees, excluding federal income taxes.

27 — Net gain from operations before dividends to policyholders and federal income taxes (Line 1 + 4-11-13-17-21-22-23).

28 — Dividends to policyholders.

29 — Net gain from operations after dividends to policyholders and before federal income taxes (Line 27-28).

30 — Federal income taxes incurred (excluding tax on capital gains).

31 — Net gain from operations after dividends to policyholders and federal income tax (Line 29-30).

The following is a description of how these income statement items are calculated.

Line 1—Premiums: Insurance companies, like most other businesses, use a form of accrual basis accounting, as opposed to the straight cash basis accounting used by most individuals on their own income tax returns. The Premiums in Line 1 therefore consist of premium received, that is, cash premiums plus any premiums waived under policies with a disability waiver of premium provision, plus the increase during the year in premiums due and unpaid (this is an asset item, titled "Accident and health premiums due and unpaid," which appears separately on page 2 and in Exhibit 13), less the increase in premiums paid in advance. Several points should be noted about premiums due and unpaid.

- The instructions permit this asset to be held on a gross premium basis, in contrast to life insurance, for which the instructions specify that only net premiums, that is, gross premium less expense loading, may be so included. Even so, some companies choose to hold this asset on a net premium basis.
- In accordance with the general conservatism used to value insurance company assets and liabilities, only the admitted portion of premiums due and unpaid is included in Line 1 Premiums. The instructions stated that the nonadmitted portion of premiums due and unpaid consists of those premiums due prior to October 1, and "any premiums in excess of one periodic premium due and unpaid in the case of premiums payable more frequently than quarterly." (Nonadmitted assets, as opposed to admitted assets, are those for which there is reasonable doubt as to whether the insurer will ever receive its value.) In other words, for monthly premium policies, whenever more than one month's premium is due and unpaid, only one monthly premium is included in admitted assets.
- Another difference in treatment between health insurance and life insurance involves the treatment of deferred premiums. Reserves for life insurance policies are normally calculated on the assumption that premiums are paid annually. Since most policies are paid on an other-than-annual premium mode, the resulting reserves overstate the company's true liabilities. To compensate for this, assets are increased by the amount of the net deferred premiums, that is, by the excess of the net annual premium over the actual net modal premiums paid by year end. In contrast, health insurance policy reserves are usually not calculated using the annual premium assumptions, so there is no need for a deferred premium offset. Some companies, however, do use the annual premium assumptions for reserves and the deferred premium offset. For these companies, the asset item in page 2 and Exhibit 13 referred to above then becomes "Accident and Health premiums deferred and due and unpaid."

Line 4—Net Investment Income: This consists of the amount of investment income (excluding net capital gains, which are credited or charged directly to the Surplus Account), less investment-related expenses, allocated to the individual health line.

Line 11—Benefits: This consists of benefits paid (including any premiums waived under policies with a disability waiver of premium provision) plus the increase during the year in claim liability, less the increase in amounts recoverable from reinsurers. Claim liability consists of claim payments due and unpaid at year end, plus any amount due for claims that were unreported as of the end of the year.

Line 13—Group Conversions: This line typically consists of group conversion transfer charges, which arise when persons covered under group health insurance policies terminate employment and convert their coverage to individual policies. Claim experience under group conversion policies, which are issued as a matter of legal right without underwriting, is almost always worse than under regularly underwritten medical expense policies. The purpose of the group conversion transfer charge is to make the individual health line "whole" with respect to these policies. In theory, the amount of the charge should be such that these policies have no effect on the individual health net gain from operations.

Line 17—Increase in Reserves: This consists of the sum of the increase in premium, policy and claim reserves. Premium and policy reserves consist of unearned premium reserves, that is, the premium for the unexpired portion of the period of time covered by the most recent premium, plus any additional reserves held on level premium policies, which are analogous to the reserves held on level premium life insurance policies. Claim reserves are the present values of amounts not yet due on claims incurred prior to the end of the year. In the case of disability income policies with benefit periods for life or to age 65, claim reserves can be quite substantial.

Line 21—Commissions: These are payments to agents or brokers under commission contracts, on an incurral basis.

Line 22—General Insurance Expenses: These are the bulk of the company's operating costs (salaries, rent, equipment, payments to managers and general agents and so on, other than investment expenses, commissions, taxes and other expenses in Line 23 below). This item will equal cash expenses, plus any increase in due and unpaid expenses.

Line 23—Taxes, Licenses and Fees: Included here are incurred state premium taxes, OASDI and workers compensation payroll taxes, the cost of any state licenses, state insurance department assessments and fees for examinations, local property taxes, and any state and local income taxes.

Line 28—Dividends: This consists of dividends paid to policyholders, (dividends to stockholders are charged directly to the Surplus Account) plus the net increase in due and unpaid dividends, plus the increase in dividend liability (the amount the company declares late in the year as the estimated liability for dividends to be paid in the following calendar year).

Line 30—Federal Income Taxes: Included here are income taxes of any foreign government, as well as those of the United States. To be consistent with Line 4, Net Investment Income, taxes on net capital gains are excluded and charged directly to the Surplus Account.

Line 31—Net Gain from Operations after Dividends and Federal Income Taxes: This item, often referred to as the "bottom line," represents net income for the year computed according to statutory accounting principles.

9.3.2 SCHEDULE H: ACCIDENT AND HEALTH EXHIBIT

The page 5 analysis of operations, which was designed for life insurance, is not particularly appropriate for health insurance. One of the main reasons involves the treatment of reserves, the increase in which appears in Line 17. The purpose of insurance reserves, whether they are policy or claim reserves, is to permit recognition of income and outgo in the proper accounting period. One of the elements of Line 17, policy reserves, can conceptually be thought of as deductions from premiums. The other element, claim reserves, would more properly be included with benefits. It is not possible to tell from Line 17 whether a large increase in reserves was due to a large increase in premiums or to a large increase in claims (or to a combination of the two). Possible confusion in this regard was undoubtedly one of the reasons for the development of Schedule H, which is especially tailored for health insurance.

Prior to 1948, a company writing both life and health insurance had to prepare two Annual Statements: the Life Blank and the Casualty Blank. The introduction of Schedule H in 1948 caused the Life Blank to be renamed the Life and Accident and Health Blank. Since Schedule H is a holdover from the Casualty Blank, much of the terminology is different from that appearing elsewhere in the Annual Statement. As mentioned earlier, Schedule H values for most individual health insurance are broken down by renewal provision: "Non-Cancellable [sic]," "Guaranteed Renewable," "Non-Renewable for Stated Reasons Only," "Other Accident" and "All Other." These are all included under the heading of "Other Individual Policies," In addition, policy data for certain special types of individual health policies are included in the "Credit" and "Collectively Renewable" columns of Schedule H.

A description of the different sections of Schedule H follows:

Part 1—Analysis of Underwriting Operations:

In many respects, this is similar to the page 5 analysis of operations, the principal differences being that net investment income and federal income tax are not included.

Line 1—Premiums written: "Premiums written" is a good example of a holdover from the days when health insurance was treated as a casualty line (although it does not have the same meaning in life and casualty company statements). In Schedule H, it equals premiums received plus the increase in premiums due and unpaid.

Line 2—Premiums earned: This equals Line 1, "Premiums written," less the increase in unearned premium reserves and the increase in premiums paid in advance. The basic concept is to recognize only the premiums earmarked for coverage during the year in question.

Line 3—Incurred claims: This equals the Benefits line from the page 5 analysis of operations plus the increase in claim reserves. In accordance with the conservative nature of insurance company accounting, this line reflects the present value of amounts not yet due on claims incurred prior to the end of the year. It seems appropriate to include the increase in claim reserves with benefits, since claim reserves are more in the nature of unpaid losses on claims that have already taken place, rather than reserves for claims that will take place in the future.

Line 4—Increase in policy reserves: For individual health insurance, this consists almost entirely of the increase in the additional reserves held on level premium (mostly noncancelable or guaranteed renewable) policies.

Line 5 thru 7—Expenses: These agree with the comparable items — commissions, general insurance expenses, and taxes licenses and fees — in the analysis of operations on page 5.

Line 9—Gain from underwriting before dividends to policyholders: This equals Line 2 less the sum of Lines 3 through 7.

Line 10—Dividends to policyholders: This agrees with the dividends line in the analysis of operations.

Line 11—Gains from underwriting after dividends to policyholders: This equals Line 9 minus Line 10.

Part 2—Reserves and Liabilities:

This section shows the breakdown of premium reserves and policy reserves into their various components. For example, premium reserves are split into unearned premiums, advance premiums and reserve for rate credits (a group insurance item). Claim reserves and liabilities are also included. Comparable figures at the end of the previous year are shown, and the increase for the year is calculated.

Part 3—Test of Previous Year's Claim Reserves and Liabilities:

The format of this section is shown below.

1. Claims paid during the year:
   a. on claims incurred prior to current year
   b. on claims incurred during current year
2. Claim reserves and liabilities, December 31, current year:
   a. on claims incurred prior to current year
   b. on claims incurred during current year
3. Test:
   a. Line 1a and 2a
   b. claim reserves and liabilities, December 31, previous year
   c. Line a minus Line b

The premise of the test is that if claim reserves and liabilities have been set at the proper level as of the preceding year end, they should be equal to the payments in the current year on account of those incurrals, plus the corresponding claim reserves and liabilities at the end of the current year. Actually, to be more theoretically precise, the current year's payments and the reserve and liability should be discounted to the end of the previous year, so that everything is valued as of the same date. A positive value in Line 3c indicates a possible reserve insufficiency, and if this occurs for several years in a row, a company should consider strengthening the actuarial basis of its claim reserves.

Part 4—Reinsurance:

This contains premiums written, premiums earned, incurred claims and commissions on reinsurance assumed and reinsurance ceded.

9.3.3 EXHIBIT 9: AGGREGATE RESERVE FOR ACCIDENT AND HEALTH POLICIES

Of the fourteen Annual Statement Exhibits, this is the only one exclusively devoted to health insurance. After reviewing Schedule H, Exhibit 9 seems somewhat redundant, since most Exhibit 9 reserves are also included in Part 2 of Schedule H. However, Exhibit 9 has higher visibility, since it appears in the main body of the Annual Statement, while Schedule H for most companies is included in the supplementary document containing the various schedules.

Exhibit 9 is analogous to Exhibit 8, Aggregate Reserve for Life Policies and Contracts. However, unlike Exhibit 8, which shows reserves for life insurance and annuities separately by interest rate and valuation basis, Exhibit 9 shows them by function and renewal provision.

The format of Exhibit 9 is as follows:

Section A—Active Life Reserve:

Line 1—Unearned premium reserve: In companies that do not write level premium noncancelable or guaranteed renewable insurance, this will generally be the largest health insurance reserve. It represents the aggregate of all unearned portions of gross premiums received, or the portion the company would be obligated to refund if it terminated all policies on the valuation date. For a random block of business, this reserve will be in the area of 50 percent of modal premiums in force.

Line 2—Additional reserves: Since morbidity rates increase with age, level premium policies that guarantee renewability require reserves similar in nature to those for level premium term life insurance ("term" because health insurance is typically renewable to some stated age such as 65). The need for such reserves arises because a portion of the current premium must be retained to provide for later periods when claims during a given year are expected to exceed premiums collected. In such situations, to meet state minimum reserve requirements, it is not necessary to hold the full morbidity reserve in addition to the gross unearned premium reserve. Instead, the minimum standard provides that the unearned premium reserve or the morbidity reserve be held, whichever is greater. Therefore, a company writing noncancelable health insurance might show no entry on Line 2, because the unearned premium reserve is sufficient to cover the entire liability. On the other hand, if the morbidity reserve is larger, the entire amount can be shown on Line 2, with nothing shown on Line 1. Yet another way of handling the situation where the morbidity reserve is larger is to show the unearned premium reserve on Line 1 and the balance on Line 2.

Line 3—Reserve for future contingent benefits: This is the reserve for the extension of maternity and obstetrical coverage and other coverages under group health insurance policies. This will generally be zero for individual health policies, but for companies that write policies with a return of premium benefit, this might be the appropriate place to report the reserve for such a benefit.

Line 4—Reserve for rate credits: Since this is a group insurance item, it will be zero for individual health insurance.

Line 5—Totals (Gross): This equals the sum of Lines 1 through 4.

Line 6—Reinsurance ceded: This includes any portion of the reserve in Lines 1 and 2 ceded to a reinsuring company.

Line 7—Totals (Net): This is the result of line 5 less Line 6.

Section B—Claim Reserve:

At this point, it is worth mentioning again the difference between claim reserve and claim liability. The claim liability is the amount required to pay claims falling due up to and including December 31 of the current year, while the claim reserve is the amount necessary to cover all payments due after December 31 while such claims remain in payment status. The main item in this section is the "Present value of amounts not yet due on claims," and like Section A, amounts covered by reinsurance ceded are subtracted out.

There is also a line labeled "Tabular interest on policy funds." The purpose of this item is to permit a comparison between net investment income and the tabular interest required to maintain the reserves, for those reserves that use interest assumptions in their derivation. Those insurers unable to demonstrate that they are earning sufficient investment income for this purpose would presumably be required to set aside a portion of surplus to provide for possible future insufficiency of investment earnings.

9.4 OTHER SECTIONS OF THE ANNUAL STATEMENT INVOLVING INDIVIDUAL HEALTH INSURANCE

Other areas of the Annual Statement that have relevance for individual health insurance are discussed here. In many statement items, individual health insurance items are comingled with those of other lines of business, but some items for accident and health insurance are separately identified. With the exception of Exhibit 1 (premiums, dividends applied, reinsurance commissions and expense allowance incurred and commissions incurred), and Exhibit 1 1 (policy and contract claims), the term "accident and health" refers to individual and group health insurance combined.

Assets (page 2): The only item specific to health insurance is Line 15, "Accident and health premiums due and unpaid."

Liabilities, Surplus and Other Funds (page 3): Two items specific to health insurance are Line 2, "Aggregate reserve for accident and health policies" (from Exhibit 9), and Line 4.2 "Policy and contract claims: Accident and health" (from Exhibit 11).

Summary of Operations and Capital and Surplus Account (page 4): The Summary of Operations is identical to the total company column of the Analysis of Operations by Lines of Business (page 5). The Capital and Surplus Account shows the development of current year capital and surplus, beginning with prior year capital and surplus and adding such items as net gain from operations, net capital gains, and changes in reserve on account of change in valuation basis.

Cash Flow (page 4A): This is a cash flow exhibit that traces the growth in cash and short-term investments during the year by the change in cash items.

Exhibit 1—Part 1—Premiums and Annuity Considerations: As noted earlier, this exhibit includes a separate column for individual health insurance (column 10, "Accident and health — Other"). The development of incurred premiums from collected premiums is shown (the increase in deferred, due and unpaid is added, and the increase in advance premiums is subtracted), and the results are shown separately by first year, single and renewal premiums. Since it is difficult to allocate accrual items such as due and unpaid premiums between first year and renewal, the instructions permit all health insurance premiums to be included in the renewal section, and most companies do this.

Exhibit 1—Part 2—Dividends and Coupons Applied, Reinsurance Commissions and Expense Allowances and Commissions Incurred: The practice described above for premiums, of reporting everything under the renewal section, is also used in this part.

Exhibit 2—Net Investment Income: This is defined as gross investment income (Exhibit 3) less investment expenses and taxes and depreciation.

Exhibit 3—Gross Investment Income

Exhibit 4—Capital Gains and Losses on Investments

Exhibit 5—General Expenses: Expenses are shown separately for Life Insurance, Accident and Health Insurance (group and individual combined) and Investment.

Exhibit 6—Taxes, Licenses and Fees (Excluding Federal Income Taxes): These items are also shown separately for Life Insurance, Accident and Health Insurance (group and individual combined) and Investment.

Exhibit 7—Dividends and Coupons to Policyholders: This exhibit will be blank for stock companies. For mutual companies, dividends are shown separately by provision, (that is, cash and applied to pay premiums) separately for Life Insurance, and Accident and Health Insurance.

Exhibit 11—Policy and Contract Claims: Individual health insurance figures are shown in column 11, "Accident and Health — Other." Reinsurance assumed is included and reinsurance ceded is excluded.

Part 1—Liability End of Current Year: This consists of "Due and Unpaid" plus "in course of settlement" (split into "Resisted" and "Other") plus "Incurred but unreported."

Part 2—Incurred During the Year: This consists of "Settlements during the year" plus the increase in claim liability during the year less the increase in amounts recoverable from reinsurers during the year.

Exhibit 12—Reconciliation of Ledger Assets: This contains several health insurance items, which are for individual and group insurance combined.

Exhibit 13—Assets: This includes only one identifiable health insurance item, "Accident and Health premiums due and unpaid," which is for individual and group insurance combined.

Five-Year Historical Data: This shows five years of accident and health premium income, aggregate accident and health reserves, increase in accident and health reserves, and accident and health loss and expense ratios, for group and individual businesses combined. Also shown separately for individual health are incurred losses on prior years claims and net gains from operations after federal income taxes.

Schedule O—Development of Incurred Losses: For the three main categories of individual health renewal provisions ("Non-Cancellable," "Guaranteed Renewable" and "Non-Renewable for Stated Reasons Only"), Schedule O traces, separately by year of incurral, benefits paid plus the corresponding claim reserve and liability at the end of the calendar year of incurral plus the following two calendar years. If the number increases (decreases) from year to year, this is an indication that initial claim reserves and liabilities are inadequate (overadequate). Since Schedule O does not differentiate by type of coverage, however, (disability income and medical expense are all included together), it is of limited value. State insurance examiners, in applying tests to determine the adequacy of claim reserves, ordinarily rely on Schedule H, which differentiates data by renewal provision.

Schedule S: Reinsurance is reported here in three parts with provisions for separate reporting on health insurance, group and individual combined.

Schedule T—Premiums and Annuity Considerations: This exhibit shows premiums by state, territory and country. There is a column for accident and health insurance premiums, which includes both group and individual health.

Accident and Health Policy Experience Exhibit: Further information on individual health policies is provided in this separately filed exhibit, which is used by state regulators to monitor experience on individual policy forms. For each policy form, the following information is shown:

Earned premiums; incurred losses; the ratio of losses to earned premiums; commissions incurred and the rates of commission paid, and incurred dividends for the following five categories:

1. group policies, conversions and individual policies with annual premiums of $7.50 or less per person,
2. credit (group and individual),
3. hospital, medical and surgical policies,
4. loss of time policies, and
5. all other policies.

The last three categories must also be subdivided into "Collectively Renewable," "Non-Cancellable," "Guaranteed Renewable," "Non-Renewable for Stated Reasons Only," "Other Accident Only," and "All Other." The totals for direct written business must be shown and adjusted for net reinsurance assumed less ceded to obtain the net totals, which must check with the corresponding data elsewhere in the Annual Statement.

9.5 CONTINUING EVOLUTION OF THE ANNUAL STATEMENT

The Annual Statement is a continually evolving financial reporting document. The rate of change has been slow in the past however, possibly because of the desirability of maintaining uniform standards that allow comparisons over a period of time. However, the rapid changes that are taking place in the insurance business and in the financial services industry of which it is a part have raised questions as to the effectiveness of the Annual Statement. Regulators and others have questioned the adequacy of the financial reporting in the Annual Statement. Stock companies and even some mutual companies have adopted the GAAP reporting system as the primary method of financial reporting and look upon the Annual Statement as a secondary, and less important, financial reporting approach.

This environment is likely to result in serious reconsideration of the Annual Statement requirements as they currently exist and the further likelihood of substantial changes at a much more rapid rate than in the past.

Form 1

ANNUAL STATEMENT FOR THE YEAR 1986 OF THE MASTODON LIFE INSURANCE COMPANY

ANALYSIS OF OPERATION BY LINES OF BUSINESS (Gain and Loss Exhibit) (Excluding Capital Gains and Losses)

				Ordinary			Group			Accident and Health	
	1 Total**	2 Industrial Life	3 Life Insurance	4 Individual Annuities	5 Supplementary Contracts	6 Credit Life[a] (Group and Individual)	7 Life Insurance†	8 Annuities	9 Group	10 Credit[a] (Group and Individual)	11 Other
1. Premiums and annuity considerations	285,772,776		24,718,205	546,491	xxx	(201,626)	15,052,729	1,306,879	45,243,570	(96,695)	1,203,223
1A. Annuity and other fund deposits	19,992,121			19,296,132	xxx			695,989			
2. Considerations for supplementary contracts with life contingencies	78,022		xxx	xxx	78,022				xxx	xxx	xxx
3. Considerations for supplementary contracts without life contingencies and dividend accumulations	1,676,890				1,676,890						
3A. Coupons* left to accumulate at interest											
4. Net investment income	83,342,499		22,903,137	10,826,065	344,002	25,000	1,423,008	8,039,048	4,601,028	8,000	35,173,211
5. Commissions and expense allowances on reinsurance ceded	19,362,882		324,750						503,067		18,535,065
5A. Reserve adjustments on reinsurance ceded											
6. Net receipts from reinsurance excess risk pool	26,349		26,349								
7. Totals (Items 1 to 6)	410,251,539		47,972,441	30,668,688	2,098,914	(176,626)	16,475,737	10,041,916	50,347,665	(88,695)	252,911,499
8. Death benefits	19,492,585		9,357,439	xxx		11,745	10,123,401	xxx	xxx	xxx	xxx
9. Matured endowments (excluding guaranteed annual pure endowments)	1,310,662		1,310,662	xxx				xxx	xxx	xxx	xxx
10. Annuity benefits	12,687,380		xxx	8,300,480		xxx		4,386,900	xxx	xxx	xxx
11. Disability benefits and benefits under accident and health policies	84,382,108		590,813						31,124,056	20,330	52,646,909
11A. Coupons, guaranteed annual pure endowments and similar benefits											
12. Surrender benefits	19,132,733		18,594,967	xxx			537,766	xxx	xxx	xxx	xxx
13. Group conversions	11,735		(100,636)	xxx			112,371	xxx	155,545		(155,545)
13A. Transfers on account of group package policies and contracts	xxx	xxx	xxx	xxx							xxx
14. Interest on policy or contract fund	382,157		382,157		338,921				xxx	xxx	xxx
15. Payments on supplementary contracts with life contingencies	338,921		xxx	xxx	338,921						
16. Payments on supplementary contracts without life contingencies and of dividend accumulations	2,201,525				2,201,525						
16A. Accumulated coupon* payments											
17. Increase in aggregate reserves for life and accident and health policies and contracts	109,625,874		(7,748,893)	(624,922)	(68,0645)	(24,142)	298,319	366,180	4,944,725	(74,864)	112,557,536
18. Increase in reserve for supplementary contracts without life contingencies and for dividend and coupon* accumulations	(408,618)				(408,618)						
19. Increase in other reserve	24,360,514			19,522,600		(202,942)	1,218,049	3,808,633	873,815	50,827	(910,468)
20. Total (Items 8 to 19)	273,517,576		22,386,509	27,198,158	2,063,763	(215,339)	12,289,906	8,561,713	37,098,141	(3,707)	164,138,432

(Continued)

Form 1

ANNUAL STATEMENT FOR THE YEAR 1986 OF THE MASTODON LIFE INSURANCE COMPANY (continued)

ANALYSIS OF OPERATION BY LINES OF BUSINESS (Gain and Loss Exhibit) (Excluding Capital Gains and Losses)

	1 Total**	2 Industrial Life	Ordinary				Group			Accident and Health	
			3 Life Insurance	4 Individual Annuities	5 Supplementary Contracts	6 Credit Life[a] (Group and Individual)	7 Life Insurance†	8 Annuities	9 Group	10 Credit[a] (Group and Individual)	11 Other
21. Commissions on premiums and annuity considerations (direct business only)	56,763,602		2,049,243	704,929		2,398	376,552	13,750	2,135,003	5,891	51,475,836
21A. Commission and expense allowances on reinsurance assumed	1,234,459										1,234,459
22. General insurance expenses	45,703,746		5,692,441	1,075,280		359	2,541,806	325,535	6,621,143	803	29,446,379
23. Insurance taxes, licenses and fees, excluding federal income tax	9,269,260		1,166,609	128,469		261	439,203	19,554	1,560,536	355	5,954,283
24. Increase in loading on and cost of collection in excess of loading on deferred and uncollected premiums	(182,654)		(212,119)	(1,971)		(517)	31,953				
24A. Net transfers to (+) or from (−) Separate Accounts (excluding Variable Life Insurance)											
24B. Net transfers to (+) or from (−) Variable Life Insurance Separate Accounts	703,215								703,215		
25. Reserve adjustments on insurance ceded											
26. Total (Items 20 to 25)	387,018,204		31,082,683	29,104,865	2,063,763	(212,838)	15,679,420	8,920,542	48,118,038	3,342	252,258,389
27. Net gain from operations before dividends to policyholders and federal income taxes (Item 7 minus item 26)	23,233,335		16,889,758	1,563,823	35,151	36,212	796,317	1,121,374	2,229,627	(92,037)	653,110
28. Dividends to policyholders											
29. Net gain from operations after dividends to policyholders and federal income taxes (Item 27 minus Item 28)	23,233,335		16,889,758	1,563,823	35,151	36,212	796,317	1,121,374	2,229,627	(92,037)	653,110
30. Federal income taxes incurred (excluding tax on capital gain)	2,755,000		2,002,800	185,400	4,200	4,300	94,400	133,000	264,400	(10,900)	77,400
31. Net gain from operations after dividends to policyholders and federal income taxes (excluding tax on capital gains) (Item 29 minus Item 30)	20,478,335		14,886,958	1,378,423	30,951	31,912	701,917	988,374	1,965,227	(81,137)	575,710

[a] Business not exceeding 120 months duration.   *Includes coupons, guaranteed annual pure endowments and similar benefits.   **The items in this column to agree with Page 4, Column 1.

† Includes the following amount for FEGLI/SGLI: Item 1 — 3,081,284   Item 8 — 3,036,529   Item 13 — 5,272   Item 22 — 28,422   Item 23 — 7,146

SCHEDULE H – ACCIDENT AND HEALTH EXHIBIT

	1 Total		2 Group Accident and Health		3 Credit[a] (Group and Individual)		4 Collectively Renewable		5 Non-Cancellable		Other Individual Policies					
											6 Guaranteed Renewable		7 Non-Renewable for Stated Reasons Only		8 Other Accident Only	9 All Other
	Amount	%†	Amount	%†	Amount	%†	Amount	%†	Amount	%†	Amount	%†	Amount	%†	Amount %†	Amount %†

PART 1. — ANALYSIS OF UNDERWRITING OPERATIONS

1. Premiums written	156,402,010		46,126,052		32,271				106,566,768		3,664,060		12,859			
2. Premiums earned (see note b)	155,819,537	100.0	45,917,026	100.0	160,692	100.0			106,184,454	100.0	3,544,163	100.0	13,202	100.0		
3. Incurred claims	104,076,704	66.8	39,422,898	85.9	55,405	34.5			61,990,039	58.4	2,589,402	73.1	18,960	143.6		
4. Increase in policy reserves	10,336,668	6.6	122,693	.2					10,213,878	9.6			97	.7		
4.1 Reserve adjustment on reinsurance ceded	571,214	.4	571,214	1.2												
5. Commissions*	24,637,508	15.8	1,552,575	3.4	32,497	20.2			23,052,436	21.7						
6. General insurance expenses	29,300,497	18.8	4,671,576	10.2	14,260	8.9			24,099,939	22.7	513,203	14.5	1,519	1.5		
7. Taxes, licenses and fees	6,587,426	4.2	1,378,360	3.0	4,330	2.7			5,099,380	4.8	104,467	2.9	889	6.7		
8. Total expenses incurred	60,525,431	38.8	7,602,511	16.5	51,087	31.8			52,251,755	49.2	617,670	17.4	2,408	18.2		
9. Gain from underwriting before dividends to policyholders	(19,690,480)	(12.6)	(1,802,290)	(3.9)	54,200	33.7			(18,271,218)	(17.2)	337,091	9.5	(8,263)	(62.5)		
10. Dividends to policyholders																
11. Gain from underwriting after dividends to policyholders	(19,690,480)	(12.6)	(1,802,290)	(3.9)	54,200	33.7			(18,271,218)	(17.2)	337,091	9.5	(8,263)	(62.5)		

PART 2. — RESERVES AND LIABILITIES

A. Premium Reserves:																
1. Unearned premiums	3,148,790		129,652		49,028				854,985		2,110,805		4,320			
2. Advanced premiums	504,648		32,422						472,226							
3. Reserve for rate credits	1,249,386		308,915		58,280				358,067		524,125					
4. Total premium reserve, current year	4,902,824		470,989		107,308				1,685,278		2,634,929		4,320			
5. Total premium reserve, previous year	4,320,351		261,963		235,729				1,302,964		2,515,032		4,663			
6. Increase in total premium reserves	582,473		209,026		(128,421)				382,314		119,897		(343)			
B. Policy Reserves:																
1. Additional reserves	159,549,264								159,549,264							
2. Reserve for future contingent benefits (deferred maternity and other similar benefits)**	385,752		385,752										380			
3. Total policy reserves, current year	159,935,016		385,372						159,549,264				380			
4. Total policy reserves, previous year	149,598,348		262,679						149,335,386				283			
5. Increase in policy reserves	10,336,668		122,693						10,213,878				97			
C. Claim Reserves and Liabilities																
1. Total current year	182,910,531		31,060,630		61,827				140,622,172		11,156,493		9,409			
2. Total previous year	155,877,182		23,648,018		39,593				121,782,342		10,395,464		11,795			
3. Increase	27,033,349		7,412,612		22,234				18,839,830		761,029		(2,356)			

SCHEDULE H – ACCIDENT AND HEALTH EXHIBIT (continued)

	1 Total		2 Group Accident and Health		3 Credit[a] (Group and Individual)		4 Collectively Renewable		5 Non-Cancellable		6 Guaranteed Renewable		7 Non-Renewable for Stated Reasons Only		8 Other Accident Only		9 All Other	
	Amount	%†	Amount	%†	Amount	%†	Amount	%†	Amount	%†	Amount	%†	Amount	%†	Amount	%†	Amount	%†
PART 3. — TEST OF PREVIOUS YEAR'S CLAIM RESERVES AND LIABILITIES																		
1. Claims paid during the year:																		
a. On claims incurred prior to current year	39,885,528		9,542,390		14,334				28,658,752		1,662,340		7,712					
b. On claims incurred during current year	37,157,827		22,467,896		18,837				14,491,458		166,032		13,604					
2. Claim reserves and liabilities, December 31, current year:																		
a. On claims issued prior to current year	115,649,033		15,485,766		2,064				91,939,982		8,220,939		282					
b. On claims Incurred during current year	67,261,498		15,574,864		59,763				48,682,190		2,935,554		9,127					
3. Test:																		
a. Line 1a and 2a	155,534,561		25,028,156		16,398				120,598,734		9,883,279		7,994					
b. Claim reserves and liabilities, December 31, previous year	155,877,182		23,648,018		39,593				121,782,342		10,395,464		11,765					
c. Line a minus Line b	(342,621)		1,380,138		(23,195)				(1,183,608)		(512,185)		(3,771)					
PART 4. — REINSURANCE																		
A. Reinsurance Assumed:																		
1. Premiums written	15,150,202		9,401,589						2,071,694		3,664,060		12,859					
2. Premiums earned (see note 1)	14,761,120		9,411,713						1,792,042		3,544,163		13,202					
3. Incurred claims	13,118,506		8,816,664						1,693,480		2,589,402		13,960					
4. Commissions																		
B. Reinsurance Ceded:																		
1. Premiums written:	55,696,336		24,325,959						31,370,377									
2. Premiums earned (see note 1)	55,742,929		24,372,552						31,370,377									
3. Incurred claims	30,773,952		19,630,282						11,143,670									
4. Commissions	13,998,309		678,114						13,320,195									

[a] Business not exceeding 120 months duration

† In each column of Part 1, show the percentages of Line 2 for Lines 3 through 11 inclusive.

*Includes $ 0 reported as "Policy, membership and other fees retained by agents."

**If not included in claim reserves.

(b) Premiums earned are before adjustment for the increase in policy reserves which has been treated as a separate deduction.

ANNUAL STATEMENT FOR THE YEAR 1986 OF THE MASTODON LIFE INSURANCE COMPANY
EXHIBIT 9 – AGGREGATE RESERVE FOR ACCIDENT AND HEALTH POLICIES

	1 Total	2 Group Accident and Health	3 Credit[a] (Group and Individual)	4 Collectively Renewable	5 Non-Cancellable	Other Individual Policies			
						6 Guaranteed Renewable	7 Non-Renewable for Stated Reasons Only	8 Other Accident Only	9 All Other
A. ACTIVE LIFE RESERVE									
1. Unearned premium reserve	24,456,425	199,648	14,631	20,600,000	1,088,070	2,549,756	4,320		
2. Additional reserves*	234,246,713			43,200,000			470		
3. Reserve for future contingent benefits (deferred maternity and other similar benefits)	774,662	774,192							
4. Reserve for rate credits									
5. Totals (Gross)	259,477,800	973,840	14,631	63,800,000	192,134,783	2,549,756	4,790		
6. Reinsurance ceded	21,143,289	453,034			20,690,255				
7. Totals (Net)	238,334,511	520,806	14,631	63,800,000	171,444,528	2,549,756	4,790		
B. CLAIM RESERVE									
1. Present value of amounts not yet due on claims**	241,753,139	32,078,791	17,538	9,000,000	187,445,680	13,210,958	172		
2. Reserve for future contingent benefits (deferred maternity and other similar benefits)									
3.									
4. Total (Gross)	241,753,139	32,078,791	17,538	9,000,000	187,445,680	13,210,958	172		
5. Reinsurance ceded	30,012,024	3,429,678			26,582,346				
6. Totals (Net)	211,741,115	28,649,113	17,538	9,000,000	160,863,334	13,210,958	172		
C GRAND TOTALS (Net) (Item 2, Page 3)	450,075,626	29,169,919	32,169	72,800,000	332,307,862	15,760,714	4,962		
D Tabular Interest on policy funds	12,121,291	675,463	1,125	184,970	10,844,336	415,397	0		

* Attach statement as to valuation standard used in calculating this reserve. Specify reserve bases. Interest rates and methods
** Includes reserves for unaccrued benefits on incurred but unreported claims. Accrued benefits should be reported in Exhibit 11. Part 1, Lines 2.2 and 3.
[a] Business not exceeding 120 months duration

Chapter 10

INDIVIDUAL HEALTH INSURANCE POLICY FORMS
by Charles Habeck, F.S.A. and Mark E. Litow, F.S.A.

The well designed individual health insurance policy must satisfy several basic requirements:
- It must provide significant coverage of health care expenses or income loss.
- It must be competitive in its terms and benefits.
- It must include underwriting safeguards, especially to prevent overinsurance or adverse selection.
- It must comply with a complex array of laws and regulations.

The actuary who is asked to design or review an individual health insurance policy form should keep these requirements in mind, as well as the fact that an actuary is not a lawyer. Qualified legal counsel should always be sought; otherwise, there is greater risk of unhappy results, to be discovered either when the policy is filed and rejected, or when a claim is submitted for a loss not intended to be covered under the terms of the policy. The goal of this chapter is to provide the reader with a set of general precepts that will guide him through the reviewing process so as to avoid such unintended results.

10.1 THE BASICS

As a practical matter no policy contract is ever entirely written "from scratch." Sample language can be obtained from policies sold in the marketplace; there are no copyright restrictions. However, since marketing pressures dictate product differentiation, enhancements usually are sought for competitive reasons, even in revisions of a company's current products. Such improvements should be developed with close attention to the increased risk involved. It is at this point that the actuary's special knowledge must be applied, since the actuary is expected to be able to estimate the costs related to a variety of alternative plan provisions. But even without plan changes, the actuary must be able to interpret the contract language so as to confirm premium adequacy or to properly establish required reserves for that policy.

To better understand the structure and content of a health insurance policy form, the reader is advised to obtain several policies in each of these categories:

- major medical,
- Medicare supplement,
- long term care,
- hospital income, and
- disability income.

These policies should include the common rider benefits. To the extent possible, the same companies should be represented in each category in order that the internal consistency of a given portfolio can be observed. To be of greatest value, sample policies for study or reference should be chosen from among those recently approved in the states where the reader most expects his company to market its products.

This is especially true for health care benefits, since insurance coverage has become the vehicle for meeting social goals by mandate through laws and regulations. For disability income benefits, competition has brought about more change than regulations, creating a buyer's market where companies are pressured to liberalize. When benefit terms are liberalized, offsetting safeguards should be introduced to keep premiums competitive.

Consistency of policy language and format has become an important objective in policy design. Consistency is needed for marketing reasons so that agent training can build on prior knowledge of the product type. But it is also necessary for legal and administrative reasons, since court decisions have given special meanings to particular terminology and conditions. Administratively the wordprocessor has transformed this previously cumbersome burden of consistent language into a more tractable task. Using its wordprocessing capacities, one company reports that it is able to maintain internal consistency among sixty versions of its major medical policy, with riders and endorsements to meet the multiplicity of state requirements.

In developing a new or revised individual health product, the insurer typically will do the following:

- Identify its target market.
- Establish the scope of benefits.
- Set limits on the contractual risks.
- Confirm that regulatory requirements will be met.

The company's product development committee will usually prepare a memorandum outlining the main features and provisions of the new plan. This preliminary report will show how the plan meets all basic requirements. Comments will be obtained from all functional departments, and the proposal will be revised to achieve the necessary balance among marketing, underwriting, claims and regulatory considerations. Of these, the selling, underwriting and claims aspects are discussed more fully elsewhere in this textbook. The main emphasis in this chapter will be on basic plan provisions and regulatory requirements.

10.2 THE CONTENT OF AN INDIVIDUAL HEALTH POLICY

Once the plan features and provisions have been agreed upon, the construction of the policy can begin. The policy writer should strive for concise and understandable English, in order to convey the intended benefits accurately, as well as any limitations applicable to them. The writer should expect that any ambiguities will be resolved in favor of the insured. Careless or inconsistent design can produce a number of undesirable results including limited sales, adverse selection or higher claim costs than were anticipated.

In referring to sample policy forms the writer should note that current contract language reflects the impact of regulations on readability. Most state laws require a minimum score of from 40 to 50 points on the Flesch readability test, and may include rules on type size and format. In complying with these requirements, newer contracts will contain simplified versions of court-tested provisions. New interpretations are likely to emerge even though the simplified language version may purport to mean exactly what the original version meant.

Improved readability can be achieved through the following techniques:

- a logical sequence of ideas, with clear reference of pronouns,
- page format in two columns, with liberal use of "white space,"
- use of "we" and "you" for insurer and insured,
- use of examples,
- inclusion of table of contents and index.

An improved score can be achieved through the use of shorter sentences and shorter words, but the score by itself does not guarantee improved readability.

While policy forms of various insurers will differ in appearance and in arrangements, the parts will usually be the same for policies providing comparable benefits. Being legal contracts, policy forms have an internal structure fixed by custom, usage and law. Their essential features are dictated both by contract law and by insurance statutes that govern much of the structure of individual health policy forms.

The most important parts of a typical major medical policy are outlined in the Table 10.1. Note that this policy provides family benefits.

Table 10.1
Policy Outline for Major Medical Plan

FACE PAGE:
    Insuring clause
    Consideration clause
    Renewal provision
    Right to examine policy
    Execution
        Title
        Brief Description
    Form number

BACK OF FACE PAGE:
    Table of contents or index

SCHEDULE PAGE (inserted):
    Data on policy
    Data on insured persons
    Data on benefits
    Data on riders
    Data on premiums

BENEFIT PROVISIONS:
    Definitions*
    Eligibility
    Termination
    Conversion
    Benefit provisions
    Related provisions
    Losses not covered

BENEFIT SCHEDULES:
    Surgical schedule
    Other services

GENERAL PROVISIONS:**
    Contract provisions
    To keep policy in force
    To file a claim
    Adjustments to benefits
    Regular and customary

ATTACHMENTS:
    Copy of application
    Riders
    Endorsements

*DEFINITIONS MIGHT INCLUDE:
    You, we
    Insured person
    Injury
    Sickness
    Complications of pregnancy
    Doctor
    Nurse
    Hospital
    Convalescent care facility
    Home health care
    Home health agency
    Inpatient
    Skilled nursing care
    Custodial care
    Other coverage
    Medicare
    Regular and Customary

**GENERAL PROVISIONS DETAILS:
    Contract Provisions:
        Entire contact; changes
        Time limit on certain
            defenses
        Conformity with state laws
    To keep policy in force:
        Premium payments
        Grace period
        Reinstatement
    To file a claim:
        Notice of claim
        Claim forms
        Proofs of loss
        Time of payment of claims
        Payment of claims
        Physical exam and autopsy
        Legal actions
    Adjustment to benefits:
        Misstatement of age
        Other Insurance

For a disability income plan, the outline will require certain changes. First, provisions regarding family coverage can be deleted; these include eligibility, termination and conversions. Next, benefit schedules may not be used. Finally, some definitions must be dropped and others added. Examples of deletions are insured person, nurse, hospital, inpatient, skilled nursing care, custodial care, Medicare, and regular and customary. Examples of additions are income, current income, prior income, total disability, residual disability, elimination period, qualification period, benefit period, and social insurance benefits. Disability plans will include references to indexing of benefits, formulas for proportionate benefits, treatment of social insurance benefits and rules for applying for such benefits, recurrent disabilities, waiver of premium, rehabilitation, transplant surgery and presumptive disability.

10.2.1 POLICY FACE PAGE

Insuring Clause: This states the promise of the insurer to pay certain benefits upon the occurrence of contingencies insured against. The clause makes reference to all provisions, exceptions and exclusions appearing elsewhere in the policy. Sometimes certain exceptions, and the definitions of the terms "injury" and "sickness" form a part of the insuring clause. The general promises of the insurer are made here and precede statement of the more detailed agreements in the benefit provisions.

The insuring clause may state that the policy covers losses resulting only from an injury sustained or a sickness contracted and commencing after the policy is in force. Alternatively, this same exclusion of preexisting conditions may be accomplished by appropriate definition of the terms injury and sickness. A probationary period, usually 15 or 30 days, may be added by changing the insuring clause or definition of sickness to include the restrictions "sickness contracted and commencing more than X days after the policy date."

Consideration Clause: This states the insured's part of the agreement. The consideration for the issue of the policy is usually payment of the first premium and the insured's statements as recorded in the application.

Renewal Provision: This states the conditions under which the policy can be renewed or continued. Renewal provisions are classified as

1. noncancelable and guaranteed renewable;
2. guaranteed renewable;
3. nonrenewable for stated reasons only;
4. collectively renewable; and
5. renewable at the option of the company.

Premiums for noncancelable policies may not be changed; the renewal provisions for the other categories would usually state how renewal premiums are to be determined.

Most individual health policies contemplate a term period to age 65 for insured adult persons, or prior eligibility for Medicare benefits. "To age 65" commonly means until the end of the premium period in which the insured becomes 65. Disability income policies may be renewable after age 65 with the consent of the insurer if the insured is still at work. Grace period and reinstatement provisions may differ for terms after age 65. Some noncancelable disability income policies guarantee renewal to age 70, with conditional renewal allowed until age 75.

Notice of 10 Day Right to Examine Policy: The "10-day free look" is usually a feature of the face page for policies issued to persons under age 65. Some states require a longer period. A "30-day free look" requirement is becoming more widespread for policies issued to persons over age 65. In either case the policyholder is given the right to surrender the policy within the stated number of days after its delivery and to receive a refund of any premium paid. If exercised, the policy is then treated as if void from the start, effective at the moment it is given or mailed back to the agent or the company.

Execution Title: Custom and law call for a statement that the insurer has executed the policy as of its date of issue. The required language is usually found at the bottom of the face page, but sometimes it appears at the end of the policy. It is followed by facsimile signatures of the president and secretary, or other officers of the insurer. Some states require endorsement by a licensed resident agent. Health insurance policies usually are labeled to indicate benefits: disability income policy; major medical policy; Medicare supplement policy. A short description is often printed beneath the policy title to set forth benefits and renewal terms. This information may be required by law to clarify the terms of renewal.

Form Number: Each policy or rider must be assigned its own form number, which may include a state designation. The form number must be printed in the lower left-hand corner of the policy face page.

10.2.2 BACK OF FACE PAGE:

Readability rules call for a table of contents or an index of policy provisions; these are frequently placed on the back of the face page.

10.2.3 SCHEDULE PAGE

Most insurers prepare the policy schedule page using the information about new issues that is coded for entry into the master policy record. The policy schedule page can show, by use of the proper programs, as much information as is required, even for the most complex disability income or major medical policies. This includes data on the policy, the insured, premiums, basic benefits and rider benefits.

Policy Data: This encompasses policy number, policy date or date of issue, initial term of coverage, first renewal date and expiration date.

Insured Data: This includes the name of insured, his age on the policy date, the names and ages of dependents insured, the name of the beneficiary, the name of policyowner.

Premium Data: This includes specification of the modal premiums by benefit and rider, the policy fees, the total premium for all available payment modes, the premium payment period by benefit.

Benefit and Rider Data: This contains any variation in coverage such as the maximum amount of each benefit, length of time for periodic payments or other internal limits.

For a disability income policy, this data includes total disability amount per month, elimination period, maximum benefit period (separately for accident and sickness), partial or residual benefits, any benefits contingent on social insurance, rider benefits for accidental death and dismemberment, guaranteed insurability and COL adjustments.

For a hospital and medical expense policy, this data includes the maximum daily benefit, the maximum duration of daily hospital benefit (in days), the maximum miscellaneous hospital expense benefit, the maximum physician in-hospital expense benefit (per call), the maximum number of calls, the deductible amounts and how they are applicable.

For a major medical policy, the data includes the deductible amount (fixed or variable), the per cause or per calendar period basis, the maximum benefit, the coinsurance percentage, the maximum out-of-pocket cost to the insured and the internal benefit limits.

For a Medicare supplement policy, this data includes Part A deductible and copayment amounts (and adjustments to them each year), Part B deductible amounts (if paid), and the coinsurance percentage of Medicare allowable, usual and customary level of charges.

10.2.4 BENEFIT PROVISIONS

The benefit provisions present the details of what is payable for each contingency insured against, furnishes the definitions of terms having special meanings, and lists miscellaneous items not otherwise covered.

Benefits: Each benefit will be stated in a separate paragraph, appropriately captioned for ease of reading. Where benefit amounts vary, reference is normally made to the policy schedule page. Information concerning fixed limits may appear both in the benefit provision and in the policy schedule.

A few "schedule policies" are still offered by some insurers. These policies contain the text of a number of elective benefit provisions that are in force only if so noted in the policy schedule, along with the applicable premium for each benefit.

Less confusion results if each benefit provision is printed on a separate page. Then the policy is assembled with only those benefits selected, and once again, only these are listed in the policy schedule with their premiums.

A benefit provision is a subordinate insuring clause that specifies the parenthetical phrases in the following generalized benefit statement:

If the insured sustains (injury or sickness), (becomes disabled), suffers (a loss) which (continues) the Company will pay (the described benefit) commencing, continuing, and ending (at specified times measured from commencement of loss).

Descriptions of the various benefits are contained in Chapters 2 and 3.

Near the benefit provisions will appear explanations of provisions dealing with recurrent disabilities, recurrent or successive periods of hospitalization, waiver of premium during total or residual disability, rehabilitation or other benefits of a similar nature.

Some policies specify that certain losses shall be deemed to result from sickness, such as complications of pregnancy or transplant donor benefits. These statements may also appear in the exclusions provisions of the policy.

Definitions: Words given special meaning in a policy are defined in a separate section of the policy if they are used more than once. If used only once a definition appears near the provision where the word is used. This practice is in keeping with readability regulations, which attempt to reduce the need for cross references. Terms defined in a separate section are listed before these are used. Terms such as "accumulation period," "benefit period" and "deductible amount" may need special explanation close to the statement of benefits.

Exclusions, Exceptions and Reductions: Terms like "exclusions" and "exceptions" usually refer to events, conditions or expenses that are not covered by the policy. Limitations and reductions may refer to modifications of benefit payments for one reason or another. For instance, disability benefits may be reduced if the insured was not gainfully employed away from home at the time the loss began. Hospital daily benefits may be reduced automatically at age 65. Statutes permit such items to be shown in the benefit provisions to which they apply, or to be grouped under a single heading. In the latter case, a simpler and more inclusive caption might be "Losses Not Covered by This Policy."

10.2.5 SCHEDULE OF PROCEDURES

Surgical expense benefits may be provided in two ways. Most comprehensive major medical plans now provide unscheduled benefits, subject to deductibles, coinsurance, and reasonable and customary limits. Basic hospital-medical-surgical plans may provide a scheduled benefit, with maximum dollar allowances listed or determinable for each procedure in the schedule.

Schedules covering surgery, anesthesia, and various other types of services may be condensed or lengthy, but all should contain clear explanations of how benefits will be paid in varying circumstances. Fixed dollar or relative value schedules may be used. Fixed dollar schedules pay up to the maximum allowance stated. Relative value schedules are generally stated in units or in dollars, but will include a multiplier, such as "$50 per unit" or "150 percent of the dollar amount shown."

Benefits may be further adjusted for bilateral procedures, or more than one procedure in the same surgical field. If so, the policy language should make this clear.

10.2.6 GENERAL PROVISIONS

The policy is completed by the inclusion of a set of administrative provisions together with the uniform policy provisions stipulated by law. In a contract designed to insure a single person, the administrative provisions may cover only payment of premiums. However, policies that will insure all members of family usually require additional provisions. Note that in the outline given earlier these provisions were grouped with the benefit page.

For family coverage the policy must define the family members who are eligible to become insured persons, and also must tell how additional family members can be insured after the policy has been issued. Children eligible to be insured may include step-children or adopted children. For persons added after the policy date, the policy must specify the additional premiums to be paid and the underwriting requirements to be met. Newborn children are usually covered without evidence of insurability from the moment of birth.

Family contracts specify a date of termination of coverage for family members, typically age 65 for adults and age 21 for children, although coverage on children may extend past age 21 for those attending universities or for mentally retarded or physically handicapped, while unmarried and dependent on the insured.

Many policies now include a conversion privilege for children who reach the age of expiry, and for a divorced spouse of the insured. Conversion to a Medicare supplement policy usually does not require evidence of insurability and may be provided for those who become eligible for Medicare.

Another administrative provision of family policies allows for the appointment of a successor insured if the original insured reaches an age for which coverage is not available, age 65 for instance, or has coverage terminated due to death or for reasons other than nonpayment of premiums. In such event the control of the policy or the designation "insured " passes to the successor of the insured, provided the successor is still insured and under the age of 65.

A participating policy will include a dividend provision stating the policyholder's entitlement to a share of divisible surplus as determined by the insurer. Typically, annual dividends may be paid in cash or applied toward payment of a premium.

10.2.7 REQUIRED AND OPTIONAL POLICY PROVISIONS UNDER THE UNIFORM POLICY PROVISION LAW

General provisions required or optional under the Uniform Individual Accident and Sickness Policy Provision Law appear below. Twelve policy provisions are required by this law unless inapplicable or inconsistent with the coverage provided. The wording of the provision may be altered if appropriate, and if approved by the insurance commissioner. Contract readability laws are often responsible for alterations; however, those must be made carefully so as not to change intended meanings. The complete text of the Uniform Individual Accident and Sickness Policy Provision Law appears in Appendix 2. Appendix 3 contains a restatement of these provisions in simplified language.

A. Required Uniform Policy Provisions:

Entire Contract; Changes: This provides that the policy with the papers attached to it make up the entire contract. One exception is for a fraternal insurer that may include its Constitution and By-Laws by reference, without attachment. Officer approval is required for changes.

Time Limit on Certain Defenses: This specifies the time limit during which the policy may be contested or a claim denied because of misstatements in the application; it also specifies the time limit after which no claim can be denied on grounds that the condition existed before the effective date of coverage unless specifically excluded by waiver. Note that an alternative clause for noncancelable policies is entitled "Incontestable."

Grace Period: This specifies the grace period for the payment of premiums.

Reinstatement: This specifies the terms for reinstatement of a policy and has a provision that it shall cover only loss due to injury sustained after reinstatement or sickness beginning more than 10 days after reinstatement. The regular provision also states that no premium on reinstatement shall cover a period more than 60 days prior to reinstatement, but this proviso may be omitted from policies that are noncancelable or guaranteed renewable to at least age 50 or for a least 5 years if issued after age 44.

Notice of Claim: This specifies the place at which written notice of claim is to be given the insurer within the designated time limit after occurrence or commencement of loss or as soon thereafter as reasonably possible.

Claim Forms: This specifies that it is the insurer's obligation to furnish claim forms within 15 days of notice of a claim.

Proof of Loss: This requires that completed claim forms and other proof of loss must be furnished with 90 days of loss or as soon thereafter as reasonably possible, subject to a 1-year maximum limit.

Time of Payment of Claims: This requires that claims be paid immediately upon receipt of proof of loss with periodic benefits to be paid not less frequently than monthly, as specified.

Payment of Claims: This requires benefits to be payable to beneficiaries or to the insured. An optional facility of payment provision allows amounts up to $1,000 to be paid to a relative instead of to the insured's estate or to an incompetent. Another optional facility of payment provision permits payment directly to the hospital or to the person rendering hospital, nursing, medical or surgical services.

Physical Examination and Autopsy: This allows physical examination at reasonable intervals and for an autopsy to be performed where not forbidden by law.

Legal Action: This states that the insured may not bring suit sooner than 60 days nor later than 3 years after the time written proof of claim is required.

Change of Beneficiary: This states the right of the insured to change the beneficiary.

B. Optional Uniform Policy Provisions.

The law established other provisions to be used or omitted at the insurer's option. However, an insurer wishing to use any of these optional provisions must use either the words of the law or language approved by insurance supervisory officials as not less favorable to the insured. Optional provisions usually follow required provisions. Readability requirements have encouraged a more logical arrangement.

Change of Occupation: This allows for a reduction in benefits if the insured takes up a more hazardous occupation, and for a reduction of premium if he changes to a less hazardous one. It is seldom used.

Misstatement of Age: This allows adjustment of benefits if the age of the insured is misstated. This is common. If a policy would not have been issued, liability is limited to the return of any premiums paid.

Other Insurance With This Insurer: This allows establishment of a maximum aggregate benefit limit applicable to all policies insured by the same insurer to one insured. Excess coverage over this limit is void and premiums for any excess are to be returned. This option is common in agent-issued travel accident policies, specified loss policies and so on.

Insurance with Other Insurers (medical expense): This allows proportionate settlement of medical expense benefit claims when another coverage, of which the insurer has not been given written notice, is in force. This is rarely used.

Insurance With Other Insurers (disability): This is used to allow a pro rata reduction in disability income benefits if the insured holds policies with other insurers and has not notified the insurer. Competition has tended to drive prorating policies from the market.

Relation of Earnings to Insurance: This is permitted only with noncancelable or guaranteed renewable disability income policies as a means of preventing overinsurance. With this provision benefits can be reduced (but not below $200 per month) so that benefits under all such policies held by the insured do not exceed his average earnings during the 2 years preceding the claim. This measure is only partially effective in preventing overinsurance.

Unpaid Premium: This allows for any premium unpaid at the time of claim to be deducted from benefit payment.

Cancellation: This provision allows cancellation of the policy before its paid-to-date. It is seldom used and may be prohibited by some states.

Conformity with State Statutes: This is a provision to automatically conform the policy if it is in conflict with the laws of the state of issue. It is commonly used.

Illegal Occupation: By this provision an insurer is not liable if a loss occurs as a consequence of the insured's commission of a felony or while engaging in an illegal occupation. It is rarely used.

Intoxicants and Narcotics: By this, an insurer is not liable if a loss occurs as a consequence of the insured's being intoxicated or under the influence of a narcotic. It is rarely used.

10.2.8 ATTACHMENTS TO THE POLICY

Application: A copy of the application is attached to the policy to incorporate into the policy the statements made by the insured as to his health and insurability. Reference can be made in the policy to dependents or a beneficiary "as shown in the application" without having to enter this information on the Policy Schedule page. Alternatively, since this information is stored in the policy record, there is little extra difficulty in printing it out on the Policy Schedule.

Riders or Supplemental Provisions: Insurers often permit applicants to elect optional benefits and include them in the policy by the attachment of a benefit rider or supplemental provision. The rider states the benefit provision thereby added, the premium payable, and any applicable exceptions or exclusions. Premiums also could be stated as "shown in the Policy Schedule." A rider should incorporate, by reference, all other terms of the policy that apply to it.

Impairment Waiver Riders or Endorsements: A variety of riders and endorsements are used by insurers to modify policy benefits due to the health status of a given insured person. The underwriting process may reveal impairments that would require a waiver or impairment rider as described in Chapter 6. For example, the insured may apply for a policy containing a dismemberment benefit, but already may have suffered the loss of a limb or an eye. Such issue can be made only if a suitable rider or endorsement is attached to the policy, restating the dismemberment benefit as may be appropriate for the proposed insured. All states require that an insured sign a rider or endorsement that reduces or eliminates coverage to show his acceptance of the limitation. In most states, however, signed acceptance of such an endorsement at time of issue is not required if a prominent notice is placed on the face page of the policy calling attention to it.

Appendix 1

RESERVE STANDARDS FOR INDIVIDUAL HEALTH INSURANCE POLICIES

Table of Contents

Section 1. . . . . Active Life Reserves—General.
Section 2. . . . . Types of Individual Health Insurance Policies.
Section 3. . . . . Reserve Standards of Type A, B or C.
Section 4. . . . . Claim Reserves.
Section 5. . . . . Valuation Procedures.

Section 1. Active Life Reserves—General.

Active life reserves are required for all in force policies and are in addition to any reserves required in connection with claims. For policy Types A, B and C, described below, the minimum reserve is determined as specified herein. It is emphasized, however, that these are minimum standards and that (insert statutory reference) requires that higher, adequate reserves be established by the insurer in any case where experience indicates that these minimum standards do not place a sound value on the liabilities under the policy. For policy Type D, the minimum reserve should be the gross pro rata unearned premium.

Section 2. Types of Individual Health Insurance Policies.

A. Policies which are guaranteed renewable for life or to a specified age, such as 60 or 65, at guaranteed premium rates.

B. Policies which are guaranteed renewable for life or to a specified age, such as 60 or 65, but under which the insurer reserves the right to change the scale of premiums.

C. Policies in which the insurer has reserved the right to cancel or refuse renewal for one or more reasons, but has agreed implicitly or explicitly that, prior to a specified time or age, it will not cancel or decline renewal solely because of deterioration of health after issue; however, policies shall not be considered of this type if the insurer has reserved the right to refuse renewal provided the right is to be exercised at the same time for all policies in the same category, unless premiums are based on the level premium principle.

D. All other individual policies.

Notes:

(a) The above does not classify "franchise" as a type of policy. Such policies are frequently written under an agreement limiting the insurer's right to cancel or refuse renewal. Usually the right is reserved to refuse renewal of all policies in the group or other categories such as those ceasing to be members of the association, and this would place such policies in Type D in accordance with the last clause under C above. However, if premiums are based on the level premium principle or if the renewal undertaking for the individual meets the requirements for Type A, B or C, the franchise policy should be so classified for reserve purposes.

(b) A policy may have guarantees qualifying it as Type A, B or C until a specified age or duration, after which the guarantees, or lack of guarantees, may qualify it as Type A, B, C or D. In such case, the policy in each period should be considered for reserve purposes according to the type to which it then belongs.

(c) Where all of the benefits of a policy, as provided by rider or otherwise, are not of the same Type (A, B, C or D), each benefit should be considered for reserve purposes according to the type to which it belongs.

Section 3. Reserve Standards of Type A, B or C.

(a) Interest. The maximum interest rate for reserves should be the greater of (i) the maximum rate permitted by law in the valuation of currently issued life insurance or (ii) the maximum rate permitted by law in the value of life insurance issues on the same date as the health insurance.

(b) Mortality. The mortality assumptions used for reserves should be according to a table permitted by law in the valuation of life insurance issued on the same date as the health insurance.

(c) Morbidity or other contingency. Minimum standards with respect to morbidity are those stated in Appendix A of this regulation, which is subject to revision from time to time with respect to dates of issue of contracts.

(d) Negative Reserves. Negative reserves on any benefit may be offset against positive reserves for other benefits in the same policy, but the mean reserve on any policy should never be taken as less than one-half the valuation net premium.

(e) Preliminary Term. The minimum reserves shall be on the basis of two-years preliminary term.

(f) Reserve Method. Mean reserves diminished by appropriate credit for valuation net deferred premiums. In no event, however, should the aggregate reserve for all policies valued on the mean reserve basis, diminished by any credit for deferred premiums, be less than the gross pro rata unearned premiums under such policies.

(g) Alternative Valuation Procedures and Assumptions. Provided the reserve on all policies to which the method or basis is applied is not less in the aggregate than the amount determined according to the applicable standards specified above, an insurer may use any reasonable assumptions as to the interest rate, mortality rates, or the rates of morbidity or other contingency, and may introduce an assumption as to the voluntary termination of policies. Also, subject to the preceding condition, the insurer may employ methods other than the methods stated above in determining a sound value of its liabilities under such policies, including but not limited to the following: (i) the use of mid-terminal reserves in addition to either gross or net pro rata unearned premium reserves; (ii) optional use of either the level premium, the one-year preliminary term, or the two-year preliminary term method; (iii) prospective valuation on the basis of actual gross premiums with reasonable allowance for future expenses; (iv) the use of approximations such as those involving age groupings, groupings of several years of issue, average amounts of indemnity; (v) the computation of the reserve for one policy benefit as a percentage of, or by other relation to, the aggregate policy reserves, exclusive of the benefit or benefits so valued; (vi) the use of a composite annual claim cost for all or any combination of the benefits included in the policies valued.

For statement purposes the net reserve liability may be shown as the excess of the mean reserve over the amount of net unpaid and deferred premiums, or regardless of the underlying method of calculation, it may be divided between the gross pro rata unearned premium reserve and a balancing item for the "additional reserve."

Section 4. Claim Reserves.

(a) Reserves are required for claims on all health insurance policies, whether of Type A, B, C or D, providing benefits for continuing loss, such as loss of time for hospitalization.

(b) Claim Reserve Standards for Total Disability Due to Accident or Sickness.

(i) Interest. The maximum interest rate for reserves should be the maximum posted rate permitted by law in the valuation of life insurance issued on the same date as the date the claim is incurred.

(ii) Morbidity. Minimum standards with respect to morbidity are those stated in Appendix A of this regulation, except that for the reported claims and resisted claims and, at the option of the insurer, claims with a duration of disablement of less than two years, reserves may be based on the individual insurer's experience or other assumptions designed to place a sound value on the liabilities. Reserves based on such experience or assumptions should be verified by the development of each year's claims over a period of years along the lines of Schedule O.

(iii) For policies with an elimination period, the duration of disablement should be considered as dating from the time that benefits would have begun to accrue had there been no elimination period.

(iv) A new disability connected directly or indirectly with a previous disability which had a duration of at least one year and termination within six months of the new disability should be considered a continuation of the previous disability.

(c) Reserve Standards for All Other Claim Reserves.

(i) Interest. The maximum interest rate for reserves should be the maximum rate permitted by law in the valuation of life insurance issued on the same date as the date the claim is incurred.

(ii) Morbidity or other contingency. The reserve should be based on the individual insurer's experience or other assumptions designed to place a sound value on the liabilities. The results should be verified by the development of each year's claims over a period of years along the lines of Schedule O.

Section 5. Valuation Procedures.

The insurer may employ suitable approximations and estimates, including but not limited to groupings and averages, in computing claim reserves.

Appendix A (effective January 1, 1986)

MORBIDITY

Minimum morbidity standards for valuation of individual health insurance contracts are as follows:

1. Disability due to accident or sickness.

    Active Life Reserves:

    Contracts issued on or after January 1, 1965 and prior to January 1, 1986:

    The 1964 Commissioners Disability Table.

    Contracts issued on or after January 1, 1987:

    The 1985 Commissioners Individual Disability Tables A.

    or

    The 1985 Commissioners Individual Disability Tables B.

    Contracts Issued during 1986:

    Optional use of either the 1964 Table or either of the 1985 Tables.

    Each insurer shall elect, with respect to all individual contracts issued in any one statement year and all claims incurred in that year, whether it will use Tables A or Tables B as minimum standard. The insurer may, however, elect to use the other Tables with respect to any subsequent statement year.

    Claims Reserves:

    The minimum morbidity standard in effect for active life reserves on currently issued contracts, as of the date the claim is incurred.

2. Hospital Benefits, Surgical Benefits and Maternity Benefits (either specified or expense reimbursement).

    Active Life Reserves:

    Contracts issued on or after January 1, 1955 and before January 1, 1982:

    The 1956 Intercompany Hospital-Surgical Tables.

    Contracts issued on or after January 1, 1982:

    The 1974 Medical Expense Tables, Table A, Transactions of the Society of Actuaries, Volume XXX, page 63. Refer to the paper (in the same Volume, page 9) to which this Table is appended, including its discussions, for methods of adjustment for benefits not directly valued in Table A: "Development of the 1974 Medical Expense Benefits," Houghton and Wolf.

3. Cancer Expense Benefits.

   Active Life Reserves:

   Contracts Issued on or after January 1, 1986:

   The 1985 NAIC Cancer Claim Cost Tables.

4. Accidental Death Benefits.

   Active Life Reserves:

   Contracts issued on or after January 1, 1965:

   The 1959 Accidental Death Benefits Table.

5. For all other contracts or benefits, including major medical, the insurer should adopt a standard which will produce active life reserves that place a sound value on its liabilities under each such benefit. For all benefits other than disability, claim reserves are to be determined as provided in the Standards.

Appendix 2

UNIFORM INDIVIDUAL ACCIDENT AND SICKNESS POLICY PROVISION LAW

Table of Contents

Section 1. . . . . Definition of Accident and Sickness Insurance Policy
Section 2. . . . . Form of Policy
Section 3. . . . . Accident and Sickness Policy Provisions
Section 4. . . . . Conforming to Statute
Section 5. . . . . Application
Section 6. . . . . Notice, Waiver
Section 7. . . . . Age Limit
Section 8. . . . . Non-Application to Certain Policies
Section 9. . . . . Violation
Section 10 . . . . Judicial Review
Section 11 . . . . Repeal of Inconsistent Act
Section 12 . . . . Effective Date of Act
Exhibit A . . . . Regulation Regarding Overinsurance Provisions

Section 1. Definition of Accident and Sickness Insurance Policy.

The term "policy of accident and sickness insurance" as used herein includes any policy or contract covering the kind or kinds of insurance described in (insert here the section of law authorizing accident and sickness insurance).

Note: if the insurance law of the state in which this draft is proposed for enactment does not have a section specifically authorizing the various types of insurance which may be written, this section should be modified to define accident and sickness insurance as "insurance against loss resulting from sickness or from bodily injury or death by accident, or both."

Section 2. Form of Policy.

(A) No policy of accident and sickness insurance shall be delivered or issued for delivery to any person in this state unless:

 (1) the entire money and other considerations therefor are expressed therein; and

(2) the time at which the insurance takes effect and terminates is expressed therein; and

(3) it purports to insure only one person, except that a policy may insure, originally or by subsequent amendment, upon the application of an adult member of a family who shall be deemed the policyholder, any two or more eligible members of that family, including husband, wife, dependent children or any children under a specified age which shall not exceed nineteen years any other person dependent upon the policyholder; and

Note: In states having community property systems derived from the civil law it is suggested that in the foregoing subparagraphs the words "an adult member" be replaced with "the head".

(4) the style, arrangement and over-all appearance of the policy give no undue prominence to any portion of the text, and unless every printed portion of the text of the policy and of any endorsements or attached papers is plainly printed in light-faced type of a style in general use, the size of which shall be uniform and not less than tenpoint with a lower-case unspaced alphabet length not less than one hundred and twenty-point (the "text" shall include all printed matter except the name and address of the insurer, name or title of the policy, the brief description if any, and captions and sub-captions); and

(5) the exceptions and reductions of indemnity are set forth in the policy and, except those which are set forth in section 3 of this act, are printed, at the insurer's option, either included with the benefit provision to which they apply, or under an appropriate caption such as "Exceptions," or "Exceptions and Reductions", provided that if an exception or reduction specifically applies only to a particular benefit of the policy, a statement of such exception or reduction shall be included with the benefit provision to which it applies; and

(6) each such form, including riders and endorsements, shall be identified by a form number in the lower left-hand corner of the first page thereof, and

(7) it contains no provision purporting to make any portion of the charter, rules, constitution, or by-laws of the insurer a part of the policy unless such portion is set forth in full in the policy, except in the case of the incorporation of, or reference to, a statement of rates or classification of risks, or short-rate table filed with the (Commissioner).

(B) If any policy is issued by an insurer domiciled in this state for delivery to a person residing in another state, and if the official having responsibility for the administration of the insurance laws of such other state shall have advised the (Commissioner) that any such policy is not subject to approval or disapproval by such official, the (Commissioner) may by ruling require that such policy meet the standards set forth in subsection (A) of this section and in section 3.

Section 3. Accident and Sickness Policy Provisions.

(A) Required Provisions.

Except as provided in paragraph (C) of this section each such policy delivered or issued for delivery to any person in this state shall contain the provisions specified in this subsection in the words in which the same appear in this section; provided, however, that the insurer may, at its option, substitute for one or more of such provisions corresponding provisions of different wording approved by the (Commissioner) which are in each instance not less favorable in any respect to the insured or the beneficiary. Such provisions shall be preceded individually by the caption appearing in this subsection or, at the option of the insurer, by such appropriate individual or group captions or subcaptions as the (Commissioner) may approve.

(1) A provision as follows:

Entire Contract; Changes: This policy, including the endorsements and the attached papers, if any, constitutes the entire contract of insurance. No change in this policy shall be valid until approved by an executive officer of the insurer and unless such approval be endorsed hereon or attached hereto. No agent has authority to change the is policy or to waive any of its provisions.

Note: When enacted in states which prohibit amendment of a policy form by means other than attached printed rider upon a separate piece of paper the new law should contain (but not as a required policy provision) an added section defining "endorsement" in such a manner as to make the new law consistent with current statutes.

(2) A provision as follows:

Time Limit on Certain Defenses: (a) After three years from the date of issue of this policy no misstatements, except fraudulent misstatements, made by the applicant in the application for such policy shall be used to void the policy or to deny a claim for loss incurred or disability (as defined in the policy) commencing after the expiration of such three year period.

(The foregoing policy provision shall not be so construed as to affect any legal requirement for avoidance of a policy or denial or a claim during such initial three year period, nor to limit the application of section 3 (B), (1), (2), (3), (4) and (5) in the event of misstatement with respect to age or occupation or other insurance.)

*(A policy which the insured has the right to continue in force subject to its terms by the timely payment of premium (1) until at least age 50 or, (2) in the case of a policy issued after age 44, for at least five years from its date of issue, may contain in lieu of the foregoing the following provision (from which the clause in parentheses may be omitted at the insurer's option) under the caption "Incontestable":

> After this policy has been in force for a period of three years during the lifetime of the insured (excluding any period during which the insured is disabled), it shall become incontestable as to the statements contained in the application.)

    (b) No claim for loss incurred or disability (as defined in the policy) commencing after three years from the date of issue of this policy shall be reduced or denied on the ground that a disease or physical condition not excluded from coverage by name or specific description effective on the date of loss had existed prior to the effective date of coverage of this policy.

(3) A provision as follows:

> Grace Period: A grace period of... (insert a number not less than "7" for weekly premium policies, "10" for monthly premium polices and "31" for all other policies) days will be granted for the payment of each premium falling due after the first premium, during which grace period the policy shall continue in force.

*(A policy in which the insurer reserves the right to refuse renewal shall have, at the beginning of the above provision,

> "Unless not less than thirty days prior to the premium due date the insurer has delivered to the insured or has mailed to his last address as shown by the records of the insurer written notice of its intention not to renew this policy beyond the period for which the premium has been accepted".)

*[Amended by 1956 NAIC Proceedings II 290.]

*(Each such policy in which the insurer reserves the right to refuse renewal on an individual basis shall provide, in substance, in a provision thereof or in an endorsement thereon or in a rider attached thereto, that subject to the right to terminate the policy upon non-payment of premium when due, such right to refuse renewal shall not be exercised before the renewal date occurring on, or after and nearest, each anniversary, or in the case of lapse and reinstatement at the renewal date occurring on, or after and nearest, each anniversary of the last reinstatement, and that any refusal of renewal shall be without prejudice to any claim originating while the policy is in force. The preceding sentence shall not apply to accident insurance only policies.)

*[Amended by 1956 NAIC Proceedings II 290.]

(4) A provision as follows:

*Reinstatement: If any renewal premium be not paid within the time granted the insured for payment, a subsequent acceptance of premium by the insurer or by any agent duly authorized by the insurer to accept such premium, without requiring in connection therewith an application for reinstatement, shall reinstate the policy; provided, however that if the insurer or such agent requires an application for reinstatement and issue a conditional receipt for the premium tendered, the policy will be reinstated upon approval of such application by the insurer or, lacking such approval, upon the forty-fifth day following the date of such conditional receipt unless the insurer has previously notified the insured in writing of its disapproval of such application. The reinstated policy shall cover only loss resulting from such accidental injury as may be sustained after the date of reinstatement and loss due to such sickness as may begin more than ten days after such date. In all other respects the insured and insurer shall have the same rights thereunder as they had under the policy immediately before the due date of the defaulted premium, subject to any provisions endorsed hereon or attached hereto in connection with the reinstatement. Any premium accepted in connection with a reinstatement shall be applied to a period for which premium has not been previously paid, but not to any period more than sixty days prior to the date of reinstatement.

Note: (The last sentence of the above provision may be omitted from any policy which the insured has the right to continue in force subject to its terms by the timely payment of premiums (1) until at least age 50 or, (2) in the case of a policy issued after age 44, for at least five years from its date of issue.)

*[Editor's Note: For a statement of interpretation of this provision. see 1963 NACI Proceedings II 514-517.]

(5) A provision as follows:

Notice of Claim: Written notice of claim must be given to the insurer within twenty days after the occurrence or commencement of any loss covered by the policy, or as soon thereafter as is reasonably possible. Notice given by or on behalf of the insured or the beneficiary to the insurer at (insert the location of such office as the insurer may designate for the purpose), or to any authorized agent of the insurer, with information sufficient to identify the insured, shall be deemed notice to the insurer.

Note: In a policy providing a loss-of-time benefit which may be payable for at least two years, an insurer may at its option insert the following between the first and second sentences of the above provision:

> ["Subject to the qualifications set forth below, if the insured suffers loss of time on account of disability for which indemnity may be payable for at least two years, he shall, at least once in every six months after having given notice of claim, give to the insurer notice of continuance of said disability, except in the event of legal incapacity. The period of six months following any filing of proof by the insured or any payment by the insurer on account of such claim or any denial of liability in whole or in part by the insurer shall be excluded in applying this provision. Delay in the giving of such notice shall not impair the insured's right to any indemnity which would otherwise have accrued during the period of six months pre ceding the date on which such notice is actually given."]

(6) A provision as follows:

Claim Forms: The insurer, upon receipt of a notice of claim, will furnish to the claimant such forms as are usually furnished by it for filing proof of loss. If such forms are not furnished within fifteen days after the giving of such notice the claimant shall be deemed to have compiled also with the requirements of this policy as to proof of loss upon submitting, within the time fixed in the policy for filing proofs of loss, written proof covering the occurrence, the character and the extent of the loss for which claim is made.

(7) A provision as follows:

Proofs of Loss: Written proof of loss must be furnished to the insurer at its said office in case of claim for loss for which this policy provides any periodic payment contingent upon continuing loss within ninety days after the termination of the period for which the insurer is liable and in case of claim for any other loss within ninety days after the day of such loss. Failure to furnish such proof within the time required shall not invalidate nor reduce any claim if it was not reasonably possible to give proof within such time, provided such proof is furnished as soon as reasonably possible and in no event, except in the absence of legal capacity, later than one year from the time proof is otherwise required.

(8) A provision as follows:

Time of Payment of Claims: Indemnities payable under this policy for any loss other than loss for which this policy provides any periodic payment will be paid immediately upon receipt of due written proof of such loss. Subject to due written proof of loss, all accrued indemnities for loss for which this policy provides periodic payment will be paid... (insert period for payment which must not be less frequently than monthly) and any balance remaining unpaid upon the termination of liability will be paid immediately upon receipt of due written proof.

(9) A provision as follows:

Payment of Claims: Indemnity for loss of life will be payable in accordance with the beneficiary designation and the provisions respecting such payment which may be prescribed herein and effective at the time of payment. If no such designation or provision is then effective, such indemnity shall be payable to the estate of the insured. Any other accrued indemnities unpaid at the insured's death may, at the option of the insurer, be paid either to such beneficiary or to such estate. All other indemnities will be payable to the insured.

Note: The following provisions, or either of them, may be included with the foregoing provision at the option of the insurer:

["If any indemnity of this policy shall be payable to the estate of the insured, or to an insured or beneficiary who is a minor or otherwise not competent to give a valid release; the insurer may pay such indemnity, up to an amount not exceeding $ (insert an amount which shall not exceed $1000), to any relative by blood or connection by marriage of the insured or beneficiary who is deemed by the insurer to be equitably entitled thereto. Any payment made by the insurer in good faith pursuant to this provision shall fully discharge the insurer to the extent of such payment."]

["Subject to any written direction of the insured in the application or otherwise all or a portion of any indemnities provided by this policy on account of hospital, nursing, medical, or surgical services may, at the insurer's option and unless the insured requests otherwise in writing not later than the time of filing proofs of such class, be paid directly at the hospital or person rendering such services; but it is not required that the service be rendered by a particular hospital or person."]

(10) A provision as follows:

Physical Examinations and Autopsy: The insurer at its own expense shall have the right and opportunity to examine the person of the insured when and as often as it may reasonably require during the pendency of a claim hereunder and to make an autopsy in case of death where it is not forbidden by law.

(11) A provision as follows:

Legal Actions: No action at law or in equity shall be brought to recover on this policy prior to the expiration of sixty days after written proof of loss has been furnished in accordance with the requirements of this policy. No such action shall be brought after the expiration of three years after the time written proof of loss is required to be furnished.

(12) A provision as follows:

Change of Beneficiary: Unless the insured makes an irrevocable designation of beneficiary, the right to change of beneficiary is reserved to the insured and the consent of the beneficiary or beneficiaries shall not be requisite to surrender or assignment of this policy or to any change of beneficiary or beneficiaries, or to any other changes in this policy.

Note: The first clause or this provision, relating to the irrevocable designation of beneficiary, may be omitted at the insurer's option.

(B) Other Provisions

Except as provided in paragraph (C) of this section, no such policy delivered or issued for delivery to any person in this state shall contain provisions respecting the matters set forth below unless such provisions are in the words in which the same appear in this section; provided, however, that the insurer may, at its option, use in lieu of any such provision a corresponding provision of different wording approved by the (Commissioner) which is not less favorable in any respect to the insured or the beneficiary. Any such provision contained in the policy shall be preceded individually by the appropriate caption appearing in this subsection or, at the option of the insurer, by such appropriate individual or group captions or subcaptions as the (Commissioner) may approve.

(1) A provision as follows:

Change of Occupation: If the insured be injured or contract sickness after having changed his occupation to one classified by the insurer as more hazardous than that stated in this policy or while doing for compensation anything pertaining to an occupation so classified, the insurer will pay only such portion of the indemnities provided in this policy as the premium paid would have purchased at the rates and within the limits fixed by the insurer for such more hazardous occupation. If the insured changes his occupation to one classified by the insurer as less hazardous than that stated in this policy, the insurer, upon receipt of proof of such change of occupation, will reduce the premium rate accordingly, and will return the excess pro rata unearned premium from the date of change of occupation or from the policy anniversary date immediately preceding receipt of such proof, whichever is the more recent. In applying this provision, the classification of occupational risk and the premium rates shall be such as have been last filed by the insurer prior to the occurrence of the loss for which the insurer is liable or prior to date of proof of change in occupation with the state official having supervision of insurance in the state where the insured resided at the time this policy was issued; but if such filing was not required, then the classification of occupation risk and the premium rates shall be those last made effective by the insurer in such state prior to the occurrence of the loss or prior to the date of proof of change in occupation.

(2) A provision as follows:

Misstatement of Age: If the age of the insured has been misstated, all amounts payable under this policy shall be such as the premium paid would have purchased at the correct age.

*(3) A provision as follows:

Overinsurance: If an accident or sickness or accident and sickness policy or policies previously issued by the insurer to the insured be in force concurrently herewith, making the aggregate indemnity for (insert type of coverage or coverages) in excess of $ (insert maximum limit of indemnity or indemnities) the excess shall be void and all premiums paid for such excess shall be returned to the insured or to his estate. or, in lieu thereof: Insurance effective at any one time on the insured under this policy and a like policy or policies in this insurer is limited to the one (such) policy elected by the insured, his beneficiary or his estate, as the case may be, and the insurer will return all premiums paid for all other such policies.

*[Amended by 1964 NAIC Proceedings I 98.]

*(4) A provision as follows:

Overinsurance: If, with respect to a person covered under this policy, benefits for allowable expense incurred during a claim determination period under this policy together with benefits for allowable expense during such period under all other valid coverage (without giving effect to this provision or to any "overinsurance provision" applying to such other valid coverage), exceed the total of such person's allowable expense during such period, this insurer shall be liable only for such proportionate amount of the benefits for allowable expense under this policy during such period as

(i) the total allowable expense during such period bears to

(ii) the total amount of benefits payable during such period for such expense under this policy and all other valid coverage (without giving effect to this provision or to any "overinsurance provision" applying to such other valid coverage) less in both (i) and (ii) any amount of benefits for allowable expense payable under other valid coverage which does not contain an "overinsurance provision". In no event shall this provision operate to increase the amount of benefits for allowable expense payable under this policy with respect to a person covered under this policy above the amount which would have been paid in the absence of this provision. This insurer may pay benefits to any insurer providing other valid coverage in the event of overpayment by such insurer. Any such payment shall discharge the liability of this insurer as fully as if the payment had been made directly to the insured, his assignee or his beneficiary. In the event that this insurer pays benefits to the insured, his assignee or his beneficiary, in excess of the amount which would have been payable if the existence of other valid coverage had been disclosed, this insurer shall have a right of action against the insured, his assignee or his beneficiary, to recover the amount which would not have been paid had there been a disclosure of the existence of the other valid coverage. The amount of other valid coverage which is on a provision of service basis shall be computed as the amount the services rendered would have cost in the absence of such coverage.

For the purposes of this provision:

(i) "allowable expense" means 110% of any necessary, reasonable and customary item of expense which is covered, in whole or in part, as a hospital, surgical, medical or major medical expense under this policy or under any other valid coverage.

(ii) "claim determination period" with respect to any covered person means the initial period of (insert period or not less than thirty days) and each successive period of a like number of days, during which allowable expense covered under this policy is incurred on account of such person. The first such period begins on the date when the first such expense is incurred, and successive periods shall begin when such expense is incurred after expiration of a prior period.

or, in lieu thereof:

"claim determination period" with respect to any covered person means each (insert calendar or policy period of not less than a month) during which allowable expense covered under this policy is incurred on account of such person.

(iii) "overinsurance provision" means this provision and any other provision which may reduce an insurer's liability because of the existence of benefits under other valid coverage.

Note: The foregoing policy provision may be inserted in all (guaranteed renewable and non-cancelable as well as guaranteed renewable) policies providing hospital, surgical, medical or major medical benefits. The insurer may make this provision applicable to either or both (a) other valid coverage with other insurers and (b), except for individual policies individually underwritten, other valid coverage with the same insurer. The insurer shall include in this provision a definition of "other valid coverage" approved as to form by the (Commissioner). Such term may include hospital, surgical, medical or major medical benefits provided by group, blanket or franchise coverage, individual and family type coverage, Blue Cross-Blue Shield coverage and other prepayment plans, group practice and individual practice plans, uninsured benefits provided by labor-management trusteed plans, or union welfare plans, or by employer or employee benefit organizations, benefits provided under governmental programs, workmen's compensation insurance or any coverage required or provided by any other statute, and medical payments under automobile liability and personal liability policies. Other valid coverage shall not include payments made under third party liability coverage as a result of a determination of negligence (but an insurer may at its option include a subrogation clause in its policy). The insurer may require, as part of the proof of claim, the information necessary to administer this provision.

*[Amended by 1964 NAIC Proceedings 1 99.]

(5) A provision as follows:

Insurance with Other Insurers: If there be other valid coverage, not with this insurer, providing benefits for the same loss on other than an expense incurred basis and of which this insurer has not been give written notice prior to the occurrence or commencement of loss, the only liability for such benefits under this policy shall be for such proportion of the indemnities otherwise provided hereunder for such loss as the like indemnities of which the insurer had notice (including the indemnities under this policy) bear to the total amount of all like indemnities for such loss, and for the return of such portion of the premium paid as shall exceed the pro-rata portion for the indemnities thus determined.

Note: If the foregoing policy provision is included in a policy which also contains the next preceding policy provision there shall be added to the caption of the foregoing provision the phrase "—Other Benefits." The insurer may, as its option, include in this provision a definition of "other valid coverage," approved as to form by the (Commissioner), which definition shall be limited in subject matter to coverage provided by organizations subject to regulation by insurance law or by insurance authorities of this or any other state of the United States or any province of Canada, and to any other coverage the inclusion of which may be approved by the (Commissioner). In the absence of such definition such term shall not include group insurance, or benefits provided by union welfare plans or by employer or employee benefit organizations. For the purpose of applying the foregoing policy provision with respect to an insured, any amount of benefit provided for such insured pursuant to any compulsory benefit statute (including any workmen's compensation or employer's liability statute) whether provided by a governmental agency or otherwise shall in all cases be deemed to be "other valid coverage" of which the insurer has had notice. In applying the foregoing policy provision no third party liability coverage shall be included as "other valid coverage."

(6) A provision as follows:

Overinsurance: After the loss-of-time benefit of this policy has been payable for 90 days, such benefit will be adjusted, as provided below, if the total amount of unadjusted loss-of-time benefits provided in all valid loss-of-time coverage upon the insured should exceed (insert amount)% of the insured's earned income; provided, however, that if the information contained in this application discloses that the total amount of loss-of-time benefits under this policy and under all other valid loss-of-time coverage expected to be effective upon the insured in accordance with the application for this policy exceeded (insert amount)% of the insured's earned income at the time of such application, such higher percentage will be used in place of (insert amount)%. Such adjusted loss-of-time benefit under this policy for any month shall be only such proportion of the loss-of-time benefit otherwise payable under this policy as

(i) the product of the insured's earned income and (insert amount)% (or, if higher, the alternative percentage described at the end of the first sentence of this provision)

bears to

(ii) the total amount of loss-of-time benefits payable for such month under this policy and all other valid loss-of-time coverage on the insured (without giving effect to the "over insurance provision" in this or any other coverage)

less in both (i) and (ii) any amount of loss-of-time benefits payable under other valid loss of-time coverage which does not contain an "overinsurance provision". In making such computation, all benefits and earnings shall be converted to a consistent (insert "weekly" if the loss-of-time benefit of this policy is payable weekly, "monthly" if such benefit is payable monthly, etc.) basis. If the numerator of the foregoing ratio is zero or is negative, no benefit shall be payable under this policy. In no event, shall this provision (i) operate to reduce the total combined amount of loss-of-time benefits for such month payable under this policy and all other valid loss-of-time coverage below the lesser of $300 and the total combined amount of loss-of-time benefits determined without giving effect to any "overinsurance provision", nor (ii) operate to increase the amount of benefits payable under this policy above the amount which would have been paid in the absence of this provision, nor (iii) take into account or operate to reduce any benefit other than the loss-of-time benefit.

For purposes of this provision:

(i) "earned income", except where otherwise specified, means the greater of the monthly earnings of the insured at the time disability commences and average monthly earnings for a period of two years immediately preceding the commencement of such disability, and shall not include any investment income or any other income not derived from the insured's vocational activities.

(ii) "overinsurance provision" shall include this provision and any other provision with respect to any loss-of-time coverage which may have the effect of reducing an insurer's liability if the total amount of loss-of-time benefits under all coverage exceeds a stated relationship to the insured's earnings.

Note: The foregoing provision may be included only in a policy which provides a loss-of-time benefit which may be payable for at least 52 weeks, which is issued on the basis of selective underwriting of each individual application, and for which the application includes a question designed to elicit information necessary either to determine the ratio of the total loss-of-time benefits of the insured to the insured's earned income or to determine that such ratio does not exceed the percentage of earnings, not less than 60%, selected by the insurer and inserted in lieu of the blank factor above. The insurer may require, as part of the proof of claim, the information necessary to administer this provision. If the application indicates that other loss-of-time coverage is to be discontinued, the amount of such other coverage shall be excluded in computing the alternative percentage in the first sentence of the overinsurance provision. The policy shall include a definition of "valid loss-of-time coverage", approved as to form by the (Commissioner), which definition may include coverage provided by governmental agencies and by organizations subject to regulation by insurance law and by insurance authorities of this or any other state of the United States or of any other country or subdivision thereof, coverage provided for such insured pursuant to any disability benefits statute or any workmen's compensation or employer's liability statute, benefits provided by labor-management trusteed plans or union welfare plans or by employer or employee benefit organizations, or by salary continuance or pension programs, and any other coverage the inclusion of which may be approved by the (Commissioner).

*[Amended by 1964 NAIC Proceedings 1 100-101.]

(7) A provision as follows:

Unpaid Premium: Upon the payment of a claim under this policy, any premium then due and unpaid or covered by any note or written order may be deducted therefrom.

*(8) A provision as follows:

[Former paragraph (8) entitle "Cancellation" deleted and remaining paragraph renumbered by 1956 NAIC proceedings II 290.]

Conformity with State Statutes: Any provision of this policy which, on its effective date, is in conflict with the statues of the state in which the insured resides on such date is hereby amended to conform to the minimum requirements of such statutes.

(9) A provision as follows:

Illegal Occupation: The insurer shall not be liable for any loss to which a contributing cause was the insured's commission of or attempt to commit a felony or to which a contributing cause was the insured's being engaged in an illegal occupation.

(10) A provision as follows:

Intoxicants and Narcotics: The insurer shall not be liable for any loss sustained or contracted in consequence of the insured's being intoxicated or under the influence of any narcotic unless administered on the advice of a physician.

Note: Paragraphs (9) and (10) are suggested for states which desire such provisions.

(C) Inapplicable or Inconsistent Provisions

If any provision of this section is in whole or in part inapplicable to or inconsistent with the coverage provided by a particular form of policy the insurer, with the approval of the (Commissioner), shall omit from such policy an inapplicable provision or part of a provision and shall modify any inconsistent provision or part of the provision in such manner as to make the provision as contained in the policy consistent with the coverage provided by the policy.

(D) Order of Certain Policy Provisions

The provisions which are the subject of subsections (A) and (B) of this section, or any corresponding provisions which are used in lieu thereof in accordance with such subsections, shall be printed in the consecutive order of the provisions in such subsections or, at the option of the insurer, any such provisions may appear as a unit in any part of the policy, with other provisions to which it may be logically related, provided the resulting policy shall not be in whole or in part unintelligible, uncertain, ambiguous, abstruse, or likely to mislead a person to whom the policy is offered, delivered or issued.

(E) Third Party Ownership

The word "insured", as used in this act, shall not be construed as preventing a person other than the insured with a proper insurable interest from making application for and owning a policy covering the insured or from being entitled under such a policy to any indemnities, benefits and rights provided therein.

(F) Requirements of Other Jurisdictions

(1) Any policy of a foreign or alien insurer, when delivered or issued for delivery to any person in this state, may contain any provision which is not less favorable to the insured or the beneficiary than the provisions of this act and which is prescribed or required by the law of the state under which the insurer is organized.

(2) Any policy of a domestic insurer may, when issued for delivery in any other state or country, contain any provision permitted or required by the laws of such other state or country.

(G) Filing Procedure

The (Commissioner) may make such reasonable rules and regulations concerning the procedure for the filing or submission of policies subject to this act as are necessary, proper or advisable to the administration of this act. This provision shall not abridge any other authority granted the (Commissioner) by law.

Section 4. Conforming to Statute.

(A) Other Policy provisions.

No policy provision which is not subject to Section 3 of this act shall make a policy, or any portion thereof, less favorable in any respect to the insured or the beneficiary than the provisions thereof which are subject to this act.

(B) Policy Conflicting with this Act.

A policy delivered or issued for delivery to any person in this state in violation of this act shall be held valid but shall be construed as provided in this act. When any provision in a policy subject to this act is in conflict with any provision of this act, the rights, duties and obligations of the insurer, the insured and the beneficiary shall be governed by the provisions of this act.

Section 5. Application.

(A) The insured shall not be bound by any statement made in an application for a policy unless a copy of such application is attached to or endorsed on the policy when issued as a part thereof. If any such policy delivered or issued for delivery to any person in this state shall be reinstated or renewed, and the insured or the beneficiary or assignee of such policy shall make written request to the insurer for a copy of the application, if any, for such reinstatement or renewal, the insurer shall within fifteen days after the receipt of such request at its home office or any branch office of the insurer, deliver or mail to the person making such request a copy of such application. If such copy shall not be so delivered or mailed, the insurer shall be precluded from introducing such application as evidence in any action or proceeding based upon or involving such policy or its reinstatement or renewal.

(B) No alteration of any written application for any such policy shall be made by any person other than the applicant without his written consent, except that insertions may be made by the insurer, for administrative purposes only, in such manner as to indicate clearly that such insertions are not be be ascribed to the applicant.

(C) The falsity of any statement in the application for any policy covered by this act may not bar the right to recovery thereunder unless such false statement materially affected either the acceptance of the risk or the hazard assumed by the insurer.

Note: Section 5, or any subsection thereof, is suggested for use in states which have no comparable statues relating to the application

Section 6. Notice, Waiver.

The acknowledgment by any insurer of the receipt of notice given under any policy covered by this act, or the furnishing for forms for filing proofs of loss, or the acceptance of such proofs, or the investigation of any claim thereunder shall not operate as a waiver of any of the rights of the insurer in defense of any claim arising under such policy.

Section 7. Age Limit.

If any such policy contains a provision establishing, as an age limit or otherwise, a date after which the coverage provided by the policy will not be effective, and if such date falls within a period for which premium is accepted by the insurer or if the insurer accepts a premium after such date, the coverage provided by the policy will continue in force subject to any right of cancellation until the end of the period for which premium has been accepted. In the event the age of the insured has been misstated and if, according to the correct age of the insured, the coverage provided by the policy would not have become effective, or would have ceased prior to the acceptance of such premium or premiums, then the liability of the insurer shall be limited to the refund, upon request, of all premiums paid for the period not covered by the policy.

Section 8. Non-Application to Certain Policies.

Nothing in this act shall apply to or affect (1) any policy of workmen's compensation insurance or any policy of liability insurance with or without supplementary expense coverage therein; or (2) any policy or contract of reinsurance; or (3) any blanket or group policy of insurance; or (4) life insurance, endowment or annuity contracts, or contracts supplemental thereto which contain only such provisions relating to accident and sickness insurance as (a) provided additional benefits in case of death or dismemberment or loss of sight by accident, or as (b) operate to safeguard such contracts against lapse, or to give a special surrender value or special benefit or an annuity in the event that the insured or annuitant shall become totally and permanently disabled, as defined by the contract or supplemental contract.

Note: This provision may, if desired, be modified in individual states so as to be consistent with current statutes of such states.

Section 9. Violation.

Any person, partnership or corporation willfully violating any provision of this act or order of the (Commissioner) made in accordance with this act, shall forfeit to the people of the state a sum not to exceed $(insert amount) for each such violation, which may be recovered by a civil action. The (Commissioner) may also suspend or revoke the license of an insurer or agent for any such willful violation.

Note: This provision is to be used in those states which do not have similar legislation now in effect.

Section 10. Judicial Review.

Any order or decision of the (Commissioner) under this act shall be subject to review by appeal (writ of certiorari) to the (insert title) Court at the instance of any party in interest. The filing of the appeal (petition for such writ) shall operate as a stay of any such order or decision until the Court directs otherwise. The Court may review all the facts and, in disposing of the issue before it, may modify, affirm or reverse the order or decision of the (Commissioner) in whole or in part.

Note: This Section should be used only in those states which do not have similar legislation now in effect.

Section 11. Repeal of Inconsistent Acts.

Note: This section should contain suitable language to repeal acts or parts of acts presently enacted and inconsistent with this act. The repealing section should contain an appropriate exception with regard to section 12 of this act.

Section 12. Effective Date of Act.

This Act shall take effect on the (insert day) day of (insert month), 19 (insert year). A policy, rider or endorsement which could have been lawfully used or delivered or issued for delivery to any person in this state immediately before the effective date of this Act may be used or delivered or issued for delivery to any such person during five years after the effective date of this Act.

*[Amended by 1964 NAIC Proceedings I 101.]

*EXHIBIT A
REGULATION REGARDING OVERINSURANCE PROVISIONS

Each individual health insurance policy, delivered or issued for delivery in this State on or after (insert the effective date contained in Section 5 of

Exhibit A), which contains the overinsurance provisions authorized in (insert reference to statutory section which contains Section 3 (B) (4) of the Uniform Individual Accident and Sickness Policy Provisions Law) or (insert reference to statutory section which contains Section 3 (B) (6) of the Uniform Individual Accident and Sickness Policy Provisions Law) as amended by (insert session laws citation to Exhibit A) or, at the option of the insurer, the application for such policy, shall contain, or have attached to or be stamped or endorsed to add, a statement to the effect that benefits under the policy are subject to reduction if the insured has benefits under any other coverage of the type described in the overinsurance provision causing overinsurance as defined in such provision. If the insurer elects to include such statement in the policy, rather than in the application, the policy shall also contain, or have attached to or be stamped or endorsed to add, an additional statement to the effect that during a period of ten days from the date the policy is delivered to the policyholder, it may be surrendered to the insurer together with a written request for cancellation of the policy and in such event the insurer will refund any premium paid therefor including any policy fees or other charges.

*[Added by 1964 NAIC Proceedings I 101.]

Legislative History (all references are to the Proceedings of the NAIC).

1950 Proc. 398, 399-413, 414 (adopted).
1964 Proc. I 91, 95, 98-101. 115 (amended).

See also:
1979 Poc. I 375 (UPPL restated in simplified language) P. 185-1

Appendix 3

RESTATEMENT OF THE NAIC UNIFORM INDIVIDUAL ACCIDENT AND SICKNESS POLICY PROVISION LAW IN SIMPLIFIED LANGUAGE

PURPOSE:

This restatement of the required and most often used optional provisions of the Uniform Policy Provision Law in simplified language is intended as a guideline for the submission and approval of individual accident and sickness policies written in simplified language. Although it is intended specifically for use in those states which adopt the NAIC Model Life and Health Insurance Policy Language Simplification Act, its use as a guide for approval of policies voluntarily written in simplified language is encouraged.

The restated provisions are intended to most accurately reflect the original intent of the uniform Policy Provision Law and to duplicate its substantive requirements. The rights and obligations of both the Insured and Insurer or any case law interpreting the Uniform Provisions are not intended to be affected. They are intended as a uniform "safe harbor" for companies relying upon them. The restatements are no less favorable to the insured or beneficiary and their use is sanctioned under the authority granted by Section 3(A) of the Uniform Policy Provision Law.

The drafting notes accompanying these restated provisions are in addition to those found in the Model Law.

Although the provisions are stated in the "Insured and Insurer" format, rather than the personal "We/You" so as to conform more closely to the style of the model, the use of the personal pronoun format or the substitution of other descriptive terms where appropriate is encouraged. Minor grammatical changes may result from the personal pronoun format.

Section 3. Accident and Sickness Policy Provisions.

(A) Required Provisions

(1) Entire Contract; Changes: this policy [with the application and attached papers] is the entire contract between the Insured and the Company. No change in this policy will be effective until approved by a company officer. This approval must be noted on or attached to this policy. No agent may change this policy or waive any of its provisions.

Note: Bracketed material used when appropriate if application or other papers attached.

FLESCH SCORE without parenthetical material - 64.626

FLESCH SCORE with parenthetical material - 64.585

(2) Time Limit of Certain Defenses:

(a) Misstatements in the Application:

After 3 years from the issue date only fraudulent misstatements in the application may be used to void the policy or deny any claim for loss incurred or disability that starts after the 3 year period.

(A policy which the insured has the right to continue in force subject to its terms by the timely payment of premium (1) until at least age 50 or, (2) in the case of a policy issued after age 44, for at least five years from its date of issue, may contain in lieu of the foregoing the following provision.)

Incontestable:

(a) Misstatements in the Application:

After this policy has been in force for 3 years during the Insured's lifetime (excluding any period during which the Insured is disabled), the Company cannot contest the statements in the applications.

(b) Pre-Existing Conditions:

No claim for loss incurred or disability that starts after 3 years from the issue date will be reduced or denied because a sickness or physical condition not excluded by name or specific description before the date of loss had existed before the effective date of coverage.

Note: The restated provision uses the reference to loss incurred or disability that starts. If the policy provides coverage for hospital or medical benefits only as for disability benefits only, then one or the other may be inappropriate and companies are encouraged to delete the inappropriate phrase. The 3 year period is based on the Model, thus, in those states that have reduced the period to a lesser time; the lesser time period should be inserted. The captions "Misstatements in the Application" and "Pre-Existing Conditions" are an integral part of the provision and must be

APPENDIX 3

read in conjunction therewith. The restatement is not intended to have any affect upon or to a bar to any other defenses under the policy.

FLESCH SCORE - paragraphs (a) and (b)
With Required provision - 36.285
With Optional provision - 36.913

(3) Grace Period: This policy has a 31 day grace period. This means that if a renewal premium is not paid on or before the date it is due, it may be paid during the following 31 days. The grace period will not apply if, at least 30 days before the premium due date, the Company has delivered or mailed to the Insured's last address shown in the Company's records written notice of the Company's intent not to renew this policy. During the grace period, the policy will stay in force.

(The above is for those under which the insurer reserves the right to refuse renewal.)

Grace Period: This policy has a 31 day grace period. This means that if a renewal premium is not paid on or before the date it is due, it may be paid during the following 31 days. During the grace period the policy will stay in force.

(The above is for those under which the insurer does not reserve the right to refuse renewal.)

Note: Insert a number not less than "7" for weekly premium policies, "10" for monthly premium policies and "31" for all other policies.

FLESCH SCORE where insurer reserves right to refuse renewal - 62.681

FLESCH SCORE where insurer does not reserve right to refuse renewal - 67.531

(4) Reinstatement: If the renewal premium is not paid before the grace period ends, the policy will lapse. Later acceptance of the premium by the Company (or by an agent authorized to accept payment) without requiring an application for reinstatement will reinstate this policy.

If the Company or its agent requires an application, the Insured will be given a conditional receipt for the premium. If the application is approved, the policy will be reinstated as of the approval date. Lacking such approval, the policy will be reinstated on the 45th day after the date of the conditional receipt unless the Company has previously written the Insured of its disapproval.

The reinstated policy will cover only loss that results from an injury sustained after the date of reinstatement or sickness that starts more than 10 days after such date. In all other respects the rights of the Insured and the Company will remain the same, subject to any provisions noted on or attached to the reinstated policy.

Any premiums the Company accepts for a reinstatement will be applied to a period for which premiums have not been paid. No premiums will be applied to any period more than 60 days before the reinstatement date.

(The last paragraph of the above provision may be omitted from any policy which the Insured has the right to continue in force subject to its terms by the timely payment of premiums (1) until at least age 50 or, (2) in the case of a policy issued after age 44, for at least five years from its date of issue.)

FLESCH SCORE - 42.421

(5) Notice of Claim: Written notice of claim must be given within 20 days after a covered loss starts or as soon as reasonably possible. The notice can be given to the Company at its home office, or to the Company's agent. Notice should include the name of the Insured and the policy number.

FLESCH SCORE - 68.536

Optional Paragraph: If the Insured has a disability for which benefits may be payable for at least 2 years, at least once every 6 months after the Insured has given notice of claim, the Insured must give the Company notice that the disability has continued. The Insured need not do this if legally incapacitated. The first 6 months after any filing of proof by the Insured or any payment or denial of a claim by the Company will not be counted in applying this provision.

If the Insured delays in giving this notice, the Insured's right to any benefits for the 6 months before the date when the Insured gives notice will not be impaired.

FLESCH SCORE - 65.644

(6) Claim Forms: When the Company receives the notice of claim, it will send the claimant forms for filing proof of loss. If these forms are not given to the claimant within 15 days, the claimant will meet the proof of loss requirements by giving the Company a written statement of the nature and extent of the loss within the time limits stated in the Proofs of Loss Section.

FLESCH SCORE - 62.007

(7) Proofs of Loss: If the policy provides for periodic payment for a continuing loss, written proof of loss must be given the Company within 90 days after the end of each period for which the Company is liable. For any other loss, written proof must be given within 90 days after such loss. If it was not reasonably possible to

give written proof in the time required, the Company shall not reduce or deny the claim for this reason if the proof is filed as soon as reasonably possible. In any event, the proof required must be given no later than 1 year from the time specified unless the claimant was legally incapacitated.

FLESCH SCORE - 49. 846

(8) Time of Payment of Claims: After receiving written proof of loss, the Company will pay [monthly] all benefits then due for _____. Benefits for any other loss covered by this policy will be paid as soon as the Company receives proper written proof.

Note: Delete or change "monthly" to reflect if necessary the period stated in the policy and insert applicable term for type of benefits.

FLESCH SCORE - 66.403

(9) Payment of Claims: Benefits will be paid to the Insured. Loss of life benefits are payable in accordance with the beneficiary designation in effect at the time of payment. If none is then in effect, the benefits will be paid to the Insured's estate. Any other benefits unpaid at death may be paid at the Company's option, either to the Insured's beneficiary or estate.

FLESCH SCORE - 60.278

Optional Paragraph: If benefits are payable to the Insured's estate or a beneficiary who cannot execute a valid release, the Company can pay benefits up to $1,000 to someone related to the Insured or beneficiary by blood or marriage whom the Company considers to be entitled to the benefits. The Company will be discharged to the extent of any such payment made in good faith.

FLESCH SCORE - 40.290

Optional Paragraph: The Company may pay all or a portion of any indemnities provided for health care services to the provider, unless the Insured directs otherwise in writing by the time proofs of loss are filed. The Company cannot require that the services be rendered by a particular provider.

FLESCH SCORE - 51.853

(10) Physical Examinations & Autopsy: The Company at its expense has the right to have the Insured examined as often as reasonably necessary while a claim is pending. It may also have an autopsy made unless prohibited by law.

Note: If no right to an autopsy is desired or is not appropriate for the type of coverage the second sentence of the provision and the caption reference to Autopsy should be deleted.

FLESCH SCORE with right of Autopsy - 42. 173

FLESCH SCORE without right of Autopsy - 67.333

(11) Legal Actions: No legal action may be brought to recover on this policy within 60 days after written proof of loss has been given as required by this policy. No such action may be brought after 3 years from the time written proof of loss is required to be given.

FLESCH SCORE - 60. 863

(12) Change of Beneficiary: The Insured can change the beneficiary at any time by giving the Company written notice. The beneficiary's consent is not required for this or any other change in the policy, unless the designation of the beneficiary is irrevocable.

FLESCH SCORE - 38. 166

(B) Other Provisions.

(2) Misstatements of Age: If the Insured's age has been misstated, the benefits will be those the premium paid would have purchased at the correct age.

FLESCH SCORE - 68.692

(3) Other Insurance in This Insurer: If the Insured has more than one policy [   ]. only one policy chosen by the Insured will be effective. The Company will refund all premiums paid for all the other policies.

Note: Insert designation for limitation, i.e., Policy Form - type - form

FLESCH SCORE - 64.626

Optional Paragraph: If the Insured has more than one policy with this Company providing a total indemnity for [   ] or more than [$] the excess insurance shall be void. The premiums paid for the excess shall be returned to the Insured.

Note: Insert type of coverage or coverages and insert maximum limit of indemnity or indemnities.

FLESCH SCORE - 67.672

(7) Unpaid Premiums: When a claim is paid, any premium due and unpaid may be deducted from the claim payment.

FLESCH SCORE - 70 .145

(9) Conformity with State Statutes: Any provision of this policy which, on its effective date, is in conflict with the laws of the state in which the Insured resides on that date is amended to conform to the minimum requirements of such laws.

FLESCH SCORE - 45. 849

(10) Illegal Occupation: The Company will not be liable for any loss which results from the Insured committing or attempting to commit a felony or from the Insured engaging in an illegal occupation.

FLESCH SCORE - 38.487

(11) Intoxicants and Narcotics: The Company will not be liable for any loss resulting from the Insured being drunk or under the influence of any narcotic unless taken on the advice of a physician.

Note: Appropriate language reflecting an applicable statutory definition of drunk or intoxicated may be substituted.

FLESCH SCORE - 48.494

Note: The provisions were graded under the terms and conditions of the NAIC Model Life and Health Insurance Policy Language Simplification Act. As such, captions are not scored and it is assumed that the words "Insured, Insurer and disability" are defined in the policy.

Legislative History (all references are to the Proceedings of the NAIC).
1979 Proc. I 44, 47, 372, 374, 375-379 (adopted).

Index

Accident and Sickness Minimum Standards Model Bill, 31
Accident Medical Expense Benefits, 23-25
    all-accident, 24
    camp insurance, 25
    sports accident, 24
    student accident, 24
    travel accident, 24
Accidental Death and Dismemberment, 47, 136
Accidental Death Benefits Table
    see 1959 Accidental Death Benefits Table
Accounting
    accrual, 93-96
    date, 96
    period, 93-94
    rules, 93-115
    statement date, 94
Active Life Reserves, 201, 205
AD&D
    see Accidental Death and Dismemberment
Additional Monthly Income, 45
Admitted Assets, 173
Advance Premiums, 97
Alcoholism, 28, 29-30
All Cause Deductible, 16
Alternative Valuation Procedures and Assumptions, 100
Amortization, 97
Ambulatory Surgical Center Expense, 31
Analysis of Operations by Lines of Business, 171-174
Annual Statement, 97, 111, 169-186
Anticipated Loss Ratio, 74, 102
Antiselection, 62, 114, 126, 166
Area Rating, 59
APS
    see Attending Physician's Statement
Assets, 173
Asset-Share Model, 65, 75-77
Association Blank, 169-170
Attending Physician's Statement, 124, 125, 142, 147
Baucus Amendment, 22, 32
Benefit
    amount, 47, 166
    period, 16-17, 22-23, 35

Benefits, 173
Binding Receipt, 120, 167
BOE
  see Business Overhead Expense
Business Health Insurance, 160
Business Life Insurance, 159-160
Business Overhead Expense, 128-129, 135, 162
Buy-out Insurance, 42, 128, 162
Calendar Year Model, 75
California Relative Value Study, 12-13
Cancer Coverage, 18-19, 32
Cash Flow Method, 79
Cash Transactions, 95
CAST
  see Cumulative Antiselection Theory
Claim
  administration, 114, 141, 148-49
  completion percentage, 108
  costs, 58
  examiner, 149
    disability income insurance, 150
    medical care, 149
  evaluation, 142-43
  liabilities, 103-106, 176-77
  payment, 112, 146-47
  reserves, 103-106, 176-177, 178
    calculation, 106-111
    testing, 112-13, 176
  trend factors, 100-101
  validity, 144-46
Claim Payment Method for Estimating Liabilities
  average size, 110
  formula, 111
  loss ratio, 111
  tabular, 110
Claim Run-out Method, 106-110
Coinsurance, 17, 21, 166
COL
  see Cost of Living
Collected Premiums, 96
Commissioners Disability Tables, 99, 110, 205
Common Accident Deductible, 16
Commutation Functions, 77-79
Compensable Loss, 36
Comprehensive Medical Insurance, 14, 160

Conditional Receipt, 120, 167
Conservatism, 95-97
Consumer Price Index, 44-45, 147
Contestability (Incontestable Clause), 143-44, 151-52
Contingency Reserves, 114-15
Contingent Benefits, 105, 114-15
Continuance Tables, 62
Convention Blank, 169-70
Corridor Deductible, 14
Cost of Living, 43, 44-45, 53-54, 127, 136
Coterminal Benefits, 38
CPI
   see Consumer Price Index
Cumulative Antiselection Theory, 62, 72
Deductible, 15-16, 126, 133-34, 166
   all cause, 16-17
   common accident, 16
   corridor, 14
   family, 16
   fixed-dollar, 11
   per cause, 16-17
   variable, 16
Deferred Premiums, 98, 173
Deficiency Reserves, 100
Dental Care, 25, 28
DIR
   see Disability Income Record
Disability Income Insurance, 35-40, 127-29, 160
   business, 128-29
   monthly income benefit, 41, 45, 47, 131-32
   occupation, 130-31
   underwriting, 128-29
Disability Income Record, 147
Disabled Life
   annuities, 112-13
   reserves, 113
Dividends, 66-67
Doctor
   definition, 28-29
Drug Addiction, 28, 29-30
Due and Unpaid, 105, 112
Elimination Period, 9, 35, 62, 166
   effect, 62
Exclusion Rider, 122, 143

Exclusion Waiver
  see Exclusion Rider
Exclusions and Limitations, 27-28
  alcoholism, 28, 29-30
  cosmetic surgery, 28
  dental care, 28
  drug addiction, 28, 29-30
  eyeglasses, 28
  government owned or operated facilities, 28, 30
  government plans, 27
  hearing aids, 28
  mental disorders, 28, 30
  military duty, 27, 153
  nervous disorders, 28, 30
  nursery care, 27
  pediatric charges, 27
  preexisting conditions, 27
  pregnancy, 28
  suicide, 153
  war, 153
  workers' compensation, 27
Exhibit 9, 177-178, 186
Expense Loading Margins, 101
Expenses, 63-64
  premium calculation, 63-64
Experience, 69-72
  data collection, 69-70
  period, 71
Experimental Medical Procedures, 32
Explicit Method for Profit Margins, 67
Family Deductible, 16
Field Underwriting, 118, 166
Fixed-Dollar Deductible, 11
Formula Methods
  premium calculation, 77-79
Fund Accumulation, 66
Future Buy-out Expense Option, 43
Future-Income Option, 48
GAAP
  see Generally Accepted Accounting Principles
Gain from Operations (Net), 174
Gain from Underwriting, 176
General Insurance Expenses, 174
Generally Accepted Accounting Principles, 67, 171
  profits, 80-81

Good Health Clause, 152
Gross Premium, 57
Group Conversions, 163, 165, 172, 174
Guaranteed
   issue, 8, 139
   renewable, 60-61, 99, 125, 166, 170, 175, 180, 181
   insurability, 48, 135
Guarantee-to-Issue, 140
Health Insurance
   availability at older ages, 3, 20-33
   history, 1-4
   life insurance companies, 4-5
Home Health Care, 30
Hospice Care, 31
Hospital
   definition, 29
   expense reimbursement benefits, 10
   indemnity benefits, 7-9
      accident, 9
      Medicare supplement, 9
      elimination period, 9
      limited underwriting, 8
      marketing methods, 8
Implicit Method for Profit Margins, 66-67
In Course of Settlement, 105
Incurred
   claims, 175
   date, 104, 106
   transactions, 106-110
   unreported reserve, 105
Indexing Prior Earnings, 44-45
Individual Claim Estimates, 110
Inflation, 100, 101, 108
Inside Limits, 3, 166
Inspection Report, 123, 147
Insurance
   disability income, 127-29
   medical expense, 120-22
Intercompany Hospital Surgical Tables
   see 1956 Intercompany Hospital Surgical Tables
Interest
   discounting, 66, 110
   premium calculation, 65-66

Investment
  earnings, 66
  income (net), 173
Issue Limits, 136-37
Lapsation, 64-65
Level Premium, 101, 102, 103
  policy reserves, 101
Liabilities, 94, 103-106, 176-77
Life Companies as Individual Health Insurers, 4-5
Life Insurance, 5-6, 120-22
Lifetime Benefit Period, 39
Long-Term Care, 33-34
Long-Term Leveling Premium, 94, 101-103
Loss Ratio, 101, 102, 103, 109, 156-57, 164
  anticipated, 74, 102
  method, 77-78
Loss Ratio Guidelines, 73-75
Major Medical Benefits, 3, 13-14, 160
  accumulation period, 16
  all-cause benefits, 16
  comprehensive coverage, 14
  benefit period, 16-17
  coinsurance, 17
  covered medical expense, 15, 16
  deductible, 14-15
    all cause, 16-17
    common accident, 16
    corridor, 14
    family, 16
    fixed-dollar, 11
    per cause, 16-17
    variable, 16
  eligible medical expense, 15-17
  inside limits, 17
  maximum benefits, 17
  out-of-pocket limit, 14
Management Information Systems, 80-81
Margins, 72
Marketing, 162-63
Maternity Benefits, 10, 12, 26-27, 127, 153
Mean Policy Reserves, 97
Medicaid, 9, 33
Medical Expense Insurance, 7, 120-122, 126-27
  accident medical expense, 23-25
  dental insurance, 25

hospital indemnity, 7-9
  hospital expense reimbursement, 7, 10-11
  major medical, 13-18
  maternity, 10, 12, 26-27
  Medicare supplement, 20-23, 127, 129
  reimbursementt, 11-12
  specified disease, 18-19
  surgical expense reimbursement, 12-13
  underwriting, 125-29
Medical Expense Tables
  see 1974 Medical Expense Tables
Medical Impairment Bureau, 124
Medical Underwriting, 119-20
Medicare--Items and Services Not Covered, 21
Medicare--Part A, 20-23
  benefit period, 22-23
  copayment, 22
  deductible, 21, 22
  lifetime reserve days, 20
  spell of illnesss, 20
Medicare--Part B, 20-23
  coinsurance, 21
  deductible, 20, 21, 22, 23
  reasonable charges, 20-21
Medicare Supplement Benefits, 20, 21, 22, 23, 129
Mental Disorders, 28, 30
MIB
  see Medical Impairment Bureau
Midterminal Policy Reserves, 97
Minimum Loss Ratio, 73-74
Minimum Policy Reserve Standards, 99, 101
Misrepresentation, 143-44
Modal Loading, 68
Model Life and Health Insurance Policy Language Simplification Act, 225
Model Rate Filing Guidelines, 102
Morbidity, 61, 99, 101, 205-206
Mortality, 97, 99
Multiple-Line Sales, 160
NAIC
  see National Association of Insurance Commissioners
NAIC Cancer Claim Cost Tables
  see 1985 NAIC Cancer Claim Cost Tables
National Association of Insurance Commissioners, 27, 31, 73-74, 95, 96-98, 99, 100, 101, 169
  Accident and Sickness Minimum Standards Model Bill, 31

accounting standards, 94-115
Loss Ratio Guidelines, 73-75
Minimum Policy Reserve Standards, 95, 97, 99, 100, 101
Model Rate Filing Guidelines, 102
Unfair Claims Practice Bill, 155
Uniform Individual Accident and Sickness Policy Provision Law, 196, 207-224, 225-31
Negative Reserves, 100
Nervous Disorders, 28, 30
Net Premium, 77-78
Net Valuation Premium, 96
New York Regulation 62, 74-75
NIAAF
see Not Issued as Applied For
1956 Intercompany Hospital-Surgical Tables, 100
1959 Accidental Death Benefits Table, 100
1964 Commissioners Disability Table, 99, 110
1974 Medical Expense Tables, 100
1985 Commissioners Individual Disability Table A, 99, 110
1985 Commissioners Individual Disability Table B, 99, 110
1985 NAIC Cancer Claim Cost Tables, 100
Nonadmitted Assets, 173
Noncancelable, 61, 166, 170, 180
Nonmedical Underwriting, 119-20
Non-Renewable for Stated Reasons Only, 60, 166, 175, 181
Not Issued as Applied For, 119, 122-23
Nursery Care, 27
Nursing Home Care, 9, 33
    custodial care, 9
    intermediate care, 9
    skilled care, 9
OASDI
    see Old Age, Survivors, and Disability Insurance
Occupation Classes, 71
Old Age, Survivors, and Disability Insurance, 1, 9, 20, 22, 39, 46, 132, 134-36, 146, 155
Out-of-Pocket Limits, 14, 166
Overhead Expense Benefit, 41
Own Occ
    see Own Occupation Definition
Own Occupation Definition, 37, 145, 154
Paramedical Underwriting, 119
Partial Disability, 36, 145, 154
Participation Limits, 136
Pay-out Pattern, 107

INDEX

Pediatric Charges, 27
Per Cause Deductible, 16-17
Percentage of Premium Method, 76
Persistency, 64-65
Policy
  claims, 114
    investigation, 114
    settlement, 114
  experience exhibit, 181
  forms, 187-89
    attachments, 198
  reserves, 98-103, 176-77
  year model, 75, 76
Policyholder Dividends, 114-15
Pools for Substandard Medical Expense Insurance Risks, 32
Preexisting Conditions, 27, 59-60, 142, 145, 152
Preliminary Term Modifications, 100
Premium
  calculation, 61, 75-79
  guarantees, 60
  rating, 58, 103-105
  reserves, 96-98
  revenues, 94
  waiver, 46-47
  net valuation, 96
Premiums
  advance, 97
  deferred, 98, 173
  earned, 175
  uncollected, 98
  unearned, 96-97, 175, 177
  written, 175
Prepaid Revenues and Expenditures, 94
Presumptive Total Disability, 36, 154
Prior Monthly Earnings, 51
Profit
  objective, 66-67
  study, 66-67
Prospective
  premiums and claims, 102
  reserve, 102
  revenue shortfall, 102
  tabular claim costs, 102
Qualification Period, 50

Rating
   classes, 60
   systems, 61-72
Recovery Benefits, 55
Recurrent Disability, 83, 154
Reformation of Policy, 141, 150
Regulation, 62, 73, 74-75
Rehabilitation, 54-55, 150
Reinstatement, 138-39
Relative Value Schedule, 12, 146
Renewable Provisions, 12, 60, 138, 191-92
   conditionally, 60
   guaranteed, 60-61, 166
   noncancelable and guaranteed, 61, 166, 180, 181
   non-renewable for stated reasons only, 60, 166
   optionally, 166
Rescission, 143-44, 149, 151
Reserve
   for rate credits, 94
   method, 100
   modification, 100
Residual Disability, 49-54, 121, 136, 147
   benefit formula, 49
Retrospective
   loss ratio, 101
   net premiums, 102-103
   premiums and claims, 101-102
   reserve, 101, 102
Return on Equity, 66, 67
Return on Investment, 66, 67, 76
ROE
   see Return on Equity
ROI
   see Return on Investment
Sales Compensation, 163-65
Schedule H, 97, 112, 170, 171, 175-78, 184-185
Schedule O, 112
Selling, 159-63
   regulations, 165-66
Sensitivity Testing, 76
Skilled Nursing Facility, 20
SNF
   see Skilled Nursing Facility
Solvency, 98-99
Specified Disease Benefits, 18-19

INDEX

State of Issue, 58
State Owned or Operated Facilities, 28-30
State Cash Sickness Program, 160
Statutory Accounting Principles, 103, 170
Suicide, 153
Summary of Operations, 179
Supplementary Benefits, 43-49, 160
Surgical Expense Reimbursement Benefits, 12-13
Surplus, 114, 179
Taxes, Licenses and Fees, 174
Total Disability, 36, 154
Uncollected Premiums, 98
Underwriting
   disability income insurance, 127-29
   field, 118
   guaranteed issue, 139
   guarantee-to-issue, 140
   life insurance, 120-22
   marketing strategy, 120-22
   medical, 119-20
   medical expense insurance, 120-22, 126-27
   Medicare supplement insurance, 129
   nonmedical, 119-20
   paramedical, 119
   renewability, 148
   replacement, 139
Unearned Premium Reserve, 177
Unfair Claims Practices Bill, 155
Uniform Individual Accident and Sickness Policy Provision Law, 196, 207-224, 225-31
Unisex, 58-59
Unpaid Revenues and Expenditures, 95
Unreported Claim, 114
Valuation
   date, 104
   net premium, 96-97
Variable Deductible, 16
Vesting, 164
Waiting Period, 35
Waiver of Premium, 46-47, 113